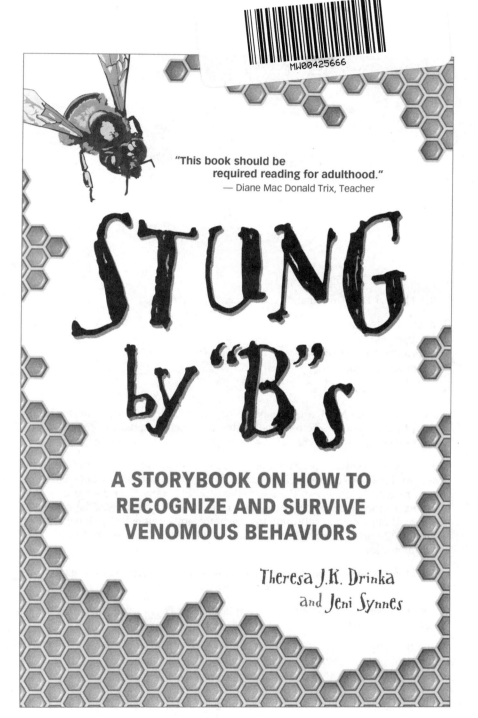

"This book should be
required reading for adulthood."
— Diane Mac Donald Trix, Teacher

STUNG
by "B"s

A STORYBOOK ON HOW TO
RECOGNIZE AND SURVIVE
VENOMOUS BEHAVIORS

Theresa J.K. Drinka
and Jeni Synnes

Bbalm Publishing • Waupaca, WI

For our children and grandchildren.

© 2011 Theresa J. K. Drinka and Jeni Synnes

BBALM PUBLISHING
N3371 Bailey Street
Waupaca, WI 54982-9186
www.stungbybs.com

ISBN: 978-0-9837643-0-4

The stories and vignettes presented in this book are told from the perspective of the people we interviewed. Identifying characteristics of the stories have been altered to protect the confidentiality of the storytellers and the subjects in their stories. Any resemblance to real people or events is accidental and unintended. The content in this book is not meant to substitute for psychotherapy or other professional services. If you feel the need for such services, you are encouraged to consult with a mental health professional.

For information about professional presentations or consultations, go to:
www.stungbybs.com

Cover and interior design ©2011 TLC Graphics, *www.TLCGraphics.com*
Cover design by Monica Thomas, Interior design by Erin Stark

Flying Bee, File #: 12706519: *www.istockphoto.com* / © kimberrywood
Honeycomb, File #: 10390272: *www.istockphoto.com* / © derrrek
Photography by John Morser, Visual Perspectives

Printed in the United States of America

Table of Contents

Foreword

While seeing a patient at my home office, I was distracted by a mysterious buzzing sound. Between patients, I went to the front door to pick up my mail and noticed a bee bonking itself against the window as if it was trying to get out. When I came back in, there were about 50 bees doing the same thing on the window. I became frightened at the possibility of a swarm of bees taking over my home. Yikes! I was feeling so violated when I learned that these bees were living in my chimney and may have been lurking there for some time, waiting to strike! Hmmm, I thought, this is a fascinating metaphor for what this book is truly about. People who are right amongst us ready to cunningly strike, and we don't even know it until it's sometimes too late.

Clients with Cluster B Personality Disorders are known to clinicians as very difficult and complex individuals to work with and treat because of their subtle, manipulative, "stinging" behaviors. These venomous behaviors can challenge even the most experienced analyst to maintain a therapeutic approach. When working with patients who exhibit these behaviors, I've struggled to not react with defeat or anger. Sadly sometimes I lost the struggle, only to recognize I'd been "stung" after the fact, which was at times very painful. This book shows the reader how to become aware of these subtle, manipulative, stinging behaviors so as to keep from becoming a victim of the "stings." Most typically what we see in the literature is how to work with Cluster B Personality Disorders in the

context of therapy. That "Stung by B's" is attempting to teach the reader how to personally recognize and deal with the impact of Cluster B behaviors makes this book clearly stand out as it addresses this issue on a more personal basis. And, that Theresa Drinka and Jeni Synnes so scholarly write about this subject in a very readable and easy to identify with manner makes this a true gem not only for the lay reader, but for clinicians too! Rather than focus on how to diagnose these disorders, they show how to identify patterns of behavior that we have all experienced in those we work with and live around.

I recall hearing that a primitive tribe had been taught by their ancestors that when the belly of the sea sucks the water into it, it's time to run up into the hills to higher ground because the sea will spit back out the water with a vengeance. So, when the tribe saw the tide recede during the 2004 Indian Ocean tsunami, although they didn't know the science of earthquakes and tsunami's, they had learned an important ancestral story that saved their lives. I loved hearing this, as I've felt that there is something so rich and valuable in stories—often wisdom that can save our lives and help us survive. Drinka and Synnes so beautifully gift us these stories for survival in this book. They share stories that contain wisdom that can help us to survive serious Cluster B behaviors. Through real stories they show how to label the behaviors and increase our awareness so as to not become victims any longer.

DEBRA A. HILL, MD
Private Practice Adult, Adolescent & Child Psychiatrist and Psychoanalyst

Volunteer Clinical Faculty, UCI Neuropsychiatric Institute, Irvine, California

Acknowledgements

We offer special thanks to our husbands, Paul Drinka and Paul Synnes, who dared to edit multiple versions of this book. They encouraged us to consider additional ideas and challenged us to dig deeper. We greatly appreciate their patience and honesty, especially through our low times and most difficult conversations.

We also give special thanks to the editors of the book. Elizabeth James performed a skillful edit of our work in progress, providing invaluable advice on many fronts. Jill Andersen applied her professional editing skills to the final version.

Thank you to the artistic talents and insights of Monica Thomas for the cover design. Hats off to Halle for seeing the honeycomb. Thank you to Erin Stark for making our book more readable with her masterful interior design.

Tami and Tom and the helpful people at TLC Graphics demonstrated their professionalism as they guided us through the maze of the publishing business. We thank them for their patience and encouragement.

Sharon Sizemore Martin and Jessica Hanson braved through early versions, giving us thoughtful insights on content, and the encouragement to continue when we were ready to give up. Thank you, Sharon and Jessica.

We are also grateful to Carol Payne, Joseph Drinka, Ellen Lawrence, Diane Mac Donald Trix and Ann Stephani, who shared

their professional and personal insights during the many phases of writing this book.

We are indebted to the many people throughout the country who had the courage and strength to share their stories. We would like to acknowledge each one of you. Although the details of the stories have been modified and your names must be confidential, we want you each to know that your contribution to this book was invaluable.

Last but not least, we thank all the members of our families who endured our ongoing struggles as we navigated the illogic associated with "B" behaviors.

An Introduction to "B"s

"The easiest person to deceive is one's self."
EDWARD G. BULWER-LYTTON

A Gary Larson cartoon portrays God making a skillet dinner, with our planet in the skillet. Various seasonings such as birds, insects and trees surround God. However, God is also shaking in a seasoning called "jerks." This seasoning is full of aggressive and manipulative behaviors that will cause pain, suffering, frustration and confusion. People often use the metaphor of being stung to describe being figuratively blindsided or injured by someone who lies and manipulates, or who is selfish, irresponsible or arrogant. In this book we describe both those who sting and those who've been stung by these behaviors. Many of the people who are stung in the following stories were expecting a honeybee, when instead they were surprised and stung, often repeatedly, by a more aggressive bee.

Oh, Those Bees

We all know and love domesticated honeybees. They are docile creatures that perform magic on our food and flower crops. We welcome these bees into our gardens and try to protect them if

they are threatened. Numerous writers throughout history, including Aristotle, Plato, Shakespeare and Tolstoy, have used honeybees as symbols of socialized human society.[1]

Although difficult to distinguish from the domesticated honeybee, the Africanized honeybee is a more aggressive hybrid, having earned the nickname "killer bee." Africanized bees were bred to produce greater amounts of honey. However, their vicious stinging habits need to be managed.[2]

While honeybees can function as a metaphor for the workings of a communal society, Africanized bees can function as a metaphor for more-frustrating behaviors that suggest certain maladaptive personality traits. Maladaptive personality traits come in three varieties: odd, manipulative and anxious. The group of personality traits known as cluster B personality disorders is defined by manipulative behaviors. Each of the four personality disorders within the B cluster is characterized by specific patterns of manipulative behaviors.

We have no way of knowing whether people with manipulative behaviors have cluster B personality disorders. We can only observe their behaviors, and it is to our advantage to watch for patterns in those behaviors. *In this book we refer to those who repeatedly execute manipulative behaviors that lead to social dysfunction as "B"s.* Encounters with these "B"s surprise and sting us when we least expect it.

Like Africanized bees, people who consistently exhibit "B" behaviors can be dangerous. Occasionally, we mistake an Africanized bee for a domestic bee and get stung, often more than once. We immediately think of ways to defend ourselves, like wearing protective clothing or recognizing the characteristics, habits and

[1] Wilson, *The Hive*, 4.
[2] Schneider et al., "Seasonal Nest Usurpation," 356–364.

appearance of aggressive bees. However, the attacks from both the Africanized bees and the human "B"s include erratic and surprise elements that predispose us to being stung.

Like Africanized bees, "B"s are overly defensive, they usurp territory, and they surround themselves with guard/rescue bees to protect themselves and justify their manipulative behaviors. While Africanized bees cannot survive prolonged periods of forage deprivation, "B"s have difficulty surviving prolonged periods in which they are not the focus of attention. Both leave venom in the victim that festers after they are gone.

The impact of a sting will differ if you are in a formal or casual relationship with the perpetrator, and whether the relationship is a short- or long-term one. Also, the impact of the sting will be greater if the perpetrator is someone you trust or depend on. When several of these variables interact, they can increase the effects on the unfortunate ones who get stung.

Beware! People often behave strangely around aggressive stinging "B"s. *Sometimes people even beg to be stung.* The novel *Perfume: The Story of a Murderer* by Patrick Suskind is a graphic example of a mass of people who wanted to believe in someone so much that they were intoxicated by the irresistible scent of a sadistic murderer, viewing him as wonderful. One of the final passages in the book depicts the masses captivated by the killer's scent, a graphic metaphor for how we sometimes behave around people who skillfully exhibit stinging behaviors.

Aggressive stinging "B"s buzz in our worlds of work, family, friends and acquaintances, and also within government and health and human service systems, where manipulative behaviors can have a profound negative effect on their targets. There are many consequences of encounters with stinging manipulators. They can leave us more cautious and less trusting of the human race. They can also cause us to question our competence or sanity. High-functioning "B"s will use their intelligence, physical attractiveness, talents or power to attract people. Because they are selective about whom they sting and whom they charm, aggressive stinging "B"s thrive, and are sought after and actually rewarded for their maladaptive behaviors.

As social workers, we have spent many years observing stinging behaviors in our clients, and the effects of stinging behaviors on our clients. The inspiration for this book arose as we thought of our own lives, and the times we have been unexpectedly stung by someone with manipulative behaviors: a coworker, friend, or someone who was just passing through our lives. Over the years, we have informally counseled friends and acquaintances who sought our guidance after being caught off guard and stung by someone they trusted. As we spoke with our friends and colleagues, we realized that they had stories to share. They, in turn, asked their friends and acquaintances for more stories. As our volume of stories grew, we decided to write this book.

Although we have read many books, articles and blogs about "emotional bloodsuckers," "prima donnas at work," "backstabbers," "nasty people," "bullies" and other such characters, the volume of stories that we collected in a short time from friends and acquaintances surprised us. We encourage you to read books about manipulators and to apply the principles from those books. However, we feel that many people learn best from reading everyday stories by others. We will elaborate on themes by using true-life vignettes and narratives that exemplify a variety of stinging behaviors.

The stories in this book are not about our clients or client relationships. They are all based on stories told by friends and acquaintances. Although this book is about people who exhibit manipulative behaviors and reactions to these people, it is more specifically about how these behaviors affect us in ways we don't realize. This book is about the repeated stings we experience throughout life; how to recognize different types of stings; how to prevent them, when possible; and how to treat them when we get stung.

Although all of the stories are told as the narrators experienced them, details have been modified to protect the innocent and the guilty by disguising the people and circumstances. The stories reflect archetypal situations that should be familiar to you. The manipulative behaviors depicted in these stories are so universal, that when we tell them during workshops, attendees often ask how we knew what was going on in their home, school or workplace. The themes of the stories were so common that they thought we were talking about them. We have no intention of maligning or embarrassing anyone. Any resemblance to people known to the reader is unintended and purely coincidental.

None of the stories we gathered for this book are about mass murderers. Some of the stories had major consequences but many seemed minor. However, the fact that people remembered seemingly minor stories after so many years makes them significant. Taken collectively and over time, occurrences like these wear people down, sicken them, cause them to leave the jobs they love, precipitate divorces and suicides, compel people to stop trusting each other, and subsequently cause them to stop caring about making the world a better place.

The stories told in this book recount a variety of experiences that occurred in many different settings. Although you may not be able to relate to all of the stories, we hope you will find many stories that speak to your experiences and give you reasons to think about how you might change your responses to "B" behaviors.

Our purpose is to help you recognize stinging behaviors early and give you time to plan strategies for survival. Our intent is also to help you recognize the patterns of "B" behaviors. We hope our examples will give you the insight to recognize that you have been stung. We hope the power of this recognition will stimulate your courage to reject the role of victim by taking a proactive approach to your future encounters with potential "B"s.

It is our belief that the majority of people in the world want to trust people, find joy, and get along with others. The inherent benevolence in the majority of the population creates a play-ground for those who are adept at using stinging behaviors to manipulate for their advantage. We believe that awareness of the patterns used by these manipulators will allow you to maintain control and make better choices about how to avoid stings and how to respond if you are stung. Hopefully, this book will help prevent multiple stings and aid the healing process when stings are inevitable.

CHAPTER ONE

Definitions of Cluster B Personality Disorders and Examples of "B" Behaviors

*"All charming people have something to conceal,
usually their total dependence on the appreciation of others."*

CYRIL CONNOLLY

We Have All Been Stung

Manipulative behaviors catch us off guard, assailing us at work and in our personal lives. If the behavior is a single episode and it never repeats, it might be due to someone having a bad day. When the behaviors repeat, they begin to form a pattern on the continuum of "B" behaviors. When these behaviors target others, they erode trust and prevent individuals and groups from reaching their potentials.

The primary theme of this book is learning to recognize patterns of manipulative behaviors. Sometimes the patterns are subtle, and sometimes there are long time periods between the behaviors. However, when someone exhibits a pattern of manipulative behaviors, it's likely that their behaviors will recur, either

1

directed at you or at others. This chapter describes cluster B personality disorders and the continuum of "B" behaviors, from occasional maladaptive behaviors to psychopathy.

TONY

"The police chief had resented me ever since I became president of the local police officer's union. During my probationary year, after promotion to lieutenant, the chief made things very difficult, telling me I was the least-qualified person to achieve that position. The chief forced me to take extra classes and do extra assignments.

"One day, after my probation ended, the chief proposed that every police officer would have to attend three mandatory training sessions on their days off. I told the chief that I thought this was unfair for the officers. For the first time in my recollection, the chief listened to me, talking *with* me and not *at* me. I actually felt that I was getting through to the chief as we arrived at a compromise agreement. The chief and I shook hands on our deal. For the first time in many months, I left work happy to have arrived at a mutual solution to a departmental problem.

"I emailed the police officers to let them know that they were exempt from attending the training when they weren't working. The next day, I was still exuberant, and whistled as I drove to work. At our morning briefing the chief made the announcement that every police officer would have to work three extra days at the chief's discretion.

"This clearly voided our verbal agreement. I thought that I had connected with the chief in a way that would make everyone's lives better, and the chief 'rewarded' me by figuratively stabbing me in the back."

ABOUT THIS CASE STUDY ——————————————

Tony's story portrays an example of the maladaptive and manipulative behaviors that commonly affect our wellbeing. Although some of the behaviors the chief exhibits are manipulative and Tony recognizes a pattern to the behaviors, it's not possible to tell, by reading Tony's story, if the chief has a personality disorder. Simply because someone exhibits a pattern of "B" behaviors doesn't define them as having a personality disorder, nor does it make them a psychopath. "B" behaviors occur on a continuum defined by repetition and destructiveness. Often the destruction is psychological, subtle and not immediately obvious to others. Perhaps it is these two latter qualities that are the most devastating. We will return to Tony and his chief later in the book.

Classifying Maladaptive and Manipulative Behaviors

Mental health professionals use a variety of tools to recognize patterns and classify maladaptive behaviors. Classifying behaviors guides them in diagnosing and treating specific mental disorders. The fourth edition of the *Diagnostic and Statistical Manual of Mental Disorders* (DSM) published by the American Psychiatric Association is the guidebook that is most often used in the United States. The DSM defines a personality disorder as "enduring patterns of inner experience and behavior that deviate markedly from the expectations of the individual's culture, pervasive and inflexible, having an onset in adolescence or early childhood, stable over time, and leads to distress and impairment."[3] By using the criteria

[3] American Psychiatric Association, *Diagnostic and Statistical Manual-IV*, 685.

provided in the DSM, a mental health provider diagnoses a personality disorder when, at a minimum, maladaptive behaviors are *reliable, repetitive, predictable*, and *destructive* in an important area of a person's life.

Another interesting characteristic of people with personality disorders relates to how they solve problems. When faced with a disagreement with another person, someone without a personality disorder will attempt to operationally define the problem and describe the actions required to solve the problem. He will subsequently evaluate the solution based on whether each party was satisfied with the outcome. However, someone with a personality disorder views a disagreement and immediately defines it in a very personal manner. This person's evaluation of and solution to the problem will be based on protecting his identity (how he sees himself) rather than solving the real problem.

As an example, if my son married your daughter and my fear of losing my son makes me anxious, if I have a personality disorder I might "solve" the problem in my mind by thinking of you as lesser than I am (less sophisticated, less intelligent, less important) or even by accusing you of not respecting my son. In this way I can justify my belief that my son could never choose you as a parent over me. Rather than solving the original problem, this approach to problem solving often creates new problems.

There is evidence that genetics are responsible for at least some cluster B disorders. Combinations of genetic and environmental factors are common. However, there is still controversy about what percentage of cluster B disorders is inherited and what percentage is a part of a person's early childhood environment.

Like queen bees, people who exhibit repetitive maladaptive behaviors and those who develop personality disorders have only the predisposition for acting a certain way. Bees become queens because of what they are fed. Some people are born with the potential for developing personality disorders but likely adopt defined patterns of manipulative and maladaptive behaviors because of how they are raised. Some children who are raised by a "B" will accept the "B's" behaviors and counter them with other "B" behaviors. Other children reject the "B" behaviors of their caregivers and discover ways to protect themselves.

Cluster B Personality Disorders

The DSM-IV divides personality disorders into three clusters: A, B and C. Cluster A contains withdrawn types with paranoid and bizarre beliefs. Cluster C contains anxious types who might be avoidant, dependent or obsessed with perfection. Cluster B contains types that are referred to as "immature" or "manipulative."

Four personality disorders are included in the B cluster. Characteristics associated with these disorders include those listed in Table 1.

TABLE 1: Characteristics of Cluster B Personality Disorders

Antisocial Personality Disorder:

callous, deceitful, impulsive, reckless, irresponsible, often charming

Narcissistic Personality Disorder:

grandiose, interpersonally exploitive, envious, lacks compassion, feels entitled, arrogant

Borderline Personality Disorder:

appears vulnerable, impulsive, unstable sense of self, unstable emotions (rapidly switches between over-idealizing and devaluing), self-destructive, often paranoid

Histrionic Personality Disorder:

flirtatious, overly dramatic, vague, shallow emotional expression, demands center stage

Difficulties in Diagnosing Cluster B Personality Disorders

Cluster B personality disorders are complex and particularly difficult to diagnose. It takes a skilled therapist to make a correct diagnosis. Alexander Lowen states that one of the reasons for this difficulty is that narcissism underlies each of the four cluster B disorders, but manifests itself differently in each disorder.[4] People with antisocial personality disorder are deceitful and get their charge from playing games at others' expense. People with nar-

---

[4] Lowen, *Narcissism*, 13-23.

cissistic personality disorder require constant adulation from others but lack compassion for them. Those with borderline personality disorder get their attention from others in self-destructive ways, sometimes by claiming persecution and sometimes by suicide threats. Those with histrionic personality disorder are emotionally flamboyant, appear needy, and dress provocatively.

Certain behavior patterns are unique to each disorder, and some behavior patterns can be found in more than one disorder. Although the pairings are not absolute, Table 2 depicts frequently observed behaviors that are shared among cluster B personality disorders. For example, persons with antisocial personality disorder and persons with narcissistic personality disorder might recognize and understand the feelings of others but lack compassion for those feelings. Those with antisocial personality disorder often take their lack of compassion into a criminal realm, whereas those with narcissistic personality disorder usually stay within the boundaries of the law.

While persons with histrionic personality disorder and persons with borderline personality disorder both are emotionally unstable, those with histrionic personality disorder have a better sense of who they are. Persons with borderline personality disorder and persons with histrionic personality disorder are both often seen as drama queens or kings. People with borderline personality disorder, however, will likely create more chaos with their drama patterns than those with histrionic personality disorder. Those with borderline personality disorder are more likely to distort reality and can become paranoid. However, paranoia is also prominent in those with antisocial personality disorder.

**TABLE 2: Shared Behaviors Among
Cluster B Personality Disorders**

	Antisocial	Narcissistic	Borderline	Histrionic
Regard self as superior	X	X	X *at times*	X
Lack compassion	X	X		
Shallow			X	X
Inconsistent			X	X
Capricious			X	X
Seductive	X		X	X
Needs attention		X	X	X
Emotionally unstable		X	X	X
Drama king/queen			X	X
Paranoid	X		X	

Many individuals who consistently exhibit manipulative behaviors do not fall neatly into one of the four disorders that constitute the B cluster. Instead, they often exhibit behaviors from two or more disorders. Such persons may be given more than one diagnosis within the B cluster. They could also be given the diagnosis of personality disorder not otherwise specified (NOS), or they may be given no diagnosis.

Another reason it is difficult to diagnose cluster B personality disorders is because behaviors typical of the disorders might result from alcohol or drug abuse. This makes diagnosis more complicated because it's difficult to determine if the behaviors are stemming from a personality disorder, substance abuse or both.

Problems with Treatment

There are individuals with cluster B personality disorders who also have other psychiatric disorders, like major depression, mania or anxiety. While depression, mania and anxiety disorders can be effectively treated with medication and psychotherapy, medications don't seem to work for the cluster B personality disorders, and psychotherapy has to be extremely specialized to be effective. A therapist must clearly delineate which symptoms can and cannot be treated with medications. Some clinicians might hesitate to make a diagnosis of a personality disorder because effective treatment involves a time-consuming process of changing the way life events are perceived and acted upon.

Sometimes a therapist chooses to treat a lesser diagnosis because of limited treatment options or inadequate reimbursement rates. While certain kinds of therapy can help, the individual with the cluster B disorder must feel compelled, by force or crisis, to get treatment. That is difficult for those who have problems with self-reflection or who aren't in distress. The majority of therapists are neither paid enough nor do they have enough time to provide successful treatment for those with cluster B disorders who do come for treatment. And yes, sometimes even the therapist is conned by these individuals. This is why you might see two therapists testifying on opposite sides at a trial for someone with a cluster B personality disorder.

Divergent Opinions

Michael Jackson was a multitalented performer who was revered by many adoring fans. He also had a very troubled personal life. As portrayed in the media, he apparently exhibited some borderline behaviors: an unstable self-image leading to facial surgeries; impulsiveness in spending; feeling misunderstood; unusual social functioning; and substance abuse.[5] He was embedded in chaos, even after his death.

Shortly after Jackson's death, a website for physicians revealed some interesting insights into the complexity inherent in understanding these behaviors. A plastic surgeon wrote a short piece commenting on Mr. Jackson's facial surgeries.[6] She suggested that he might have had body dysmorphic disorder, a condition in which a person experiences severe emotional distress and obsessive tendencies over a relatively small or nonexistent physical defect. Physicians, including psychiatrists, responded to her blog, and one post suggested that Jackson had Klinefelter's syndrome, a genetic condition where a male has an extra X chromosome. Most of the blog posts expressed sympathy for Jackson, blamed others for not protecting him, and suggested that the medical profession had failed him. A few physicians stated that Jackson was probably quite persuasive in requesting his facial surgeries. Several posts said that Jackson was responsible for his own behavior. Three of the 37 posts alluded to a personality disorder, including borderline personality disorder.

Maladaptive personality traits often co-exist with other medical problems. Medical problems are the primary reason that people with maladaptive personality traits and disorders seek out a

[5] As referenced in the documentaries *The Jacksons: An American Dream*, Arthur, 1992, and *Living With Michael Jackson*, Bashir, 2003.
[6] Walden, "A Nip and a Tuck: Michael Jackson," blog entry 7/14/2009.

healthcare provider. All of the blog comments made by physicians are speculative but they point out the complex thinking that must go into making any diagnosis and the difficulty of sorting out medical problems from psychological ones.

The Difficulty of Quantifying Cluster B Personality Disorders

The behaviors characteristic of cluster B personality disorders are widespread throughout the population for every age and also for every occupation, including physicians, ministers, social workers, bankers, nurses, attorneys, teachers, politicians, business executives, laborers, waiters, clerical workers, and on and on. Unfortunately, the research on incidence of these personality disorders is conflicting and doesn't always reflect these disorders' negative impact on society.

As Martha Stout pointed out in her book *The Sociopath Next Door*, most antisocial personalities are not in prison.[7] Instead, they are in your family, your neighborhood, your church, your school, and anywhere else you might go. People with patterns of antisocial behaviors love walking on the edge and playing games with people they have already stung. The bigger the challenge, the more aggressively they play the game, and they can be so seductive.

A study conducted by Nelson, Robinson and Hart found that children learn to be mean and manipulative toward their playmates as toddlers.[8] In a survey of 328 preschoolers that asked the children to rate their peers, the authors found as many as 20 percent of preschool girls displayed behaviors such as telling their friends not to play with someone. This would be followed by a threat, such as uninviting them to a birthday party if the playmates didn't do what

[7] Stout, *The Sociopath Next Door*, 82.

[8] Nelson, Robinson & Hart, "Relational and Physical Aggression of Preschool-Age Children," 115–139.

was asked. While this was not a long-term study, the authors have published subsequent data on teenagers that found the same results. Whether or not this type of behavior is indicative of similar behaviors later in the lives of these children is not known. We are concerned about the children who are the victims of the mean behavior. How did they handle these manipulative behaviors, and how do their experiences play out in adulthood?

Blanco et al. studied antisocial and histrionic personality disorders in young people and found that 3.5 percent of the college students had histrionic personality disorder and 4.7 percent had antisocial personality disorder. Of the non-college individuals, the numbers were 4.4 percent and 8.5 percent, respectively. Blanco et al. also found that very few of the young people had sought treatment for their disorders.[9] They did not look at narcissistic or borderline personality disorders.

Gross et al. found the lifetime prevalence of borderline personality disorder in primary care to be 6.4 percent.[10] A study by Stinson et al. found that 6.2 percent of adult Americans had suffered from narcissistic personality disorder sometime in their lives, and that number included 11.6 percent of men in their twenties.[11] Twenge and Campbell studied what they referred to as the growing epidemic of narcissism, and found that narcissistic personality disorder appears to be increasing in the American culture. They found large increases in narcissism among students from the 1960s onward. They predicted that, if Americans in their 20s continue on the same trajectory, more than half will develop narcissistic personality disorder by the time they are 65.[12]

---

[9] Blanco et al., "Mental Health of College Students," 1433, 1435.

[10] Gross et al., "Borderline Personality Disorder in Primary Care," 53.

[11] Stinson et al., "Prevalence, Correlates, Disability," 1036.

[12] Twenge, *The Narcissism Epidemic*, 36.

The true incidence of cluster B personality disorders in the population is unknown for several reasons. People who have these disorders have little to no self-insight and seldom seek treatment for a personality disorder. They might see a therapist because they are depressed or because they think that someone is taking advantage of them. If an individual with relatively better coping skills does seek treatment for his cluster B personality disorder, it's likely that a crisis in some significant area of his life has propelled him into treatment. Perhaps he has encountered some pressure within his social system, e.g., his spouse has threatened to divorce him if he doesn't get help.

Repeatedly being stung by people with cluster B personality disorders can have long-term effects. The largest group seen by counselors is likely composed of people who have been stung by those with these disorders. Individuals seeking help are often caught in situations, marriages, workplaces or friendships in which they have been affected or are being controlled by someone who has an undiagnosed cluster B personality disorder.

Mental health professionals with counseling practices do see some of the more severe cluster B personality disorders in people with the poorest coping skills. However, those visits are usually mandated by the court system.

ALEX

"I am a prison counselor, so if someone with a cluster B personality disorder comes to see me, it is because that person is in distress and will drop out of treatment as soon as the distress has passed. When prisoners with cluster B disorders are required to see me, the prisoners revel in the fact that I've been forced to see them, and later they enjoy talking about how ineffective and worthless I am. Outside of prison that game quickly gets stale, and the person with the cluster B disorder would stop seeing a counselor."

Continuum of Severity: From Behaviors to Severe Personality Disorders

Another factor making it difficult to diagnose cluster B personality disorders is that behaviors that define these disorders exist within a wide range of intensity. An article in the *Journal of Personality Disorders* provides a helpful classification of borderline personality disorder by dividing it into three groups that speak to a continuum of severity.[13] Group one is self destructive with low levels of antisocial, paranoid and aggressive behaviors. Group two has more paranoia, and group three has severe antisocial and aggressive traits.

Princess Diana, as portrayed in the book *Diana in Search of Herself: Portrait of a Troubled Princess*, was described as having an unstable sense of self and ricocheting extremes of love and devaluation that typify borderline personality disorder. The book also mentions specific self-destructive behaviors such as throwing herself down a flight of stairs when she was pregnant and

[13] Lenzenweger et al., "Refining the Borderline Personality Disorder Phenotype," 325.

bulimia.[14] If these behaviors actually occurred, her behaviors would fall within group one.

At the extreme, Adolf Hitler had an unstable sense of self, extreme paranoia, extreme aggression and no conscience. Hitler would be as far into group three as you could get. Although these two people displayed their personality characteristics in very different ways, each of them likely had a fear of abandonment and an identity disturbance that were at the core of their behaviors. They each re-created an identity. Hitler established himself as savior of the Germanic population and slaughtered millions of innocent people. Diana established herself as a benevolent person by being a loving mother and a spokesperson for various charities.

We view the "B" behaviors as a *sometimes-progressive* trajectory: from occasional "B" behaviors that everyone exhibits from time to time; to repeated patterns of "B" behaviors that have some social consequences; to defined groupings of specific thinking, feeling and behaving that are enduring, pervasive and cause distress in important areas of a person's life; to defined groupings of specific thinking, feeling and behaving that cause severe distress injury or death to individuals or segments of society. Individuals can move back and forth on this trajectory.

Some behaviors are considered acceptable in certain circumstances, such as lying to avoid hurting someone's feelings. In some microenvironments, lying is recognized and accepted as part of doing business. Lying behaviors that are malicious, like lying that threatens someone's reputation, livelihood or other significant aspect of life, are at the middle and far end of the intensity scale. Most cultures would consider such behaviors as unacceptable.

---

[14] Smith, *Diana in Search of Herself*, 129, 173–85, 364, 366.

We also believe that each of the cluster B personality disorders is related, so that individuals with these disorders often exhibit some symptoms characteristic of each of the four cluster B disorders. Persons with consistent and specific patterns of "B" behaviors cross the line into the realm of personality disorders. The inner circle represents the psychopath. A psychopath might exhibit a pattern of extreme behaviors from one or all of the disorders within the cluster B personalities. Those who are bereft of conscience can justify anything. These people have the potential to exhibit behaviors severe enough to be considered psychopathic.

People wonder if anyone who exhibits a few of the behaviors typical of the cluster B personality disorders can turn into a psychopath. Charles Manson, a convicted murderer, picked up young women who were runaways, lured them into his cult, and pressured some of them to become murderers. Somehow he instinctively knew which ones he could convince to cross that line. Although all of us allow some of our maladaptive and manipulative traits to surface from time to time, most of us have the ability to self-reflect and to correct our behavior. We also surround ourselves with friends and loved ones who will give us honest feedback.

Theoretically, anyone with a cluster B personality disorder (diagnosed or not) could turn into a malignant psychopath. Those who consistently exhibit more-extreme versions of these cluster B behaviors need more external pressure to self-correct than people who occasionally exhibit a few of the mild cluster B behaviors. They also have to be able to form a trusting relationship with someone who is willing and able to give them honest feedback.

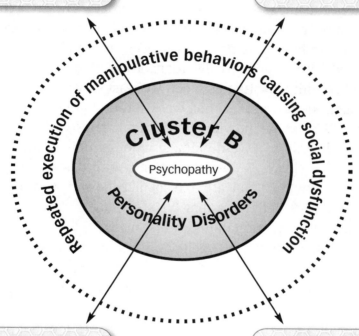

Occasional Narcissistic Behaviors

arrogant, materialistic, entitled, interpersonally exploitive, aggressive when insulted, no interest in emotional closeness

Occasional Histrionic Behaviors

overly dramatic, seductive, vague, shallow, suggestible, craves attention

Repeated execution of manipulative behaviors causing social dysfunction

Cluster B

Psychopathy

Personality Disorders

Occasional Antisocial Behaviors

initially charming, deceitful, impulsive, irritable, reckless diregard for others, irresponsible, no remorse

Occasional Borderline Behaviors

impulsive, unstable sense of self, unstable emotions (rapidly switches from over-idealizing and devaluing), rageful, self-destructive, often paranoid

FIGURE 1: Increasing Incidence and Severity of "B" Behaviors

If Personality Disorders Are So Hard to Diagnose, How Can We Identify and Avoid These Stinging Behaviors?

In this chapter we have discussed the difficulties in diagnosing and treating cluster B personality disorders and the range of behaviors encompassed within these disorders. The fact remains that most people who consistently exhibit patterns of destructive manipulative behaviors have never been, nor will they ever be, diagnosed with personality disorders. Their manipulative behaviors will continue to sting us when we least expect it.

Through the rest of this book we will refer to these individuals as "B"s. "B"s can be individuals with undiagnosed cluster B personality disorders or individuals who exhibit some of the manipulative cluster B traits consistently and destructively. It is most important that you learn to recognize the wide severity range of manipulative behaviors that "B"s employ and also come to understand their permutations and nuances.

When you encounter "B" behaviors it's normal to try to figure out the cause of your pain. Typically, coworkers, acquaintances or friends will roll their eyes if you suggest a diagnostic label because many of us are taught, "If you can't say anything nice, you shouldn't say anything at all." However, this does not prevent us from observing "B" behaviors, looking for patterns, and tallying the potential damage from doing nothing.

It's not our intention to label or diagnose cluster B personality disorders in the people portrayed in our stories. Rather, we are interested in how these manipulative behaviors affect others. We are also interested in the social and communication patterns that "B"s introduce into groups. It is likely that through the course of your life, people who regularly exhibit "B" behaviors will adversely affect you. The ability to recognize characteristic "B" patterns of behavior will help you plan strategies to cope with them.

Before we continue, we will give more detailed examples of some typical "B" behaviors.

Antisocial (a.k.a. Sociopathic) Behaviors

Those with antisocial (also referred to as sociopathic) behaviors exploit people and situations. Individuals consistently exhibiting this pattern of "B" behaviors tend to be deceitful opportunists, superficial, glib and impulsive. They will bend social norms to their advantage. Erich Fromm coined the term "malignant narcissism" to describe sociopathy.[15] Otto Kernberg pointed out that the antisocial personality was fundamentally narcissism without morality, and that malignant narcissism includes a sadistic element, creating, in essence, a sadistic psychopath.[16] However, not all persons with antisocial behaviors are murderers or rapists. There are many ways to get your kicks when you have either a limited conscience or no conscience at all.

In 2008 Bernie Madoff confessed to using an intricate Ponzi scheme to defraud investors, many his purported friends.[17] The fact that the fraud continued for many years and involved $50 billion provides some appreciation for how long someone with "B" behaviors can go on stinging before he gets caught. The Washington Post reported that Madoff boasted he had close ties to the Securities and Exchange Commission regulators.[18] The Post also reported that an SEC staffer who was onto Madoff's scheme in 2004 was reassigned to another case. Madoff's victims clamored

---

[15] Fromm, *The Heart of Man.*

[16] Kernberg, "Factors in the Psychoanalytic Treatment," 51–85.

[17] "Bernard Madoff Biography," biography.com/articles/Bernard-Madoff-466366

[18] Goldfarb, "Staffer at SEC Had Warned of Madoff," washingtonpost.com

to be included in his "high-returns" scheme, and most claimed to be shocked to find out how they had been duped, even though few questioned their extraordinary returns.

Few schemes are as pervasive or elaborate as Madoff's. When those with antisocial behaviors get caught, however, they are never sorry for what they did. They are only sorry for their own suffering as a consequence of getting caught. Clifford Irving wrote an auto-biography about Howard Hughes that was purely fiction and then lied about it. He spent 17 months in jail for fraud. Years later, in an interview on CBS, Irving admitted he had done it, paid the price and declared it to be over. In response to Mike Wallace asking him if he had any regrets, Irving replied, "If you put a tightrope across the canyon and you walk it and it breaks, you don't regret what prompted you to walk the rope. You regret that it broke."[19]

We often think that most people who consistently exhibit anti-social behaviors are either in jail or belong in jail. But many of these people are functioning as members of our communities, businesses, churches, schools, clinics and so forth. Less heinous or pervasive acts by people who consistently exhibit antisocial behaviors can also be devastating to smaller groups than those hurt by Madoff. Often, there are early clues to antisocial behaviors that we can attend to or choose to ignore. The following is an example that should have provided an early clue to a group get-ting acquainted with their new boss.

[19] "Bernard Madoff Biography," biography.com/articles/Bernard-Madoff-466366

MARNIE

"One of the first times I encountered my former boss, he was meeting with members of our group and telling the story about a conference at a swank hotel. His flight had been cancelled, so he was forced to spend an extra night in the hotel. The hotel happened to be the site of a major film awards ceremony. My boss went on to say that the lobby and conference center were filled with actors. As he had a lot of time on his hands, he wandered around the hotel. He stumbled upon the pressroom, and on a whim he took a notepad and pretended to be a reporter and interviewed several actors. He described the outfits and tattoos in detail. Everyone around the table was howling because as he described the situation, it was very funny.

"I remember being amazed that this high-powered executive would do such a thing. I admired him for having the guts to do what he did. I didn't think anymore about the story until years later, when my former boss was forced out for inappropriate behavior with a subordinate colleague. It was clear that he had lied multiple times, and I was left wondering if there was any truth to the story that this charming man told about the awards night. With the clarity of hindsight, I now realize that story, true or not, should've been a warning sign that I had chosen to ignore."

Narcissistic Behaviors

Like antisocial behaviors, narcissistic behaviors are superficial and exploitative. Where antisocial behaviors tend to be impulsive, however, narcissistic behaviors are not. Those who consistently exhibit narcissistic behaviors have an image they want to portray and intentionally surround themselves with people who will reflect the image they have of themselves. If you are someone who heaps praise on such a person, you will have your foot in the door. This is only if that person values your praise, however. If you aren't a person who is prone to effusive praise, or if the narcissist views you as a potential threat, you risk becoming dust under his feet.

Narcissistic behavior can be overt or covert. According to Eleanor Payson, people with narcissistic traits can pursue their grandiose needs by being arrogant and haughty or they might disguise their haughtiness.[20] A covert narcissist might seek power under the guise of being a benefit to humanity but will require eternal loyalty and appreciation for what he does for you. According to Payson, some covert narcissists see themselves as great but never do anything to achieve the greatness to which they aspire.[21] Some narcissists will wall themselves off from others and choose a lonely existence because they believe they are so great that no one could truly appreciate how special they are.

Those with narcissistic traits selectively display "B" behaviors to people they consider to be inferior or threatening. Narcissists tend to have excessive pride in their achievements and a disdain for the achievements of others. People with narcissistic behaviors who are high-functioning are interpersonally exploitative, don't display their emotions, and seldom cry. They don't like to show a weak side, so they will likely cover up their personal illnesses because they believe they've achieved perfection, and don't like seeing themselves as vulnerable. They spend an inordinate amount of time and energy making sure that they put only their best foot forward.

---

[20] Payson, *The Wizard of Oz and Other Narcissists*, 27.
[21] Ibid., 28.

GILBERT

"As a young man I ran a bill collection agency. My friend, another bill collector, was lamenting that he had been trying to collect a bill from a famous author who was known for not paying his bills. I bet him that I could collect the money. My friend, fed up with the struggles he had with the author, told me that if I could collect the money, I could keep it. So one day while this man was teaching a class, I burst into the lecture room and marched down the aisle as he was speaking, and demanded the money. The author paid up and I kept the money."

ABOUT THIS CASE STUDY

Believing that you are too important to pay your bills is a narcissistic behavior. In Gilbert's story, the author only did the right thing when he was faced with being viewed publicly as imperfect.

SETH

"I was an administrative assistant and the office historian. During a period of organizational change, I thought it would be useful for employees to recall our department's history. I collected old photos of group functions and made a display on a bulletin board in the conference room. Each time I went into the conference room, several of the pictures were lying face down on the ledge. This puzzled me until I realized that each picture contained only one common group member, Sonia. Over the next few years, I watched Sonia remaking her image from a slightly overweight brunette who displayed no sense of fashion into a sleek, fashionable redhead. Years later, I discovered that

Sonia's desire was to become the head of the company. Sonia wanted everyone to remember her not as she was but as she wanted to be. Only later did I come to understand this little incident as a warning, because on her journey to the top, Sonia stepped on everyone who got in her way.

"I recall another occasion when Sonia needed major surgery. On the day of her surgery, some of her colleagues decided to bring her flowers. When they walked into her room a few hours after surgery, Sonia was awaiting them dressed in her street clothes in full makeup, even though she was several days from discharge."

ABOUT THIS CASE STUDY ————————————————————

Because of her narcissistic traits, Sonia couldn't allow herself to be seen as imperfect, weak, or in any way less than her coworkers.

Borderline Behaviors

People who consistently exhibit borderline behaviors tend to be complex and difficult to understand. Despite an underlying narcissism, they often have an unstable self-image, fear abandonment, and may be paranoid. People who consistently exhibit borderline behaviors might charm you into helping them. At the same time, they might appear to others as stubborn, negative, easily slighted, chronically offended or indignant. They are difficult to befriend because they are continually pulling you close and just as quickly pushing you away. They often appear needy as some crisis, real or imagined, is always looming. They thrive on chaos. They may appear depressed one minute and elated or even maniacal the next. One way to distinguish them from those with manic depression is the rapid speed with which people who exhibit borderline behaviors switch between the two states.

Someone who exhibits these behaviors might lead you to tread lightly so that you don't upset them. They will also leave you feeling manipulated. People with a strong need to take care of others are attracted to people with borderline behaviors. Sometimes those with a strong need to take care of others also exhibit borderline behaviors. These include professionals who frequently overstep their professional boundaries and go the extra mile for preferred clients or patients but not for others.

In the movie *Holy Smoke*, Kate Winslet plays a cult member with borderline behaviors and Harvey Keitel plays a deprogrammer who exhibits narcissistic pride in his achievements. Keitel's character is hired to get Winslet's character to denounce the cult. Winslet's character first seduces Keitel's character to have sex with her, subsequently pushes him away by telling him that he is old and ugly, and then seduces him again. For most of the movie, Keitel's character actually thinks that he's helping her, when, in fact, Winslet's character has the upper hand. Borderline behaviors can be subtle and very seductive and leave you feeling disoriented. This movie also shows how someone with narcissistic behaviors can be attracted to a person with borderline behaviors.

The film *Fatal Attraction* is another Hollywood portrayal of borderline behaviors. Glenn Close's character lures in Michael Douglas's character by using sex and stroking his narcissism, after which she takes him on a rollercoaster ride that ends dramatically with her death after she destroys his life.

TROY

"I had a friend, Ashley, and when she had surgery I would walk her dogs. She drank too much and I knew it, but we started dating. We dated for two years, and our relationship was full of highs and lows. During the highs, Ashley and I would have great sex, and things would seem stable. During the lows, Ashley would drink heavily, become difficult, and threaten suicide whenever I suggested breaking up with her. At a holiday party at my parent's home, Ashley got drunk and stood at the top of the stairs and shouted, "Troy won't have my baby!" I was horrified. When Ashley would call and threaten to hurt herself, I would be concerned and we would get back together.

"Our whole relationship was defined by these cycles. Sex with Ashley was great, and she used it to manipulate me. It kept me coming back. Finally, I saw a pattern in what she was doing and ended our relationship. She never actually hurt herself, and as we stayed in touch in later years, she never acknowledged her manipulative behavior."

Histrionic Behaviors

Persons who consistently exhibit histrionic behaviors also have narcissism at their core and feel unappreciated when they aren't the center of attention. Their self-esteem depends on the approval of others. Those with histrionic behaviors are dramatic performers, provocative and have flowery speech patterns. Many television news pundits have adopted histrionic behaviors, portraying insignificant news events as terrible tragedies or dastardly deeds. Like narcissistic and antisocial "B"s, people with patterns of histrionic behaviors have shallow emotions, even though they act like they don't. Unlike narcissistic and antisocial "B"s, those with histrionic behaviors believe that relationships are more significant than they really are.

Various blogs reveal that many people with histrionic behaviors have discovered the Internet. A histrionic "B" could never have enough friends on Facebook, and the more followers a histrionic "B" can attract on Twitter, the better she can feel about herself. Histrionic "B"s who are inclined to be sexually provocative can be involved in all kinds of pornographic websites, dating services and social chat rooms. It doesn't matter if they are married or have a real relationship. What matters is that their newfound friends think they are special and beautiful and wonderful. Since histrionic "B"s typically draw attention to themselves by their appearance, they are likely to send photos over the Internet, and some of those photos can be highly inappropriate. Like narcissistic "B"s, they will become very upset by any remark that they perceive as critical of them.

Many reality show contestants exhibit histrionic behaviors. In 2008, the governor of Illinois was arrested for political corruption.[22] Shortly afterward, the former governor and his wife dressed and acted in a way that kept them at the center of attention. As their spotlight was waning, they each participated as contestants in reality shows.

In 2009 news outlets reported on a couple that achieved brief fame for crashing a White House State Dinner while striving to be on a reality television show. The couple demonstrated a need to be the center of attention. When confronted, they offered evidence that they had an invitation. The materials they offered as proof, however, were reported as vague. People who knew the couple stated that the couple had a history of crashing high-profile events.[23]

[22] Highlights: Rod Blagojevich, chicagotribune.com
[23] Thomas, di Nies & Dwyer, "White House Crashers," abcnews.go.com

Some politicians exhibit histrionic behaviors. When a would-be politician makes vague comments about everything, even when he doesn't know what he is talking about, he might be a histrionic or narcissistic "B." When a politician makes himself present everywhere, suggesting he might be a candidate without actually announcing his candidacy, suspect that he might be a histrionic "B."

GEORGIA

"I counseled an employee who exhibited negative body language at meetings. He would cross his arms, make sour faces and roll his eyes when he disagreed with someone on the team. His body language would negatively affect the direction of the team's problem solving. The day after I counseled him, the employee returned to work and said that he had stood in front of his mirror all night and was unable to see any of the negative body language that he had been accused of and didn't know what I was talking about. The more I tried to explain, the more confused he seemed to be. He was not able to key into my specifics, and therefore it was impossible for him to identify how he could correct the problem."

JOHN

"Sam, the vice president of the union, had a reputation for helping people. He did extraordinary things for other people that no one else would do. When a dispute occurred within the union regarding meeting attendance, he volunteered to work on rewriting the policy. So I put him in charge of the rewrite but then he refused to help. Instead of writing the objectives, he just kept saying that he disliked the policy. He would go round and round and was never able to come up with specifics about what he disliked or how to fix the problem. I would find a solution and suggest he write it up this way, and then we would go back to the beginning. Finally, I told him to come up with a solution. He quit the union.

"Sam then started volunteering to help people, especially women. Women would say, 'Oh, do you know Sam? He is amazing.' He seemed to find his niche, where he could be the center of attention, be liked and save people without following specific rules."

STEWART

"I had a female colleague who dressed very suggestively at work. This was a law office where serious business was conducted. She had accused several clients of coming on to her but gave no specifics. One day she told me that her physician had made a pass at her during a physical exam. I was increasingly afraid of her and realized I should never be alone with her out of fear that she would accuse me of something."

ABOUT THESE CASE STUDIES ——————————————

The persons encountered by Georgia, John and Stewart demon-strated the vague thought patterns that are consistent with histrionic behaviors. Stewart was smart to keep his distance from his colleague. The difficulties of discussing these patterns with those who have them can be very frustrating for anyone trying to supervise or advise them. These patterns can be espe-cially destructive to a group effort.

Changing Behaviors

Sometimes seemingly normal people appear to drastically change their behaviors. Imagine an individual who exhibits narcissistic behaviors and is proud that he is a level ahead of you on the orga-nizational ladder but is cordial and even appears to try to help your career. One day you are promoted to the next level and are now his equal. He suddenly feels threatened by you and begins to actively undermine your position in the organization by telling lies about your job performance or even implying that you engaged in unlawful behavior. Is this person just exhibiting occa-sional narcissistic behaviors or has he stepped over the line and become a narcissistic or antisocial "B"?

EILEEN

"I helped a woman I had known peripherally throughout my career get hired into our company. She was knowledgeable and strong, and I thought she would be a good fit for our organization. Once she started, we got along well. I shared information with her, and she seemed receptive. Eventually we were asked to share leadership on a project. She then verbally attacked me in public, switched positions, and always took an opposite position from mine. It became impossible to accomplish anything because of the roadblocks she was creating. I was starting to feel a bit crazy because the ground kept shifting. I felt like she used me to get into a leadership position and then she tried to step right over me."

ABOUT THIS CASE STUDY

Eileen was blindsided by a "B" who was determined to get to the top at all costs. High-functioning "B"s are skillful at hiding their stinging behaviors from people they want to impress. If this "B" offered some clues to her future behavior, Eileen didn't notice them until it was too late.

MANDY

"In one of my workshops a team physician was extremely gregarious and engaging. He appeared to have high-level knowledge of the subject and always had an answer that appeared to take the best interests of the team into consideration. Months later, at a conference in another part of the country, one of the nurses from the previous workshop approached the podium where I was standing. She wanted me to know that the team physician who was behaving in such a benevolent and mature manner at my team workshop was the biggest problem on the team. He berated other team members and wouldn't work with the team to solve complex problems."

ABOUT THIS CASE STUDY ⸻⸻⸻⸻⸻⸻⸻⸻

High-functioning "B"s can readily mask manipulative behaviors as learned "professional" behaviors. Many high-functioning "B"s are fascinated with psychology and take workshops and courses to help them increase their proficiency at reading the behavior of others. In our workshops it's common for "B"s to let everyone else know that they have all the answers.

"B"s of Many Colors

While some "B"s are caught in illegal acts, many "B"s function as upstanding citizens. Truman Capote, as portrayed in the movie *Capote*,[24] had been meeting in prison with Perry Smith, one of the murderers of the Clutter family. Capote had been interviewing this man periodically and easily drew comparisons between his own upbringing and the killer's. He finally realized that there was very little separation between his socially acceptable life and Smith's life in prison. Capote, who had some awareness of his own lying, overly dramatic and alcoholic behaviors, turned to Perry Smith and said, "We grew up in the same house; you went out the back door and I went out the front." Capote and Smith had similar upbringings and had developed similar traits. Perhaps he realized there was a fine line between his success and Perry Smith's fate.

[24] *Capote*, Miller, 2005.

"B"s who are relatively high-functioning members of society can be very bright and cunningly nasty. It is equally interesting how "B"s can behave badly and then turn around and appear totally charming. Usually such individuals cannot see their true selves because something in their developmental past creates a wall that prevents self-reflection.

The Seductiveness of "B"s

The ability of "B"s to draw people in to their stinging nests is legendary. A tragic example of this phenomenon is the story of Jim Jones, the founder of the Peoples Temple, a cult masquerading as a religious sect. From the time he realized (in his early 20s) that he could push Marxist beliefs by disguising them as a religion, Jim Jones was on a roll. He started the process by creating an idealized public image as a savior for downtrodden blacks and other disenfranchised members of society. On his journey, Jones became politically active and had contact with many elected officials and important people, including Walter Mondale, Rosalyn Carter, Harvey Milk and the mayor of San Francisco, George Moscone.

In the 1970s Jones began preaching that he was the reincarnation of Jesus of Nazareth, Mahatma Gandhi, Buddha, Vladimir Lenin and Father Divine.[25] In the PBS documentary *Jonestown: The Life and Death of Peoples Temple*, former Temple member Hue Fortson, Jr. quoted Jones as saying, "What you need to believe in is what you can see...If you see me as your friend, I'll be your friend. If you see me as your father, I'll be your father, for those of you that don't have a father...If you see me as your savior, I'll be your savior. If you see me as your God, I'll be your God."[26] Over the years, defectors from the cult told their stories of Jones' abuse,

[25] The Jonestown Institute, http://jonestown.sdsu.edu
[26] *Jonestown: The Life and Death of Peoples Temple*. PBS documentary, 2009.

sexual misconduct and lies. Jones was successful in persuading his friends in high places, however, that these stories were not true.

When Congressman Leo Ryan and an entourage of reporters finally were convinced to visit the cult in November 1978, Jones had Ryan and the others killed. Following the murders, Jones and his inner circle both encouraged and then forced more than 900 cult members to drink grape flavored cyanide. In the *Witness to Jonestown* documentary, it is made clear that Jones was a person who could quickly size people up and immediately know what was important to them.[27] Jones instinctively knew which buttons to push to gain someone's allegiance. But by the time the person figured out what had happened, it was too late.

"B"s want to convince others that they (the "B"s) are extraordinary and that people should do extraordinary things to get them what they (the "B"s) want. A classic behavior of "B"s is to draw you in by zeroing in on your vulnerabilities and heaping praise on you so that you feel special and engage with them. They convince you that you need them to help you get what you want. Then after luring you into their "B's" nest, they will make sure you give them what they want, e.g., praise, information about a competitor, or a blind eye to their misdeads.

"B"s might also try to convince you that they are special in some area and that you need to make special adaptations for them, such as changing rules or altering boundaries to get them what they want. An example of something they might ask you to do is to ignore a company policy requiring a background check— because it would take too long, so they might not accept the job. Sometimes they establish themselves as special or as having something you want. Then they ignore you, so you go out of your way to get them to like you or to even notice you.

---

[27] *Witness to Jonestown.* MSNBC documentary, 2008.

OLIVIA

"As a manager, potential employees who appear exceptionally competent challenge me. When someone who is self-assured, clever and engaging enters the picture, I'm amazed at how I can end up breaking my own rules and becoming my worst enemy. I guess I'm a sucker for people who seem highly qualified and ask for special accommodations. A candidate might make herself seem so special that I can't afford not to hire her. On occasion I have gone to human resources (HR) to increase a candidate's starting salary, proving to the candidate that he is special enough for me to bend the rules.

"One candidate wanted a salary that was only a few hundred dollars higher than what we could pay. She would not sway, and I ended up begging HR to make an exception. HR would not, and she didn't take the job. It took me a long time to realize that she was not the right person for the job, and if she really wanted the job, she would've accepted the minor difference in salary. Whenever we made exceptions for candidates because we thought they were extraordinary, they almost always ended up wreaking havoc."

ABOUT THIS CASE STUDY

Olivia clearly learned from her past mistakes, realizing that being asked to bend the rules for someone might be a clue to their future behavior.

Why Do We Fall for "B"s?

The stories of "B"s reveal a lot about why we succumb to their behaviors. Sometimes "B"s simply tell us what we want to hear. Other times, hanging out with someone we think is important, cool, good looking or at the forefront of something new reflects well on us, so we are drawn to these people. Many "B"s are skilled enough to cover their "B" behaviors in front of certain people who they regard as special. For the people needed to complete their manipulative schemes, "B"s will don whatever mask is required for the occasion. Fortunately, it is the rare "B" who can play the game forever, and if you are astute, you will notice slips in behavior, attitude or demeanor. Unfortunately, highly skilled "B"s will surround themselves with a group (some who are also "B"s) to protect themselves.

Perhaps an individual exhibits none or only a few "B" behaviors until he feels threatened by something you do or say, or even by the look on your face. Some people who get stung by a "B" survive and learn from their experience. Others might find themselves so entwined in a relationship with a "B" that they don't know how to extract themselves or to even question what really happened. They may downplay the experience, think they imagined it and start to feel a little crazy. And still others, unaware that they have been stung, unwittingly step into the "B's" nest.

Most of us are susceptible to specific "B" behaviors. We refer to these vulnerabilities, unique to each of us, as our Achilles' heels. A clever "B" has an uncanny ability to recognize our vulnerabilities. A narcissistic "B" understands the value of praise. If a "B" values you either because he needs you or thinks you are special and by associating with you he too will be special, he will praise you. If you see yourself as an underdog or victim and a narcissistic "B" praises you, you are likely hooked. Histrionic, borderline and antisocial "B"s often enter an interaction as a victim. If you happen to enjoy rescuing people, you can be quickly drawn in to their drama. Beware! All of them can just as quickly turn from victims to persecutors.

SUMMARY

IN THIS CHAPTER WE PRESENTED A BRIEF DESCRIPTION OF the cluster B personality disorders and outlined common "B" behaviors. We have demonstrated how difficult it is to diagnose and treat a cluster B personality disorder and have therefore chosen not to diagnose those who exhibit "B" behaviors. We proposed that "B" behaviors occur on a continuum. All people occasionally exhibit "B" behaviors. Some exhibit them more than others and their "B" behaviors form specific patterns. The behaviors of these "B"s might stay in the mild range or progress to cause severe consequences for others. We presented this chapter as a necessary background for the rest of the book, which focuses on the recipients of "B" behaviors.

In subsequent chapters we will identify some of the many permutations of "B"s and share stories from persons with diverse backgrounds. We encourage you, the reader, to observe the patterns in these behaviors. While the stories come from different settings and involve different players, they have similar themes and patterns. The stories are disguised and should be viewed as archetypal stories to remember as you encounter similar behavioral patterns.

It's easy to dismiss the behavior of a "B" as a minor annoyance. Perhaps it is helpful to think of ground bees that build their nests in inconspicuous places where you least expect them. Passing by, you might get stung and, not knowing where the sting came from, you might be unsure if you were stung at all. You might decide to ignore the sting and go on with your business. It's only when you step directly on the nest that you will be stung with the nest's full force. Hopefully, early recognition of the patterns of "B"s will help you avoid multiple stings. By identifying the patterns of the stinging "B"s at an early stage, you can counter the manipulative behaviors and make a difference for yourself and those around you.

CHAPTER TWO

Where It All Begins

"At times truth may not seem probable."
NICOLAS BOILEAU

Lessons Learned from Childhood

An article described an actress who sustained a facial scar at age five when someone slashed her with a knife while she was playing in her front yard. This prompted a discussion with three little girls. We asked Mia, age five, if anyone had ever been mean to her. She said that somebody had pushed her down on the playground the day before, but Mia seemed to dismiss it like it was an everyday occurrence. Gabriela, age seven, said that her friend had stolen her birthday money during her birthday party, and last week this same friend had scratched Gabriela's face with a piece of ice when they were playing at school. Gabriela went on to say, "She is still my friend." Isabel, age eight, could not remember anyone having been mean to her.

Several weeks later Mia was talking to her mother and out of the blue said, "Do you know what is weird about Evi? She told me she never wanted to talk to me again. But Evi came over to me later and hugged me." Is Mia becoming aware that behavior

isn't always straightforward? That people sometimes say one thing while doing the opposite and that some people can't be trusted?

Does anyone make it through life unscathed by manipulative behavior? The answer is no. It's likely that no one escapes being betrayed, having their trust violated, being stung by someone they are familiar with, or being caught in a nasty game played by someone they might not even know. Out of curiosity we asked some adults if they remembered being stung or manipulated early in life. Some respondents also reflected on lessons they learned from their experiences.

DARCY

"I was in third grade during the Great Depression. A group of kids was taking swimming lessons at the high school. Everyone was taking the bus, and there was a small fee. I didn't have any money but knew that my parents had a twenty-dollar bill under their mattress, and I took it for bus money. After swimming, I returned to my locker and found that the change from the twenty dollars was gone. I never knew for sure who stole the money but I believe that it was the one girl I did not know very well. I was sure that none of my friends had taken it.

"Over 60 years later I can still remember the girl's name. My parents punished me by making me give them the savings bond that I had been contributing to for years, because they needed the money. I am still haunted by the unknown person who stole the money and was never held accountable."

MICHELLE

"I remember being stung over fifty years ago. I was in second grade walking home from a violin lesson one January afternoon. Two boys jumped out from a snow bank, threw me to the ground, and stomped on me while throwing snow in my face. One of the boys warned me to stop taking violin lessons. Even at age seven, I thought it was strange, because I had heard this boy play the violin and I thought that he was quite good. Although I was frightened by this incident, I never reported it to an adult. However, as a result of this assault I tried to convince my mother to stop paying for my violin lessons. I didn't do this directly, of course, fearing I would be forced to tell her about the attack. Instead, I tried to avoid practicing the violin, hoping that my mother would tire of nagging me and let me quit. To my mother's credit, she was relentless in her crusade to keep me practicing. Aside from some name-calling, this boy never assaulted me again. Since he was a grade behind me, I was able to ignore him until high school.

"In high school we were both part of an ensemble, and this boy and I were often assigned to play violin duets together. The pieces were difficult and required a lot of practice. The boy was always friendly in our high school encounters but he never apologized for his previous behavior.

"I would have forgotten this seemingly minor incident except that years later, I discovered that the same boy who assaulted me had been incarcerated as an adult for the sexual assault of a child. I now wonder if his assault on me was an indicator of his future behavior. I also wonder about the boy who accompanied him on that snowy day in January. Was he a willing participant? And what happened to him? And finally, what would have been different if, instead of hiding the incident from my parents, I had told them the truth? Would they have brushed off the episode or would they have spoken to the violin teacher or perhaps to the boy's parents? There is no way to know the answers to these questions."

ABOUT THIS CASE STUDY ———————————————————

This story highlights how important it is for adults to sense hurt in children. It's common for children to avoid talking to adults about their classmates' hurtful behaviors. It's the wise parent or teacher who can sense a child's distress and help them open up and discuss a variety of responses to malicious behaviors.

One of the most fascinating things about some of the stories we collected is that, while seemingly insignificant in the grand scheme of a person's life, these violations of trust made indelible marks on peoples' psyches. People who shared their stories quickly recalled events that had happened 20, 30, 50 and even 70 years before. Although many people prefaced their stories by saying that they were trivial, they had little trouble recalling them. It is one thing for a child to recall an insult that happened this week on the playground. It is another for an adult to remember an affront that occurred 50 years ago.

Some people that we interviewed appeared to understand manipulative behaviors at an early age, and most who remembered stories admitted to becoming less trusting or acting differently as a result of being stung. Other people related childhood stories of being stung to later being manipulated as an adult. It's interesting to see how many of the themes from childhood recur as adults, only in more-complex forms.

CROSBY

"I remember being in first or second grade, walking home from the neighborhood elementary school, when a kid, probably two years older than I was, made me stand in a hole where a stump had just been removed. It was a big hole, and the boy told me if I left the hole without his permission, he would beat me up. I recall standing in the hole, crying, while kids that I knew from school paraded by on their way home. I felt terrified of this older kid and I felt humiliated being seen by the other kids this way.

"After I had some professional and life experience under my belt, I started working in a small department in a large company. My boss could best be described as Dr. Jekyll and Mr. Hyde. He acted as though all his employees were his young charges and his job was to mold us. He loved to come to the rescue. If something stressful or intense was happening, he wanted to be in charge of fixing it and be the reason for its success. He could seem like the best boss because he would bend over backward for you. When I think of it, it often involved him breaking a rule.

"He would tell you to take some time off even if you were out of time off because he acted like he wanted to care for you or save you. But the very next day, he would make you feel like you were going to the principal's office. He had a way of making you feel small. He made me doubt myself, and I never felt confident in his presence. He would build staff up just to knock them down. There was definitely some intimidation. When I would go in to my office I would take note of whether his office was dark, and if it was, I felt instant relief. If I heard he would be out for the day, a huge weight would be lifted. If his light was on, I felt dread. I also felt trapped because my wife and I were expecting our first child, and I needed this job.

43

As a child standing in the hole, I felt totally alone, and these incidents with my boss resurrected those feelings of helplessness. Fortunately, the workers in our department were united in that we were all onto our boss. This mutual support from the people that I worked with who were also suffering is the only thing that made that job tolerable."

ROXANNE

"When I was in grade school I had two best friends, and the three of us always hung out. One day my two 'friends' teamed up and tried to push me to the ground. They would knee me in the back when we were on the bus. They began sharing intimate secrets that I had told them by writing them in the frost on the windows of the bus. One of these girls was in a vulnerable state, because her house had just burned down. The other seemed to be the ringleader.

"Years later, the ringleader cheated on her fiancée and ran off with the guy with whom she had cheated. Then she married her ex-fiancée. Their marriage didn't last long. I still live in the same small town, so as an adult I have maintained a very superficial relationship with the ringleader to avoid personal discomfort. This woman is a friend of my other friends, and none of my other friends believes she is capable of doing the things I witnessed. This ringleader has an ability to manipulate her way into any group. As a result, if I want to be in the group, I have learned that I need to get along with this woman on some level."

MADISON

"When I was in fourth grade I transferred to a new elementary school and started to make friends. One of my new friends told me that I could join her group if I would agree to stop being a friend to some of the girls who were already my friends. I silently refused and was never part of the group that went on to become the most popular group in middle school and high school. In seventh grade, a boy I considered a friend wrote me a note in math class asking me to go steady with him. When I said no, uncomfortably, he stopped being my friend. In ninth grade, a boy in my class walked up to me on a bus, totally unprovoked, stood right in my face, and told me that I was the most ugly person he had ever seen. I simply walked away.

"Although these were all notable events in my early life, none was life altering. I felt there was an element of choice involved in each of these situations. Choosing my group of friends, choosing my boyfriend and choosing to walk away from someone calling me ugly all felt like what I had to do to stay true to myself."

ABOUT THESE CASE STUDIES

Madison recognized that the behaviors directed at her were manipulative. Roxanne and Madison recognized that they could choose how to react to stinging behaviors. If we focus on identifying our choices in a situation, we can go a long way toward coping with the aftermath of manipulative behaviors directed at us.

MIRANDA

"I had a longstanding friendship with a really nice neighborhood boy I had grown up with since kindergarten. We played together outside of school. In sixth grade my feelings became a crush. At a Campfire Girls meeting after school, our patrol of five girls, all friends, was discussing boys we liked. With laughing high spirits, I said, 'I think he's going to ask me to go steady!' (Of course, at that age I hardly understood what 'going steady' meant. It was a term I had heard my mother use.)

"One girl in the group lived across the street from me, and we had been friends since kindergarten. She, the boy, and I were all in the same class at school. So the next day at school in front of everyone, she told him what I had said! I was embarrassed and astonished that someone I considered a friend would do such a mean thing! Of course I denied it. I still remember my burning red face and humiliation. Later, she had the audacity to ask me why I denied it! She told me I shouldn't have lied but should've said, 'Could be.' I was not that sophisticated at age 10! The episode totally ruined my friendship with the boy. I was too embarrassed to talk or play with him again, even though we continued to live in the same neighborhood and went to the same junior high and high school. We would just say 'Hi' when we saw each other, and I had a crush on him for years.

"The amazing thing is that I continued to be friends with the girl. I even offered to be her campaign manager when she ran for office in junior high. She accepted but subsequently dropped me for a more 'popular' girl in the 'in' crowd. Perhaps the boy and I were both victims of her meanness. He was such a nice boy, and after the campaign manager thing, I decided she wasn't a friend. I was still nice to her but I had figured out that she would do whatever she could to get ahead. Not long after this happened, her family moved to a fancy new house with glitter in the ceiling in a different neighborhood.

"I learned not to spout off in front of a group. I still trust people and share confidences but I am more careful about whom I trust. I also learned that not all people are kind. I think we naturally expect people to be like we are, and it's surprising that people can be so cruel to those who have done them no harm—even to those who have been loyal friends—for no apparent reason. This girl was a smart, cute girl but also the daughter of a strange mother (who was too proud to buy anything on sale), a social climber. The mother committed suicide in later years. The girl became a psychologist and never married. Another friend of mine in the neighborhood went to Harvard with her and kept in touch over the years through other acquaintances. Reports are that she became more of a self-centered user and less of someone you would want for a friend."

ABOUT THIS CASE STUDY

The saying "Keep your friends close and your enemies closer" might be an apt description of Miranda and Roxanne. Roxanne's and Miranda's stories are examples of continuing to be friends with your abuser. They both realized the need to be much more cautious in the future about what they shared with these people. Although these are difficult lessons, they likely served them well in later friendships.

DELIA

"At age fourteen I received a scholarship to attend a school 500 miles from home. My mother was supportive but my father didn't want me to leave home because it meant that my mother would have to go to work to supplement my scholarship. My parents gave me a ride to school but when it came time to return home for Thanksgiving, my father told me I could take the train and he would mail me a free pass because he worked on the railroad. When I boarded the train with the pass, I had no money. Many miles out of the station, the conductor informed me of a change in the regulations several years before, making my pass only good for half fare. I told him I hadn't known about the regulation change and I didn't have any money. He let me ride the train for free.

"When I reached home I informed my father, and he insisted the pass was good for full fare and would not listen to me. When it came time for me to return to school, my father put me on the train, again with no money, and I had to hide from the conductor for the remainder of the trip. When it came time to return home for Christmas, I repeated my performance in both directions, trying to find new ways to elude the conductor to keep from being thrown off the train. I was terrified and was very angry with my father for putting me through the fear and humiliation.

"Many years later, after my father had died, I applied for a healthcare position in a city near the one where I grew up. During the interview process, I had lunch with a group of physicians and sat across the table from one of them. As we spoke, I told him where I grew up, and he asked me what my last name was. When I told him, his face turned white and he gasped as he remembered my father. I suddenly realized he had been my father's physician, and when I asked him what was wrong he could only utter, 'Your father was the most unusual person I have ever met.' I wanted to ask him why but I really didn't want to know what I think I already knew. I couldn't believe that after all that time, my father's maladaptive behaviors still had the potential to affect my life."

ABOUT THIS CASE STUDY———————————————————————

Delia's story is a good example of how physically escaping "B" behaviors doesn't necessarily prevent them from continuing to sting you.

BRENT

"I was 12 years old, living in a rural area and going to parochial school. My class only had 13 kids in it. Nine were girls, so there weren't a lot of boys I could choose for my friends. My best friend was one of the boys in class. He had the same sense of humor, and we lived close to one another. One day we were goofing off in the boy's bathroom, pushing each other. He pushed me into the door of the bathroom and the door slammed the wall and broke the plaster. I was a good Catholic boy and was concerned about being involved in this destructive act. I felt guilty enough to suggest to my friend that we should tell our parents and the nuns. He led me to believe he was going to do that but he didn't, and I took the fall for the entire incident. It was traumatic to know my best friend would not back me up and share the blame.

"Within the next year, that incident caused us to part ways. I questioned why he didn't go along, and he brushed it off, so I decided he wasn't much of a friend if he didn't share the blame. If he had confessed to it, I would have felt better. He also suggested I was weak for having confessed. I was courteous to him after that but over time avoided hanging out with him and wouldn't do anything with him after school.

"Now that I think about it, we also had a falling out because I did kind of seek my revenge by making fun of him in social circles with him present. I can remember two incidents. At that time everyone was wearing short hair. He had big ears, and I called him "Elephant Ears." He liked a girl in class, and to his face I made fun of him, saying he couldn't get the girl.

"I learned three things from this experience. The first is I don't expect people to share my values but some people can undermine you if they perceive that you don't share their values. Secondly, I was surprised by my retaliatory behavior when I chose to get back at my friend by putting him down. It didn't take me long to feel terrible that I had tried to make him feel bad. I was surprised that I was capable of doing that. The third thing it taught me was about my personality, that when I get pushed hard enough, I might overact, especially when I am out of my comfort zone.

"When I recall being betrayed in my youth, it is this incident and a similar one in which I had the same reaction that come to mind. This was one of the first times I got in touch with my feelings and wasn't pleased at what I discovered. As a young person it was significant at the time, and is still significant now as a reference for later experiences. This was probably normal behavior for children and I am downplaying it because this kind of thing happens all the time. I still try to tell the truth but realize the end result will not necessarily be favorable."

MARGO

"It was summer, and I was at the fair with a girlfriend I had met in high school. I carried what little money I had in a coin purse that meant a lot to me because it had belonged to my grandfather. I wanted to go on a ride but my friend did not, so I handed her the purse and asked her to hold it. When the ride was over, I asked my friend for the coin purse but she denied I had given it to her. I never got it back and felt very hurt.

When I was younger I used to suffer injustices and stuff all of my feelings. However, as I have matured I have worked very hard not to ignore my feelings. I am currently in a position where my boss is very controlling and has put me in jobs where I am less able to speak up. I am counting the days until my retirement. I have marked the date on my calendar when I plan to speak up in front of everyone and tell the boss what I think of her manipulative behaviors. When I retire I am going back to school to finish my degree, and I look forward to that."

BETTY

"It was in high school when Gerald, a classmate, pretended to be my friend just to get close to one of my girlfriends. At that age I had not realized that people had the potential to be deceptive and could play games with other people just for fun. The realization that people could be unconscionably cruel was shocking to me. The ground was constantly shifting with Gerald. I wavered between feeling special, safe and secure to feeling trampled and abused. It became obvious to me later that others could see Gerald's character flaws before I could. Once I was with Gerald walking down the hallway at school and as we passed one of the English teachers, the teacher said to me, 'Guilt by association.' At the time it left me feeling confused but then I felt bitter because the teacher was unfairly associating me with Gerald's bad behaviors.

"In my youth I always wanted people to like me. I considered it the highest compliment to have people say, 'You are such a nice person.' It was a hard lesson and one I had to learn multiple times, that being too accepting and too open left me vulnerable to the games and manipulation some people use to charge their batteries."

ABOUT THESE CASE STUDIES

The stories of Brent, Margo and Betty demonstrate different approaches to being stung by "B"s. As we progress through life, experiencing more "B" behaviors, a common reaction is to dismiss these behaviors as normal. This sense of acceptance is an interesting form of denial or avoidance. By regarding "B" behavior as normal, one must ask where you draw the line in terms of severity of "B" behaviors. Betty's recognition that the problem doesn't only lie with the "B" is significant. She is aware that there is something within her, perhaps the need to please, that leaves her vulnerable to the stings of a "B."

Approaching the "B's" Nest

Numerous authors have described the drama of becoming trapped in the buzz of the "B's" nest. Eric Berne developed the theory of "transactional analysis" and popularized it in the book *Games People Play*.[28] Berne notes that all humans require strokes—basic units of social recognition—and that any stroke is better than no

---

[28] Berne, *Games People Play*, 29.

stroke. This means we will engage in any situation in a way that will get others to recognize us and help validate our identity. In the story "Ain't It Awful," Berne introduced the three-handed game played by an aggressor, victim and confidant.[29] The victim complains to the confidant that something is terribly wrong. As soon as the confidant offers a solution that will rescue the victim, the victim attacks the confidant (rescuer), essentially becoming the persecutor and changing the confidant's role to victim.

Dr. Gregory Lester, a psychologist who specializes in treating personality disorders, added the dimension of personality disorders to Berne's theory. Lester enhanced Berne's theory by noting that people with personality disorders adopt one of the roles of persecutor, victim or rescuer to play out their perceived identities.[30] Rather than staying in one role, they often shift between the three roles. When interacting with a "B," you are never quite sure which role you are dealing with at any given moment. It's this behavior that often makes you think you're crazy when a "B" stings you.

Lester describes a human drama triangle that develops when at least one of the players in an interpersonal interaction has a personality disorder and enters the drama as a persecutor, victim, or rescuer. The person with the personality disorder has the goal of validating his identity by drawing others into one of the other two roles in his drama triangle. For example, if the person with a personality disorder enters the triangle as a victim and you are someone who doesn't like to see anyone suffer, you might be tempted to assume the role of rescuer or guard and help or protect the victim. If the person with the personality disorder enters the drama as persecutor and you are unwittingly drawn into the drama, you have likely defined yourself as the victim.

[29] Ibid., p. 85.
[30] Lester, *Personality Disorders*, 24–26.

In the popular movie *A Christmas Story*, about a young boy's neighborhood friends growing up in the 1940s, the narrator states that there are three kinds of people in the world: "Bullies, toadies, and hapless victims."[31] Although using these terms helps us to understand the "B" behaviors, the reality is more complex because the "B" may not first appear as a bully, a persecutor or an aggressive "B." Instead of looking like Scut Farkas, the scary-looking bully in *A Christmas Story*, "B"s might adopt the demeanor of an impeccably dressed business executive, a beautiful woman, an ordinary Joe just like you, a pious minister or a caring volunteer. The "B" will portray himself as one person to the people he wants to impress and as someone else to those he doesn't care about. "B"s can appear aggressive like killer bees, helpful like honeybees, or hapless like injured bees.

The Perpetrators

The stinging "B" can be a stranger, friend, lover, coworker, or anyone else who crosses your path. A "B" will assume whatever role is necessary to draw you into the buzz of the "B's" nest. A high-functioning "B" has an innate ability to quickly size you up and determine how to use you to validate his identity. Are you apt to fight back or just accept the aggressive "B's" behaviors? For some "B"s, stinging behaviors lie dormant and only manifest themselves when under stress.

Dr. Martin Kantor believes that some of these stinging behaviors can be a self-protective response to stress.[32] Some people who repeatedly exhibit stinging behaviors may have low social status. Many other aggressive "B"s, however, are high-functioning, and their high social status allows them to wield power over others.

[31] *A Christmas Story*, Clark, 1983.
[32] Kantor, *The Psychopathy of Everyday Life*, 154.

They can be professional as well as non-professional, well-educated or not. The stressors that they perceive as being somehow threatening, either physically or conceptually, can trigger their stinging behaviors. The behaviors often manifest as a change in the person's typical behavior, at least as observed by those who aren't being targeted.

The stinging behaviors are usually directed at only certain people in a given circumstance so that everyone is not exposed. Often the perpetrator directs his or her manipulative behaviors toward the victim in private. When others are not subjected to the stinging behavior, they seldom believe it occurred. The perpetrator is often extra nice to associates of the victim. In this way, the "B" behaviors can be very destructive to the integrity of a group because some group members experience them and others do not.

The Protectors

Some people repeatedly adopt roles as guards or as victims for those who display "B" behaviors. The toadies, rescuers or guards exist to protect the "B." In an article about teams, Drinka and Streim noted that the equivalent of rescuers or guards in a team protect the "B" in three ways.[33] They can be "conduits" by transferring messages from the "B" to others who may or may not be the intended target of the message. They can be "receptors" and accept a "B's" message without question. This is because the messages are consistent with what they believe, or because the individual giving the messages exhibits qualities prized by the receptor. They can also be "reflectors" and divert praise to the "B" who initiated the message. This is a reminder that the "B" is valued. Rescuers or guards are often unwilling participants in building

[33] Drinka & Streim, "Case studies from purgatory," 543.

a "B's" nest. However, if a rescuer transmits information to a "B" with the purpose of stinging someone else, he is also behaving like a "B."

We have all likely been pushed into the proverbial snow bank, or stomped on, or stabbed in the back, or stung many times. We, personally, have watched our children and husbands suffer the same fate. We informally counsel friends and coworkers on a regular basis, and have come to see patterns in the manipulative behaviors that are often executed with great skill in a variety of seemingly safe settings by seemingly honorable people. Quite frequently these behaviors are encouraged, or at least tolerated, by many who are receptors for manipulative behaviors.

Fulfilling relationships with people involve trusting them enough to let them into your life. The difficulty in encountering manipulators is in knowing when the line of trust should end and distrust should begin. The storytellers in this chapter learned different lessons from having their trust violated by people who exhibited manipulative behaviors. They selectively learned the following:

- Stings are often repetitive
- Support from significant others makes maladaptive behaviors easier to bear
- Ways to maintain a relationship with someone they don't trust
- How to keep their feelings hidden in order to survive or tolerate a difficult situation
- How to avoid those they distrust
- How to track those they distrust
- Retaliation doesn't necessarily make you feel better

- Escaping a situation doesn't make the feelings go away
- Choosing your reaction to manipulative behavior gives you a sense of power

SUMMARY

SOME OF THE STORIES IN THIS CHAPTER INVOLVED a single sting, but the only thing to be learned from a single sting is that it hurts. It's only when you observe a pattern of multiple stings that you can be fairly certain you are dealing with a "B."

Multiple stings have a cumulative effect and can leave the victim feeling confused, helpless and guilty for crossing the perpetrator's path. Along with the distrust, the storytellers also experienced a myriad of feelings that accompanied their betrayals, including anger, frustration, disbelief, fear, loss, entrapment, humiliation, immobilization, pain, and a search for meaning. These repeated themes are evident in all of the stories we include in this book.

A number of our storytellers expressed joy at their persecutors' misfortunes. Years later, some storytellers still kept track of their persecutors. Others expressed sadness, guilt or self-doubt. All of these feelings and behaviors speak to the deep wounds created by manipulative "B"s. Our memories of early abuses, no matter how seemingly slight, are the basis for judging aggressive "B"s in later years.

Admittedly, individuals who repeatedly exhibit manipulative stinging behaviors intrigue us. Those who are the targets of stinging behaviors, however, and those who knowingly or unknowingly support these behaviors also fascinate us. We wonder why so many people tolerate manipulative behaviors. Perhaps they are unable to recognize these behaviors until it's too late. Perhaps the perpetrator is in a formal power position. Perhaps the perpetrator's behaviors are valued and revered in segments of our society, and some have come to see the behaviors as normal.

Many of the classic nursery rhymes taught us that there are evil-acting people in the world, and if we are good like Hansel and Gretel or Snow White, we will eventually prevail. It is also interesting to watch popular teen movies like *The Breakfast Club*, *Mean Girls* and *High School Musical*. While manipulative behaviors are portrayed early on in the movies, by the end of the movie the "mean" characters usually reform or at least the hero or heroine triumphs. *Mean Girls* ends with Lindsay Lohan's character realizing that she's been selling out to be popular so she goes back to her smart, simple, no-makeup self. She reconciles with the other girls (who also learn their lessons) and when she's elected prom queen, the coveted title of the mean girls, she breaks up the plastic crown and gives a piece of it to each of the mean girls and also to some of the more "nerdy" girls. Unfortunately, the messages "everyone is basically good and can be transformed" and "truth and goodness will triumph" don't necessarily apply to our encounters with "B"s. While these teen movies project a feel-good message, they don't necessarily represent life events.

As we gathered our stories, our thoughts were with Mia, Gabriela, and Isabel—the girls we introduced at the beginning of this chapter—and how we could teach them to recognize and survive painful behaviors. After a trip to the zoo, one of them noted that the most colorful frogs were the most poisonous. We thought this observance could also be applied to some "B"s. Part of a child's socialization is learning how to recognize and then coexist with aggressive "B"s without being stung by them. Some appear to learn better and earlier than others. How five-year-old Mia's ability to spot stinging

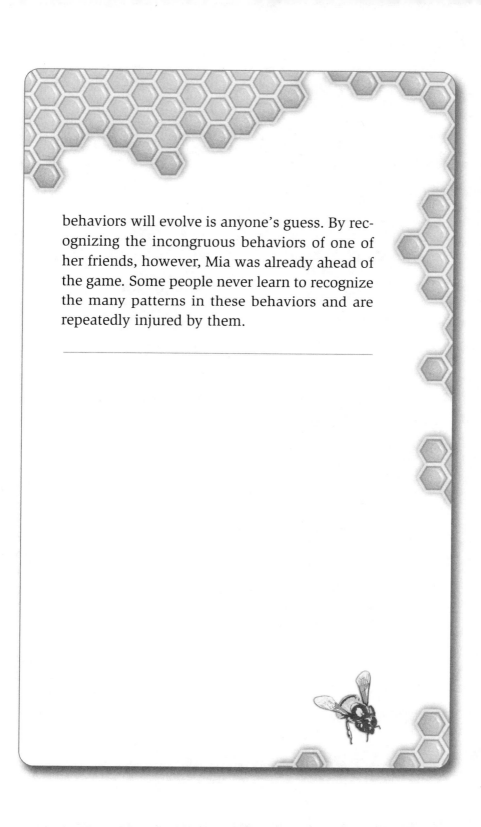

behaviors will evolve is anyone's guess. By recognizing the incongruous behaviors of one of her friends, however, Mia was already ahead of the game. Some people never learn to recognize the many patterns in these behaviors and are repeatedly injured by them.

CHAPTER THREE

Gifts from Stranger "B"s

"Some cause happiness wherever they go; others whenever they go."
OSCAR WILDE

People We Don't Know Can Sting Us

We have all had encounters with strangers who behaved like "B"s. Our responses to such people probably varied based on whether we felt threatened, whether we knew it would be a one-time encounter, whether we felt rushed, or whether the behaviors made us doubt ourselves. Perhaps a clerk made us angry and we raised our voice or got red in the face. Perhaps someone was being particularly difficult and we glanced up to notice a wry smirk on the person's face. Perhaps we left an encounter with a bad feeling that lasted for days, weeks or even years. These are the experiences that haunt us with the feeling that we should have responded differently, had a faster comeback, reported the person's unacceptable behavior, or kept our reaction in check.

Initial encounters with stranger "B"s have several elements that make these encounters particularly stunning. First, the stings of stranger "B"s seem to come from nowhere. This element of surprise makes the sting feel like you accidentally touched a hot

stove. While some "B" stings heal quickly, others can leave an irritation that superficially heals but resurfaces at a later time. Another element of stings by stranger "B"s involves a lack of knowledge about the person who stings you. Because you have not been able to observe a pattern of behavior, you feel more vulnerable after the sting. When you are surprised, it's difficult to know how to respond or even if you should respond. While you might be surprised by a "B's" sting, the sting may actually be the result of you surprising the "B." Remember, some of the most vicious attacks by "B"s occur after they have been caught off guard.

Between the printed media, television and the Internet, we are bombarded by outrageous stories of "B" behaviors. Because of this phenomenon, perhaps we risk becoming immune to the less outrageous behaviors of stranger "B"s, believing that these manipulative behaviors are normal. We are all a mere heartbeat away from stepping on a "B's" nest, and if we do get stung without warning, it's likely we won't know how to react.

The Surprise Factor

JILL

"The other day when I pulled out from a stop sign to turn left, I looked both ways before I proceeded. As I approached the middle of the intersection, however, a truck came like a bolt of lightning from my right. As soon as I saw the truck, I braked. Instead of proceeding, the man driving the truck stopped right in front of me and he glared at me. I thought his behavior was strange since he had the right of way. I surmised that he knew he was going way too fast and when faced with the potential consequences of his behavior, he chose to blame me with his glaring eyes."

CLARK

"I was taking a bus into the city with a friend when I was 13. I had just received a new watch for confirmation. There were three or four other boys on the bus who were cutting up the seats with box cutters and small knives. When my friend and I exited the bus, the boys followed. The boys put their knives up to my face and to my friend's face and demanded my watch. I threw my watch as hard as I could at the ground in an attempt to break it. I remember being mad at these boys but not scared. This incident made me less trusting of people."

ANNETTE

"I was on a trip with some of my female coworkers, and we were waiting outside the hotel for a taxi. The doorman was busy, so I walked up to the driver of the next taxi in line and bent down to ask if he could take us to the airport. I saw his hand in his pants and realized that he was masturbating. I instantly stood up and stepped back. Just as instantaneously, I thought that I really didn't see what I thought I saw. The doorman must have seen my reaction and the look on my face because he asked me what I had seen. I didn't want to tell him because I doubted myself at that point. As the doorman persisted in asking me what I saw, I finally told him. He yelled at the taxi driver, telling him he had been warned before and to never return to his hotel. It amazed me how quickly I doubted myself and what I had seen."

ABOUT THESE CASE STUDIES ───────────────────

In addition to experiencing shock, anger and diminished trust, it is extremely common to question yourself when you encounter the behavior of a stinging "B." Whether you are stung out of the blue or encounter multiple stings, if you repeatedly question yourself rather than the person who stings you, regard it as an observable pattern and realize that you are likely dealing with a "B." It's also a warning to examine your own vulnerabilities and patterns of response.

The Public Relations Attorney

MIGUEL

"There is a very wealthy church on the land adjacent to my property. The church is attempting to rezone its land from residential to multifamily because it's planning to build apartments on the property. Since this rezoning would totally change our neighborhood and eliminate the possibility of building single-family homes, the neighborhood is fighting against it. I have been organizing the neighbors and handing out leaflets to keep people informed.

"Without an appointment, Pamela, a public relations attorney hired by the church, showed up at my house. She immediately started talking about the work I had done distributing leaflets, talking to the mayor, and talking to the neighbors. She even admitted to looking me up on the Internet and praised me for some volunteer work that I was doing. The first thing she said to me was, 'You are pretty well known. I Googled your name and found out you have been involved in a lot of community events.' I'm sure she knew about all of my involvements.

"Pamela started stroking my ego by saying I had single-handedly convinced the mayor to vote against the project. She wanted to know about my family. I said I wouldn't talk about my family. She said, 'No problem.' I said I saw the issue as a developer building an apartment building on land that is zoned for private homes. It affects my property value. I said there would be a road change and the traffic would come right next to our house.

"Then Pamela asked me if I wanted the road to go away, implying that she could make it happen. I told her I searched her name on the Web and I knew her specialty was bringing large boxes to residential areas. She retorted with, 'Oh Miguel, I think of myself as someone who can bring all the sides together and mediate.' She again asked, 'Do you want that road to go away?' I asked her what she meant. She offered the removal of the road if I agreed to support the zoning change. Pamela is an attorney and her brother is a Washington lobbyist. She was milking me for information. I can't imagine what underhanded things she is capable of."

ABOUT THIS CASE STUDY

In this story Miguel tried to stay out of the "B's" nest. Although he saw Pamela as a persecutor, he managed to stay out of the role of victim. When Pamela shifted her role to that of rescuer or guard bee, Miguel could have accepted, effectively cementing his role as victim. However, he refused that role and for the time being was able to avoid getting stung. Both Pamela and Miguel knew the game was not over.

Adult Education

FELICITY

"I agreed to conduct a lecture on collaborative practice and communication for a large conference, and was honored when asked to coordinate my lecture with an expert in the field. My co-presenter emailed his presentation and I emailed a draft version of mine to him. After not hearing from him for days, I sent an email and left a phone message asking him to set a time for a phone conference so we could coordinate our talks. He then emailed me, saying he thought my talk was too long, that there was overlap, and then he suggested we both decrease our number of slides. I subsequently cut the number of my slides by two-thirds and sent them to him, saying I was sending a revised version of my talk so we could have a base from which to converse. I gave him my cell phone number and my time schedule.

"A week went by and I did not hear from him. I subsequently sent him an email asking him to please call me. After not hearing from him by the next day, I left a message on his cell phone asking him to call me. Finally, I called the conference planner, saying I could work with anyone, whether they agreed with me or not, but I could not work with someone who refused to communicate. I bowed out of giving the lecture because I didn't want the hassle, and felt that the issue was not worth fighting for. I was left feeling that those being trained by this man were being duped. Somehow it reminded me of my father, who would give us rules by which he did not abide."

FELICITY, AS A YOUNG GIRL

"I was three and a half when my sister was born. One day, as she lay screaming in her crib, I was ready to give my sister a spanking with my dad's belt when I felt the belt ripped from my hand and applied to my backside. Although I learned that it was wrong to spank my sister, I couldn't understand why my father let her cry because every time I cried I was spanked with the belt. I only remember not understanding the rules and why they applied to me but not my sister."

ABOUT THIS CASE STUDY

Felicity was right to disengage from the conference's "communications guru." In many ways, Felicity's experience with the expert was a repeat of her experience with her father as a young girl. In each case the rules were not universally applied and each situation was a learning experience. If Felicity had a longer-term business relationship with the expert speaker, she would have to address his arrogant behaviors with him.

REBEKKAH

"For the past several years I have been teaching art classes to adults who want to learn my various techniques. Zoey had taken many classes from me, and it was a running joke in my classes that every time I stepped back from talking to another student I would step on Zoey. She followed me like a shadow. I had a lot of space when I taught, so I allowed the students to attend another one of my classes without paying so that they could complete their work. I didn't expect to have to teach these repeat students like Zoey because I had already given them the information they needed.

"Zoey had questions about everything and she never finished her projects so she started showing up at all of my subsequent classes, commandeering time from me that I needed to give to the paying students. Eventually I moved to a building with limited space. Zoey called about taking a particular class but since I already had as many students as I wanted to teach, I told her the class was full. She said she would come anyway and work independently. I repeated that the class was full and I had no room for her.

"Ten minutes before my class ended, we were discussing what we had made. Zoey arrived with her hands full of bags, saying she had brought me presents. Zoey then proceeded to pull out junk for which I had no use. She said, 'Oh, if you can't use it, then give it away.' The women who had paid for my class were getting agitated and started preparing to leave. Suddenly Zoey looked around and said, 'This class isn't full. You said your class was full.' I retorted that several people had left early.

"Finally, the people attending the class left and Zoey stayed on, wanting me to show her some things on her projects. I told her I had just been on my feet for five hours and that I was leaving. It was like she didn't hear me because she again said she wanted some help on her projects. I restated that I was leaving. She finally left. The next day I mailed her a postcard saying if I say my class is full then it is full and there's no room for her. She later called me to say she thought she was doing me a favor by coming late because she didn't think she would disrupt anything. I have decided to take Zoey off my mailing list, and if she calls to take a class, it will always be full."

ABOUT THESE CASE STUDIES

Zoey was exhibiting attention-seeking behaviors. Rebekkah wondered why she attracted so many people to her classes who seemed off balance. In fact, Rebekkah is fascinating, funny and very talented. It would be expected that "B"s are attracted to her like bees to honey. If Rebekkah noticed them and paid attention to them, they could consider themselves special. If Rebekkah were a "B," she might also feel special at having so many admirers. This was not the case, however, and Rebekkah felt some were taking advantage of her and were an annoyance to her other students.

The Neighbors

ROSALIND

"From the first day we moved into our house, the kids who lived behind us would cut through our backyard via their backyard gate to get to our next-door neighbor's house. Pretty early on we talked to the parents, and they agreed they would move their backyard gate so the children would come out behind our neighbor's home instead of ours. We were concerned about the liability of having children cutting behind our house due to building materials being stored in our backyard. Three years went by and the neighbors never followed through on the agreement. During this time there were incidents that occurred with their kids.

"One time one of the kids came to our front door crying, saying he had slipped on ice in our backyard. Another time I actually watched one of the kids flip over the back gate into our yard and land on his face. He ran to our house screaming because he had landed on stinging nettle and it was all over his mouth. I spoke to the parents again and was sympathetic about the incident but reintroduced the discussion about moving the gate. I asked them to please, for the children's safety, not allow them into our backyard. I offered other solutions besides moving the gate. These suggestions were ignored, and the kids started walking the long way around to get to our next-door neighbor's house. This is when our next-door neighbor started to act up.

"Our next-door neighbors had two children and we shared a driveway. When I would come home from work, the kids would sit and wave and chat with me for a while. But after the final conversations about the backyard gate (and not allowing their friends to cut through to their house), everything just flipped. When I would come home from work, the kids stopped talking to me and the dad would shuffle them into the house when I drove into the driveway. This seemed strange and a bit sad.

"Not long after the family started ignoring me, my husband came home from work and waved at the father who was outside standing in his yard. When my husband pulled into our garage, he found the father standing at his car door, refusing to let him out of the car. Our neighbor starting yelling at my husband, saying, 'I can't believe you are making these kids walk around on this busy street to get to our house. Who the hell do you think you are?' My husband removed himself from the situation to avoid any escalation of the conflict. I considered confronting our neighbor after this because my husband was really rattled. I talked it through with others who knew our next-door neighbor peripherally, and everyone recommended I just let it go. They all seemed to agree that something was not quite right with him.

"For the next year, all interactions between their family and ours stopped. One day our neighbor was coming out to get his paper while I was outside and I said hello. He waved his arm without looking at me, as if gesturing to dismiss me. I will never forget the feeling of relief I experienced the day I drove home to find a for sale sign posted in their

72

front yard. Having someone like this in your life, even if they are on the sidelines, can be utterly exhausting and very stressful."

ABOUT THIS CASE STUDY

Rosalind's story highlights the surprise of stepping on a "B's" nest. It also demonstrates that if you are trying to solve a problem with someone who insists on confusing the situation and escalating the drama, it's a good indication that a "B" is somewhere in the interaction. In this case it was probably both neighbors who exhibited "B" behaviors. It would be standard "B" behavior for the neighbors to not follow through with their agreement and then to blame Rosalind and her husband for the problem. This seems to indicate her next-door neighbor placed the neighbors across the fence in the role of victim while simultaneously becoming the guard/rescuer "B" and classifying Rosalind as the persecutor. Ignoring someone when you disapprove of what they are doing is also a common narcissistic "B" behavior.

Rosalind and her husband wanted to stay out of the chaos but they were unable to ignore it because the neighbors were trespassing on their property and making them potentially liable for mishaps. No solution Rosalind proposed was good enough. The ultimate solution was achieved when the neighbor who was stirring things up moved away and exited the "B's" nest. If he had stayed, this situation could have escalated to the point of violence.

ROGER

"When I was in my mid-twenties, I used to help my father with his yard work. One Sunday morning I had to get over and mow his lawn because I had a plane to catch that afternoon and I would be out of town for a week. At nine o'clock I started the mower. About five minutes later, a neighbor came storming out of his house in his robe and slippers and climbed the hill to where I stood. I turned off the mower, and he got right up in my face and started screaming at me to stop mowing. He said the people in 'this neighborhood' don't mow their lawns until noon on Sundays. He referred to me as the 'lawn boy' and again ordered me to stop. I tried to explain I had to catch a plane and couldn't return at noon to finish the job. I swear that if it had been a cartoon, he would have had steam coming out of his ears.

"He stomped back into his house, and I didn't really have much of a choice, so I started the mower back up and finished the job. My father came home to a series of screaming voicemail messages from the neighbor. He played them for us, and we both had a good laugh because there was no neighborhood rule about mowing your lawn on Sunday morning. The neighbor had made that up."

ABOUT THIS CASE STUDY

In this case the neighbor adopted the perfect persecutor stance, and Roger avoided the "B's" nest by passively refusing to become the victim. Roger's humor was a useful tool when dealing with this stranger "B."

Mad Drivers

LILY

"I was alone, driving in an unfamiliar area of the city, and saw the exit a little bit later than I should have. I signaled and eased in ahead of a driver next to me and waited for the light to change. The man in the car behind me laid on his horn and began to shake his fists and then got out of his car and walked up to my car. All of the drivers in the cars around me froze in position. I rolled up my windows and just kept looking straight ahead. Just then the light changed and all of the cars, including mine, took off as fast as we could."

AMANDA

"I was driving on a freeway in a very rural part of the state. I had not seen another car for many miles. In the rearview mirror I noticed a large SUV approaching very fast in the passing lane. I just assumed he would pass me. Instead, he slowed down and stayed alongside my car for the next 25 minutes. I put my visor to the side and just kept driving the same speed. Finally, another car came up behind the SUV, and the SUV accelerated and disappeared from my sight."

ABOUT THESE CASE STUDIES

The two previous stories illustrate how frightening even a brief encounter with an intimidating and potentially antisocial "B" can be. Although the strangers' approaches were different, they each attempted to intimidate. It would have been a mistake for either Lily or Amanda to make any kind of contact with either of the drivers. In the first case there were witnesses but in the second case there were not. In either case, even eye contact would have engaged these strangers, with potentially dire consequences.

The Marketer

CHAD

"I answered the phone, and a marketer from the local newspaper tried to convince me to buy a subscription. When I politely declined, the marketer persisted in trying to convince me I needed a subscription. He would not give up and so I hung up on him. Five minutes later, the phone rang again. I recognized the marketer's voice, and he said, 'How is your mother?' and I said, 'None of your business.' He said, 'I know your mother isn't feeling well. I just talked to her, and I know where she lives.' In fact, my mother had not been feeling well, and I started to believe he really did just speak with her. He was leading me on, and I tried telling him he was making this stuff up, but he just kept pushing my buttons. He kept leading me on with generalized statements, and finally I started believing everything he said. After a few minutes, I hung up.

"I called my mother, and she wasn't there. She had been sick, and I was so worried that I immediately drove over to her house to discover she was just fine and he had never spoken with her. I immediately called the newspaper to report the marketer's behavior. They called back a few days later to tell me he was no longer working for them."

ABOUT THIS CASE STUDY

This is a perfect example of a chance encounter with antisocial "B" behaviors. This type of "B" is very astute at playing mind games by laying out bait and picking up subtle cues. In this case the worried inflection in Chad's voice indicated to the marketer that he had hooked Chad into his sick game. Unlike the previous two stories, this stranger "B" was able to draw Chad into the victim role by engaging him in a conversation. The notable lesson here is how quickly engagement occurred. Chad was wise to disengage by finally hanging up. It was a credit to Chad that he was also able to produce consequences for the "B's" behavior by calling the newspaper.

Trying to Get in Shape

REBA

"I was exercising at the fitness center, doing one round of 10 quick repetitions on each machine. As I was preparing to leave the fitness center, a woman who was twice my size got in my face, yelling that I had to sanitize the machines after each use. As all heads turned toward us, I tried to explain that I had sanitized my hands before I started and if I spent a lot of time on a machine, I would sanitize it. She wouldn't let me speak and kept yelling in my face. I quickly left the facility to keep myself from giving her the finger. After that, I cancelled my membership and bought a treadmill."

ABOUT THIS CASE STUDY ————————————

If the woman at the fitness center had really wanted to instruct Reba, she would've done so in private. Instead, she chose the elements of surprise and intimidation to publicly devalue Reba. It's difficult to prepare yourself for such a sudden attack. It's also difficult to decide on a subsequent course of action. If Reba had continued her membership with the fitness center, she would have risked another unpleasant encounter with this aggressive stranger. Even if Reba had reported this woman's behavior, any future encounters would be potentially unpleasant. Reba's path of least resistance gave her peace of mind.

Public Servants

CAMPBELL

"As an elected public servant, I made an appointment with a U.S. congressman to discuss some environmental issues. When I arrived at his office, his assistant grilled me, asking me who I was, saying 'You aren't the chairman or the highway commissioner or the sheriff.' He implied that I was not important enough and was wasting his time. I later called Washington and spoke with the congressman's chief of staff in personnel. When I complained that I was being discriminated against, he warned me not to go there. This man worked for a very powerful congressman and likely reflected the congressman's attitude toward his constituents."

 **NELL**

"As the result of working on a successful funding initiative for a charity, our team won a state award. I had never met the governor and felt honored to be invited to a special reception. As I walked up to meet the governor, he greeted me by saying, 'Congratulations, Nell, what does your husband do?' As he said this, he wouldn't let go of my hand. I was speechless and as my face turned red, I finally said I didn't have a husband. The governor was married but had a reputation as a womanizer. I went outside and burst into tears. Later I mentioned this to a friend who had been in politics for years, and he just laughed it off, saying the governor comes on to every pretty woman. I was amazed that something so subtle could reduce me to tears. A party that was in my honor ended up giving me the creeps."

ABOUT THESE CASE STUDIES

From these two cases it would seem that intimidation through disrespect is the norm in the world of politics. Campbell was likely right in her assumption that the congressman's staffer, who was a stranger to her, reflected the congressman's views. Being prepared, restating your case and refusing to back down are tools you can use in such a situation. Sometimes even the most prepared people with the best intentions don't stand a chance against the misuse of power, especially when they are strangers and don't have "favored" status.

Despite the governor's reputation as a womanizer, Nell was caught off guard by the surprise subtlety of his overture toward her. Nell's story demonstrates that it might not be the words "B"s use but their subtle behaviors—a look, a touch, a hand-

shake—that can catch you off guard and sting you when you least expect it.

"B" Behavior in the Medical System

JUDY

"I had just had my first baby, and it was the day we were to be discharged home. I had a surprise visit from an acquaintance whose daughter coincidently had a baby the same day and was a few rooms away from mine at the hospital. While this acquaintance was visiting, a doctor came to give me my exam to release me from the hospital. The doctor saw I had company so she said she would return in a few minutes. Hours passed and no one came, so I walked out to the nurses' station to find out what was happening.

"A nurse heard my question and turned to me, yelling, 'You should have told your company to leave when the doctor was there. Now you are just going to have to wait.' She had such anger and hatred in her voice. I felt like I had been punched in the gut. Tears welled in my eyes and the resident standing next to me kindly said he would find someone to discharge me from the unit. After I had my final check by the doctor, the nasty nurse came back all sweet and kind to take my baby's picture for the hospital website. I wanted her as far away from my baby and me as possible. I wanted to report her but was so overwhelmed by new motherhood that I never took the time."

ABOUT THIS CASE STUDY

In this case the harsh words from the nurse shocked Judy. This situation was a double surprise because the nurse was a stranger to Judy, and Judy never expected such condescending arrogance from a professional caregiver. In a normal situation, Judy might have given the nurse feedback. However, the nurse exploited her vulnerability. A clue that this was "B" behavior was the fact that the nurse didn't apologize to Judy when she had the opportunity to do so.

Deflecting Blame Back to the Patient

MARISSA

"A specialist in my health network diagnosed my pains, saying I was 'physically out of shape.' Six years later, I was taken by ambulance to a specialty hospital outside my network where they diagnosed my disorder. My primary-care doctor arranged a follow-up appointment with a specialist in my network. To my surprise, the same specialist who had dismissed my condition six years earlier entered the exam room, screaming, 'I saw you six years ago and determined then that you were fine.' I reported that I had felt better within a week of receiving the medication from the doctors who diagnosed my condition, and that the pains I had felt for years had disappeared.

"The specialist bombarded me with questions about smoking, drinking and exercise. It was clear that he didn't believe the responses that I had already given to the nurse. The specialist didn't listen to my replies. When he finally said that my diagnosis was not a real disease, I became angry and told him that that was not what the most recent research showed. When he started to deride the Internet, I showed him a research article that was published in a prominent research journal.

Throughout the visit he continued to deride me and tell me that my condition didn't exist. He recommended I taper the medicines I had been given—the ones that I felt were helping me.

"Because of the specialist's defensive demeanor, I could only assume he was upset because another physician had diagnosed a condition that he had missed. I left the clinic confused and angry. A short time later, I switched clinics after reading a review article by a Mayo Clinic researcher verifying my condition as not only real but commonly under-diagnosed in women. I wanted to send the article to the specialist who had been so dismissive but I thought he wouldn't read it anyway, so I never did."

ABOUT THIS CASE STUDY

This story is an example of how a physician can demonstrate arrogant and aggressive behaviors when he feels insulted. There was an episode of a popular television sitcom about a takeout restaurant known for its soup. When the chef didn't like a customer or felt insulted, he would refuse to serve the customer. The arrogant behavior of the chef was funny when it involved soup but such arrogance is dangerous when it involves an unfeeling physician. Encountering this stranger "B" twice allowed Marissa to see a pattern in his aggressive arrogance.

ANNABELLE

"I had seen Dr. Whopper once, and hoped to develop a rapport. I respected his intelligence and knowledge. When I was charged for the visit after I was told I wouldn't be charged, however, I decided to write this letter:

Dear Dr. Whopper,

I was experiencing some physical challenges and knew I needed to speak to and see a specialist. Having heard of your practice, I decided to call and see if you were on my health plan. I was told that you had applied to be part of my health plan. I said I would call back when your application had been accepted. At this time I was told by the person handling scheduling that you were only requiring the co-pay I was currently being charged for this type of visit. I was also told I was not expected to pay for this visit whether my healthcare provider picked up your practice or not.

During my visit with you, I expressed my concerns again about how payment would be handled, and you told me not to worry about it. I also discussed the pros and cons of developing a relationship with you with the thought that you possibly wouldn't be picked up by my insurance, because I wanted to use a doctor who was in my plan. Again, you told me not to worry.

I discovered that you are a knowledgeable, caring and professional doctor. You took your time with me and gave me options. I felt I was in good hands and was delighted to find such a doctor close to home. However, at this time I am not sure I will be continuing my relationship with your practice. Today the woman in billing told me she spoke with you, and you denied ever saying that I wouldn't have to pay for this visit and that you have already discounted the visit. I am not looking for a discount. The amount of money I am being billed is $77.54.

Surely it's not the money but the principle. I don't appreciate being told one thing and then being told it was never said. I'm feeling as though my integrity is being questioned. Furthermore, I'm now concerned about how I will be treated as a patient. I did schedule an MRI of my spine on your recommendation. I haven't *yet decided whether or not I'll keep this appointment. If I choose not to keep it (I would then call to cancel), you will now understand the reason why.*

Sincerely,

Annabelle Crimb

"In Dr. Whopper's letter of response, he reiterated my concern that his office had changed its story regarding billing, and also reiterated my concern about continuing to receive proper medical care, given what had transpired. He then proceeded to tell me he was sorry that their billing policies confused me. He blamed it on the insurance companies changing their processes in order to pay out as little as possible. He went on to say that this caused their office to use terminology that patients think they understand but really do not. He then implied that I called him a liar because I was really upset. He wrote that I should consider the account settled because he didn't want to cause me any hardship. He said that I had insulted him by insinuating that he would provide inferior care to someone who could not or would not pay. I certainly never intended to imply such things. Finally, he suggested that I have the MRI, saying that he always checks patient's results and makes follow-up recommendations even if a patient is not continuing in his care. I felt like he insulted me and then tried to make me feel guilty for writing the letter."

ABOUT THIS CASE STUDY ──────────────────

On face value you might think this was a classic case of miscommunication. But Dr. Whopper clearly distorted Anabelle's words to match his view of reality. First, he demeaned Annabelle by implying that she was confused and a liar and then he attempted to make her feel guilty. In the span of a letter, he portrayed Anabelle as a victim and a persecutor, and then he became the rescuer by saying the account was settled and that he always checks a patient's results, even if the patient is not continuing with his care. These are all typical "B" behaviors, and used together, they are very powerful.

Healthcare providers who display "B" behaviors can add to their patients' misery. Healthcare professions are perfect vehicles for those who exhibit "B" behaviors. Most healthcare profession schools have restrictive admission criteria and attract those with histories of high achievement. This predisposes healthcare professions to those who think they are special. Many of the "B"s providing healthcare accomplish a great deal of good. However, in a system overstressed with limited resources, their "B" behaviors can take over and obscure some of the good they are capable of achieving.

We believe practitioner abuse of patients is not the norm or even common. But it does occur. The busy nature of healthcare does not excuse practitioners from being respectful of their patients. Some of the healthcare "B"s favorite behaviors are those of overt and covert intimidation and devaluation. A patient's weakened state makes her more vulnerable to abuse. When the physician is a stranger to you, it's more difficult to assess that physician's behaviors.

When patients recover their health and compare disrespectful incidents by practitioners to their real-life traumas, they might dismiss the incidents as unimportant. And although patients are frequently asked to complete surveys about their care, the questions might not relate to their actual experiences. It is extremely important as a patient to be your own advocate, to ask questions and to refuse to be abused, or to engage someone to advocate for you. If you plan to have an ongoing relationship with a practitioner who dismisses your concerns, it's important that you give respectful feedback to that provider. Depending on the response, you might want to engage another practitioner.

More Good Deeds

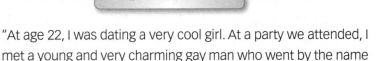

GENE

"At age 22, I was dating a very cool girl. At a party we attended, I met a young and very charming gay man who went by the name of Voijecz. I knew he was gay so he posed no threat of manly competition. He seemed to actively seek my friendship, and I figured he thought I was an interesting person. I remember Voijecz was eloquent, insightful and artistic, with something of a tragic nature. He mentioned he was an orphan who was adopted as a young boy. Over the next few years I ran into Voijecz around town, and we continued our conversations.

"When I was 24 I began an internship in Chicago, and one day Voijecz called me to tell me he had cancer, was receiving treatment in Chicago, and needed a place to stay. My girlfriend and I let him stay with us for about a month. One day my girlfriend and I were traveling back to my hometown for the weekend, and Voijecz asked if he could accompany us. As we arrived at my home, Voijecz immediately befriended my mother, who loved art. Voijecz had brought a painting with him that he was working on and prospectively sold it to my mother for $2000. Voijecz ended up staying at my parents' home for six weeks. During that time my brother returned from school and noticed Voijecz was not making progress on the painting. Some of Voijecz's friends came to visit and made comments about him being 'full of it.' Becoming suspicious, my brother took the painting to an appraiser when Voijecz was gone one weekend, and the appraiser said it was worth only $300.

"When Voijecz returned, my brother confronted him and called him a con artist, and Voijecz left, taking his painting and the $2000 with him.

I remember my mother being quite sad about the whole affair. Within a week after Voijecz's leaving, we received word that he had cut his wrists but didn't die. As I reflect back, I recognize what a tremendous con man Voijecz was. I now realize the reason he came to Chicago was that he had conned so many people in the town where I went to medical school, he had to leave for a while. He was able to con my mother by zeroing in on her interest in art. I was also a receptor for his bullshit. He made me feel special and good about myself. He always had this sadness about him. Likely one of the reasons he was able to con me was I felt sorry for him, he was so sad. He was not obviously arrogant. He played right into the dark recesses and flaws of my ego. When I look back, I'm amazed at how stupid I was."

GENE, AS A YOUNG BOY

"I was five years old when my seven-year-old neighbor, Richard, stole my soldiers from my Fort Apache. Shortly after that Richard showed up with the soldiers, saying they were his. I went to my father who talked to Richard's father, and Richard brought the soldiers back. To me, Richard always seemed a bit sinister."

ABOUT THIS CASE STUDY

As a young boy, Gene's sinister friend manipulated him. However, that experience did not prepare Gene for being stung by a charming "B." Gene's story about Voijecz illustrates the talent and charm of an antisocial "B," the seductiveness of borderline "B" behaviors, and how easily a stranger "B" can enter the inner circle of your life. Voijecz was able to target Gene's need to care for others and to feel special. And Voijecz had no problem tapping into Gene's mother's love of art. Using the standard martyr role, Voijecz was able to quickly draw them in to help him in his "time of need." Once he had a secure place in Gene's mother's home, Voijecz took full advantage of her generosity.

The healthy skepticism exhibited by Gene's brother opened the discussion in Gene's family about the veracity of Voijecz's story. This ability to openly examine a "B's" behavior is critical to uncovering a "B's" shady business and is a very useful tool when you suspect you are in the "B's" nest. An accurate perspective on the sting often comes when someone who is not the "B's" current target examines the suspected sting.

Sometimes You Just Get Lucky

JOANNE

"I was about 15 years old, and there were functions at school that I had to attend at night. Sometimes my father would pick me up after a function and other times he was unable to do so. One night I had to walk the three miles from play practice to home. Although most of the walk was along a busy street, it was very dark and it was unusual to meet anyone else who was walking. At the halfway point in my walk, I passed a bar just as a man was walking out. I was aware of his presence but not knowing what else to do, I simply kept walking as fast as I could. Suddenly he was beside me, and we started talking. He asked me where I was going, and I said I was heading home. He asked if he could walk with me. He didn't say anything about assuring my safety; he just said he would walk me home. We kept talking, and he accompanied me to the sidewalk leading to my front door. I thanked him, went inside and never saw him again."

DANICA

"When I was in college, I met a guy at a fast-food restaurant, and we struck up a conversation. He knew my name but I never told him where I lived. Shortly after our meeting, I was awakened one night by him throwing stones at my dorm-room window. This frightened me since I had not given him any personal information. Shortly after that he started to call me and leave messages that were poems. One day after returning from the dorm bathroom I entered my room to find a wrapped gift on the floor. It was a book of all the poems he had recited on the phone messages.

"Some time passed, and one night I was walking alone back to my dorm from the library. Suddenly, this stalker was in front of me. No one else was around, and I was very scared. But in an instant, my friend showed up unexpectedly and the stalker took off. I never heard from him again. This happened over thirty years ago and it still sends chills down my back."

ABOUT THESE CASE STUDIES

In most of the stories in this chapter the stranger "B"s were kept at bay and were not allowed into the social circles of the intended victims. In two of the last three stories, however, this was not the case. Gene let his guard down and went willingly but Danica was unwillingly pulled into the victim role. Both Gene and Danica were lucky that nothing more serious happened to them. In both stories the only early clues would have been the charm exhibited by the antisocial "B"s.

Although JoAnne's story could have had a frightening ending, it did not. JoAnne had no way of knowing whether or not the man who accompanied her home had good intentions or bad. However, there was a clue that this was not a "B." He did not offer her anything other than to walk her home. He did not say or brag that he would keep her safe. And he did not try to lure her into any situation.

Unfortunately, without seeing a pattern of "B" behaviors, it's not easy to spot a stranger "B" at first glance. Danica only realized the guy she met at the fast-food restaurant was someone to fear when he invaded her personal space and his intrusive actions frightened her. The man who frightened Danica had all the game-playing behaviors of an antisocial "B," and Danica was lucky indeed to have escaped harm.

Reflecting on Stranger "B"s

JANE

"The thing I have learned about being stung by strangers is that sometimes I can put the incident into perspective and assume that maybe somebody is having a bad day. Other times I can't get the episode out of my mind. Often my blood boils knowing these actions might be repeated on other innocent people, that it probably wasn't just a singular offense. I worry that my kids or friends or family could get stung by one of these reckless jerks. These feelings can be overwhelming.

"I don't necessarily think having a doctor treat me badly is any worse than the anonymous guy who flips me off from his car. Either way, I find myself scratching my head, thinking, What did I do to deserve this? I was just minding my own business and this person feels the need to ruin my day. If it's a circumstance I can manipulate to change a future outcome for me or someone else, then I will try to do that. If it's something I can't control and pursuing it will only escalate the risk to me or others, then I try to back off and work hard to let it go."

ABOUT THIS CASE STUDY

We often try to find logical excuses for "B" behaviors, like blaming the stressed medical system for the way we're treated by medical professionals. Jane makes the observation that having a doctor treat her badly is no worse than a stranger treating her badly. This is likely true for a first encounter. However, if your relationship with a professional or anyone else with "B" behavior is to be ongoing, then you need to take steps to protect yourself from repeated stings.

SUMMARY

SURPRISE WAS THE COMMON ELEMENT AMONG THE stories in this chapter. Experiencing the sting of "B" behavior once, however, doesn't mean the perpetrator is a "B." If it's a one-time encounter, we cannot verify a pattern that would be consistent with a "B."

When the dramatic interaction is with strangers, it's easier, and perhaps more appropriate, not to engage. When a stranger stings you and you feel afraid or threatened, a rapid exit is the best strategy. However, to stop the sting, the decision to not engage involves letting the trauma go and not dwelling on it.

We might not invest as much time in trying to resolve a bad encounter with a stranger. Perhaps we are more straightforward in our dealings if it's with someone we hardly know. The short length of our relationship is a benefit if we need to withdraw. Sometimes we choose to intervene and try resolving the situation because we would like a long-term relationship with the stranger.

Some of the people we interviewed wondered if somehow they had done something to deserve the treatment they received. When the strangers we meet are "B"s, we can be fairly sure that we are not the only people they have stung. They continue to sting people because they can. Instead of trying to address the problem, many of us tolerate the behavior or feel helpless. While ignoring the behavior of stranger "B"s is often appropriate, this detached attitude becomes a real problem when the "B"s are our friends, as demonstrated in the next chapter.

CHAPTER FOUR

Friends

"The only way to have a friend is to be one."
RALPH WALDO EMERSON

The Basis of Friendships

Friendships are based on trust, and friends are some of the most important people in our lives. Maintaining a group of friends is related to having a longer and happier life. Most of us nurture our friendships and treasure long-term relationships, many of which span as far back as childhood. But maintaining a deep friendship can be hard work. You need to be prepared to roll with the ups and downs if you want it to last. It is difficult to scrutinize our friendships, but it's a good idea to ask ourselves if our friends are meeting our needs and simultaneously ask if we are putting enough care into the friendships we value. If we don't periodically evaluate our friendships, we risk being hurt at some point, and the sting of a "B" might be causing that pain.

SYDNEY

"I lived with one of my best childhood friends after college, and one day she said that she thought I was moody. I had never thought of myself that way and I could've taken offense but it was coming from someone I trusted and had known for years. After some serious self-reflection, I decided that I was moody and I tried harder to avoid letting my moodiness spill over into our friendship.

"When my friend said I was moody, she said it without judgment or malice. Not intending to hurt me, she said it as an observation. It wasn't that she didn't love me because of my behavior patterns but that she still loved me in spite of them. I frequently reflect on this interaction when deciding whether or not a relationship I'm in is healthy for me."

ABOUT THIS CASE STUDY

Sydney is making observations about a healthy friendship in which honest feedback is the thread that strengthens the relationship over time.

Friendships with "B"s

Many of us have friendships with "B"s, and we don't necessarily recommend abandoning those friendships. We only urge you to spend time managing them to avoid getting stung. Friendships with "B"s are never dull. In general, "B"s have problems feeling true empathy, so if you open yourself to such a person and don't feel as much warmth in return, you should be cautious and aware of what makes you attractive to them, and what makes them attractive to you. Also, from a "B"s standpoint, friendships are all about opportunity. The following are specific "B" characteristics to be aware of so you can determine what kind of friendship to expect:

- When a "B" with anti-social behaviors encounters someone who she perceives as a willing participant for her mind games, she'll likely choose that person for a friend. Also, if there is someone she can manipulate into believing her lies and false stories, she'll want that person for a friend.

- When a "B" with narcissistic behaviors sees someone as important to others, he'll want that person as a friend in order to increase his social status. If he needs a promotion or a job and someone can help him get what he wants, he'll want that person for a friend.

- When a "B" with borderline behaviors wants to get back at someone who was her friend, she might make friends with her former friend's friend and then try to turn that person against her former friend.

- When a "B" with histrionic behaviors wants to be the center of attention and be "loved" by everyone, he might see everyone as his close friend. But in reality, his relationships lack depth.

The Need to Review Our Friendships

When you enter into a friendship with someone who has "B" behaviors, you sometimes will intentionally keep the friendship at surface level because it serves a specific purpose. Other times you might not recognize the "B" behaviors and jump in all the way, having no clue what lies ahead. While either type of friendship might meet your current needs, when an incident happens that pulls the friendship rug out from under you, the friendship becomes a painful experience.

Children are drawn to kids who are good looking, and good-looking kids tend to be more popular. A study by Robert Feldman looked at children ages 11–16 and found that lying as a social skill can help a child get along with other kids.[34] It also showed that the best teenage liars are usually the most popular. As we get older we continue to be drawn to people who are good-looking and popular and who appear to be successful. These tendencies are further reasons why we should review our friendships from time to time to see if we really know our friends—or just think we know them.

GERALDINE

"I had a coworker who always wanted to room with Amelia, the highest-ranking person in our workgroup, whenever we attended a conference. Once I asked this coworker if she considered Amelia a close friend. She replied, 'Oh, nobody gets close to Amelia.' I thought her comment was very odd, and it said as much about her as it did about Amelia."

Friends I Thought I Knew

Not all friends are who they seem to be. The news media is full of stories of people engaging in "B" behaviors. The stories are often accompanied by interviews with people who were suspicious of the "B" behaviors and had abandoned their friendships

[34] Feldman, "UMass Researcher Finds Link Between Lying and Popularity," www.sciencedaily.com

with the perpetrator. As part of the story, there is usually an interview with someone who remained the perpetrator's friend in spite of what others said.

When "B"s get into trouble, there is commonly a person (or group of people) who remains a supporter longer than anyone else. What do "B"s tell these people? How do they draw them in? We all have different receptors that make us engage with certain people. Perhaps we need praise, need to save someone, or just want a friend. The "B"s will discover these receptors and use them to get what they want.

PENELOPE

"For many years I had a friend, Harriet, an intelligent, well-educated professional who was also gifted in the arts. Harriet's husband owned several condos around the country, and a group of Harriet's friends and I would go on vacations and stay in the condos. When she was in a good mood and things were going her way, Harriet was a lot of fun. At other times, however, she would verbally attack me for no reason.

"Once, Harriet wanted to redecorate one of her bathrooms, and we agreed that I would get the supplies. As I was setting up for us to paint, Harriet kept questioning everything I was doing: the paint colors, the undercoating, the sandpaper, everything. I figured she had given me a job to do and that I was more than competent enough to do it, so I was offended when she took over once I had purchased the supplies. She did this with almost every aspect of our relationship, even claiming some of my work as hers.

"One day I realized that she made me feel the same way my dad had made me feel when he would verbally attack me for no apparent reason. I decided that I had had enough of that as a kid and didn't need such a relationship now. So I wrote Harriet a letter and ended our friendship. Harriet has a lot of friends, and maybe they don't have the same button that I do."

ABOUT THIS CASE STUDY

As a child, Penelope had developed a high tolerance for manipulative and demeaning behaviors. Penelope's tolerance for this behavior was a perfect fit with Harriet's need to criticize. These interlocking dysfunctions allowed this friendship to develop and be maintained for many years. Luckily for Penelope, she was insightful enough to recognize that the destructive pattern in her relationship with Harriet mirrored her relationship with her father. By recognizing that Harriet's need for absolute control was destructive, Penelope found the courage to permanently extract herself from this friendship.

Perpetuating the Behaviors

MARTIN

"I had caught my best friend, Henry, in a couple of lies. So when he told me he had a crippling disease, I couldn't help but question the veracity of what he was saying. Around the time I was getting ready to confront him, Henry called and informed me that he was in the hospital. I asked if I could visit him, thinking he would say no, but he said, 'Sure, that would be great, and could you bring me some magazines?' I was pretty surprised and remember wondering how he would pull this one off. The next morning I went to the hospital with my magazines, not really expecting to find him there. But he was at the hospital and looked terrible, too. The nurse wouldn't let me stay long, so we couldn't talk much. I felt like a jerk for not believing him.

"Soon, I realized that the section of the hospital he was in was a research center advertised on TV. I decided to call the place and sure enough, they only conducted experiments, not treatments. You would think that would have pissed me off but I was relieved, knowing he was lying again. When I called him to ask what the hell was going on, he said he couldn't tell me because there were a lot of other people next to him but he'd tell me when he was released.

"I never really did hear his explanation. His only response was, 'Hey, you say you don't like the things I've done, but I'm not that bad of a guy.' Years later we are still in touch, and I just take what he says with a grain of salt."

MIKE

"My best friend, Eric, said he was going to get 'taken out' if he didn't pay his gambling debt. He said he needed $4000 within an hour, so I gave it to him and he left town. Ten years passed with no contact from Eric. He still had not repaid me, so I sent him a letter that was really just a bluff. In the letter I said I was getting an attorney so I could collect my money. Shortly after I sent the letter, a registered letter showed up with $4000 in it. I heard he had started a business and I think he sent the money because he didn't want to be sued."

ABOUT THESE CASE STUDIES

We often make decisions, consciously or unconsciously, to remain in relationships that we know are not healthy for us. We may be lonely and decide this relationship is better than no relationship. We may be conflict avoidant and fear we will hurt someone's feelings or lose our friendship if we confront a friend who is lying. We may second-guess ourselves and feel we are to blame if things don't go well. Accepting and tolerating these behaviors continues to leave us, along with anyone else who encounters a Henry or an Eric, as potential victims of deceit.

People who are not "B"s care about the wellbeing of their friends. Henry and Eric used their friends' caring attitudes as a manipulative tool that caused Martin and Mike to lose sight of their own boundaries. Henry disregarded Martin's feelings, felt no remorse and had no obvious motivation to change his behavior. Martin's decision to not hold Henry accountable for his lies likely fueled Henry's desire to continue lying.

Mike was a victim of Eric's deceit for ten years but was finally able to raise himself out of the victim role and rescue himself from a bad situation. If Eric had a conscience, he would have paid Mike back without being threatened by an attorney. Mike held Eric accountable for his lies, albeit ten years later, and Mike got what he needed to finally put this relationship to rest.

Choosing to End a Friendship

PHIL

"When I started college, I supported certain political candidates because my dad did. In my freshman year I met a kid named Kyle who opened my eyes to a broader world. He set me to reading a lot. Since he was a junior, I thought he must be like God because he had made it through two years of college. He would challenge everything I believed in. Philosophically, I did a '180' after a few years. Kyle and I started an underground paper.

"After a while, I began to see the real Kyle. He was arrogant and self-righteous, putting people down and acting like he knew more than they did. It got to be too much. Kyle's idea of exploring the world was to hitchhike to Costa Rica. He got dysentery, and his parents had to fly there to get him. Kyle and I parted ways. He went to graduate school at another university. I was in graduate school and when I returned home, Kyle and I ended up working for the same company. We didn't do things socially because I got married and had children while Kyle was still smoking dope."

ABOUT THIS CASE STUDY

At times we find ourselves idealizing someone for talents that, in hindsight, don't seem quite as amazing as they first did. Phil was drawn in by his admiration for Kyle, and this idealization was magnified by Kyle's verbal challenges that made Phil question his own beliefs. This was a perfect setup for Kyle because he needed to feel superior. As Phil matured and asserted himself as a professional equal, neither Phil nor Kyle was getting what he wanted from the relationship.

MORGAN

"I was taking a journalism class in college, and a friend from high school was also in the class. We were given an assignment to interview someone else in the class, and my friend and I interviewed one another. Several days later, I walked into the instructor's office to pick up my paper. All of the papers were lying on his desk. My friend's paper was on top, and I made the mistake of reading it. I soon realized she had written all kinds of things about me that not only weren't part of the interview but weren't even true. Some of the things she wrote were really nasty. Since I was identified in the paper, I was really embarrassed and was ashamed to face the instructor after that.

"I had always admired this friend and thought she was someone you could trust. I didn't understand why she harbored these feelings about me. I ran into her a few times after that, and each time I made excuses for why I couldn't see her. It was bad enough that she had said things about me that weren't true but the instructor had given her an A, and I got a B on my paper. It was like rewarding someone for telling lies. I had forgotten this incident for 30 years until something reminded me of it. I guess you really don't forget this stuff."

RITA

"Deidre and I instantly became best friends. As children who felt cut off from our families for various reasons, we had much in common. Deidre and I sought support and solace from each other. But when we traded stories, Deidre's examples always had to be a bit more extreme than mine. Deidre acted as though she always had it a bit harder than I. The fact that Deidre always played the martyr didn't really bother me until one day when Deidre crossed the line. She told such a bold lie about a mutual friend that I could no longer make excuses for her. Subsequently, I could only see Deidre as someone who was damaged and capable of doing evil to others. I felt she really believed the stories she told about other people.

"I started to see Deidre as someone who was capable of hurting people whose characteristics magnified her inadequacies. Her lies often targeted the most kind, generous and successful people because these were the people who had things Deidre saw as threatening to her sense of self. People with husbands, children, career success and strong friendships were the targets of her attacks."

ABOUT THESE CASE STUDIES

Morgan and Rita each learned from an unmasking experience that exposed their "friends." Like Morgan, Rita suddenly recognized the destructive patterns in her friend's behaviors. This led them to distrust and separate themselves from these unhealthy friendships. Rita clearly describes many typical behaviors of a narcissistic "B." Although there is no way of knowing, Rita's observation that Deidre might actually have believed the lies she told is interesting. Perhaps it's the belief in their own fabricated stories that makes the lies "B"s tell so believable to others.

Selective Devaluation

SAMANTHA

"I wish I could put into words the face my former friend, Julie, made at me yesterday morning at a neighborhood fundraiser. I was volunteering along with many others including Julie's husband, Len. Len and I had a pleasant exchange before Julie arrived. When she arrived, Len was ahead of her and he stopped at the table where I was working and selling tickets. Len paid, and we joked about something. Julie was behind Len, projecting the most hateful facial expression imaginable. Thinking Julie could be ill or something else was wrong, I found myself saying a friendly "Hey there," even though Julie has ignored me off and on for several years.

"Julie responded by avoiding my gaze and ignoring my words. I realized she must have actually felt fine because later I saw her with a group of people, laughing and having a good time. I keep reflecting on her face, the look of pure hatred and disgust. I believe she did it because she was behind Len, and he could not see her. Julie would never have dared to make that face in front of Len. And if someone had told Len that Julie had behaved that way, he never would have believed it."

CLAIRE

"After a night at Brenda and Clayton's house, my husband and I would get in the car to leave, and I would start venting about how horrible the experience was for me. But my husband, Elliott, would always have had a good time, joking, being silly, laughing. It almost seemed like they—especially Brenda—put him on a pedestal while they knocked me down. It was subtle, not what she said but how she said it. Often I would be alone with Brenda so Elliott wouldn't be there to witness it. This went on for years until one night, when we got in the car and I said I would never go back there. Elliott hadn't noticed any of Brenda's nasty behaviors toward me.

"Although my husband continues to have an occasional relationship with Clayton, I've distanced myself from Brenda. She was a college roommate of mine. Now that I think back to those years, I realize Brenda would constantly find ways to put me down. When we took classes together, she joked about how bad I was in that particular subject. Never once did she offer to help me, despite the fact she got straight As. I was the only one she asked to be in her wedding. At the time I was flattered that she had asked me, but later I questioned whether she chose me because I was the only one who put up with her demeaning behaviors."

ABOUT THESE CASE STUDIES ───────────────────

It is often difficult to know why a "B" sees you as a threat, but to a "B," selective devaluation can successfully keep that threat at bay. The selectiveness of the devaluation is very isolating for the recipient of the "B's" behavior. It can take the form of a simple gesture, like Julie's stare. In Claire's case, the "B" devalued her but not her husband, the person who was closest to Claire. This made it difficult for Claire to discuss the "B" behavior with her husband, who had experienced the opposite behavior from Brenda. It's possible that Claire was uncertain if it had even happened, and perhaps she blamed herself. Using selective devaluation, it is important for "B"s to demean their victims covertly and to not allow those whom the "B"s deem as impor-

tant to witness their obnoxious behaviors. This allows the "B"s to maintain their sense of self-importance and to allow others, who are not the target of their behaviors, to continue to view them in high regard.

Join Me in My Misery

STACY

"As a college student, I lived in an apartment with six other girls. Nola, one of the girls, had been my best friend since preschool.

One day, Nola called all the roommates together. She informed us that she was unhappy with her life and her living situation (us), and she was going to move out to 'avoid all of us ending up hating each other.' Nola stated that she no longer enjoyed our company and she dreaded coming home because she didn't like us anymore. She made me so frustrated that I started to cry, but Nola was emotionless. A few days later, when Nola came to remove her things, she admitted that she was selfish and she did things for herself, no matter how others were affected.

"At the time, I felt Nola was looking for a simple solution to a very complicated problem. I felt like I couldn't keep up with the level of intensity Nola needed in a friendship. She needed to have fun all the time. She liked to get drunk and party and if things were not fun enough for her, she got moody and frustrated. While inebriated, she performed dangerous acts like climbing buildings, yelling at police or driving drunk.

"Nola called me several years after she left the apartment, asking if I wanted to go out for drinks. We went out and we had the emptiest conversation. She was not interested in me or in my life but wanted to know about mutual acquaintances, including all the gossip I knew about the people we used to hang out with. At that point I made a conscious decision not to have any more contact with Nola. She had the insight that she was selfish but rather than considering it a flaw or something to work on, she just saw it as a fact."

ABOUT THIS CASE STUDY

Nola is an example of a "B" that has little empathy for others. Stacy's observation that Nola was empty is an apt description of an antisocial "B." Nola's need to engage in dangerous behavior in order to get a charge from life is also typical of an antisocial "B." It was unacceptable for Nola to see her friends happy when she was not. Nola was miserable and she attempted to get her friends to feel as miserable as she was by highlighting their flaws. Stacy gave Nola a second chance in order to be certain the friendship was not salvageable. That decision seemed to make it easier for Stacy to walk away and not dwell on a failed relationship.

Put Your Guard Up and Keep It Up

CARA

"Bill was one of the first friends I made in high school, and we had some great times together. He was intelligent and often had the right thing to say in social situations. He was well known and, needless to say, I felt pretty cool being Bill's friend. He was generous with his money and would often spend it on me. We talked for hours on the phone almost every night, and when I look back I realize how much he interfered with my studying. He was outstanding at persuading me to do things I knew I shouldn't do. Although I now feel like an incredible chump, I didn't recognize his destructiveness at the time.

"Bill would focus his attention on my best friend, Tess, and me. He would talk to me about Tess, whom he liked, and I would give him advice. He made me feel like I helped him. He also introduced me to his friend Michael, who became my boyfriend. Despite the fact that Bill was dating Tess and I was dating Michael, Bill would try to seduce me. One night, Bill and I sat by the lake in a secluded spot. I was upset because my uncle had just been killed. That didn't matter to Bill. He showed no support and kept changing the subject. Later on he wanted to kiss me. Bill was actually able to convince me that kissing him was okay, just as friends. I wasn't even physically attracted to him. I look back now and get angry and confused at how I let him control me.

"One day, Bill called in a panic. He disclosed that his dad was in the mafia and that he had to move to another state and change his name. Bill sounded desperate and talked about having to decide between staying with his mom and leaving with his dad. He said he couldn't tell his mom because she'd stop him. Bill said he couldn't talk to his brother or sister. He cried and said he didn't know what to do. I believed every word he said and spent hours over the next several months comforting him.

"Only Tess and I knew about Bill's dilemma, and Bill instructed us not to tell Michael or any of our other friends. Bill even set the date when he would leave town. How could he be lying? It was too outrageous. I was spending more and more time on the phone with him, ignoring my schoolwork. Finally, one evening my mother noticed me crying and I told her the story. She called Bill's mom, who responded by telling my mom, 'That's just Bill.' Bill never left with his father, who was not in the mafia. Tess and I wanted to see what would happen on the date Bill said he was scheduled to leave. The date came and went.

Bill never explained himself. We never confronted him. The situation was just ignored but Tess and I both became wary of Bill.

"After the mafia episode, I tried to keep my distance from Bill but since he was my boyfriend's best friend I still had contact with him. After graduation, Bill convinced us that he had a rare form of cancer in his upper arm and it would eventually be fatal. Tess only stayed with him because of his cancer.

"As I was gaining trust in my mother's judgment, I told my mother about Bill's terminal cancer. She mentioned it to a physician friend of hers, and he told me that the next time he visited I should invite Bill to the house so he could observe how Bill moved his arm, and he'd be able to tell if Bill had this rare form of cancer. After shaking Bill's hand and watching him move, this physician told me it was very doubtful that Bill could have this form of cancer and still move his arm like he did. Subsequently, Tess and I, with Michael watching, told Bill we didn't believe him. Bill and I fought. I called him a liar, hoping to God he did not have cancer. It was so hard for me to tell him he was a liar when he tried his best to convince us otherwise. Neither Tess nor Michael would fight with Bill. They were terrified of conflict and of being wrong. I showed Bill absolutely no compassion or warmth, and our friendship ended.

"Bill disappeared for a few months, only to reappear during my freshman year of college. Bill would persistently call Tess and me on the telephone. He was basically his same charming self, with just a hint of insanity. Neither Tess nor I would talk to him. However, my roommate didn't believe Bill's history and would talk to him for hours. During my sophomore year, Bill finally seemed to have disappeared. After I finished college, I was grateful he didn't know where either Tess or I lived. We both hoped he would be out of our lives forever.

"Years later, when I ran into a former high-school friend who had invited Bill to her wedding, I discovered that she had received an email saying Bill had died. The email was vague on details and basically stated that the family didn't have a lot of information. I laughed because I was sure the email was not true—which shocked my friend. She later discovered that Bill had sent the email and was alive and well. When my friend confronted Bill, he laughed it off as a joke."

ABOUT THIS CASE STUDY

Bill was constantly testing people by trying to draw them into the "B's" nest with his antisocial "B" behaviors such as lying, manipulation and game playing. For some, it took multiple stings to recognize his behavior patterns and to learn that Bill would only retreat when people didn't interact with him. People with antisocial behaviors love playing games, and when the game is over they finally move on. The important lesson is that, even years later, Cara couldn't put her guard down. Cara learned that it is extremely unlikely "B"s can change their behaviors. In Bill's case, as long as people allowed him to play his games, he would always come back for more fun.

An Antisocial "B" Claims a Friend

ANDREA

"I first met Scott when my friend Lisa and I picked him up from his home. Lisa and Scott had recently met at a local gym. Scott proceeded to tell us that he was in the process of applying at law schools and he had had an oral interview at one of the schools earlier that day. As part of the interview he was asked to tell about the strangest thing that ever happened to him. He told us the story he had told the interviewer and then explained that he made up the entire story on the spot, just for fun. He was later accepted into that law school.

"After Lisa and Scott started dating, my boyfriend and I invited them to my parent's cottage for the weekend. When we arrived, my mom offered them some beer. Scott asked what kind of beer she had. My mom listed several brands, and he responded by saying, 'No thanks, I'll just go to the store and pick up my own beer.' Scott bought beer and a lot of food even though all our meals would be taken care of by my parents. When Scott returned, he and Lisa went into their bedroom and shut the door and they stayed there until dinner.

"Scott appeared at dinnertime and saw a potato salad sitting on the counter that my mom had made. He asked me what was in it. I answered, 'I don't know for sure, but it's potato salad,' and I flippantly added, 'I guess it has potatoes in it.' I thought he was joking until he asked me more aggressively what was in it. I told him again that I didn't know what he meant. He said, 'You mean if I offered you a hundred dollars you couldn't tell me what's in the potato salad?' I couldn't believe we were having this bizarre conversation and told him I would guess it was potatoes and mayonnaise. He then demanded, 'Is it mayonnaise or Miracle Whip?' I told him to open the refrigerator to see what was in there. Then he wanted to know if it had regular salt or sea salt.

"I didn't know Scott very well and my patience for him was starting to wane. We decided to watch a movie and eat in the downstairs family room. Scott and Lisa remained upstairs at the kitchen table, refusing to join us. I don't know if Scott ate the salad. After dinner they spent the evening in their bedroom.

"The next morning, I came downstairs to find the kitchen a disaster. Scott had prepared an elaborate breakfast for himself and he left every dish unwashed and in the place he had last used it, including his own dishes that were still on the breakfast table. He and Lisa were holed up in their room again. I cleaned up their dishes later that day because it was obvious that they were not coming back downstairs.

"We had invited Scott and Lisa to spend the weekend with us but we hadn't spent more than a car ride and an unwanted trip to the grocery store with them. I knocked on their door to ask if they'd like to go canoeing with us. They said they would come along. We went canoeing and were in three canoes. In one canoe, Scott was in the front with Lisa in the back. Scott spent almost the entire canoe ride sitting backward in the canoe and splashing his paddle like a child. Lisa just laughed at his immature behavior.

"The ride home was the last straw. Scott was badgering my boyfriend about how much money it would take for him to let someone else sleep with me. My boyfriend neither engaged with Scott nor answered his questions. It felt like Scott was trying to get my boyfriend and me to argue with each other. The weekend getaway had become two of the longest days of my life. I was so relieved when I finally dropped Scott off at his house. Lisa and I were good friends and coworkers. I was worried about seeing her the next day at work because I thought for sure she would feel embarrassed about Scott's behavior. I was prepared to say it was okay because I didn't want to jeopardize our friendship.

"When I got to work, Lisa was talking to Scott on the phone. She hung up while laughing and saying how funny Scott can be and commented on how silly he was over the weekend. I felt shocked that she wasn't going to acknowledge his rude behavior. My heart started to race. Finally, I had to say how embarrassed I felt in front of my family because I had invited such a rude and ungrateful guest to their home. Lisa started to cry and said that after her last relationship ended, she promised herself she would never ask a man to change for her again. She accepted Scott's behavior. Our friendship ended over this exchange. I tried to talk it over but Lisa would not discuss it.

"Lisa married Scott and moved with him to another city, where he started law school. I remember seeing a letter she wrote to a coworker about her relationship with Scott. She said she felt like during her whole life she'd been missing a part of herself and she finally found her perfect match. A few years later I ran into a mutual friend and I asked if she was in touch with Lisa. She affirmed that she was and that she was going to Lisa's upcoming wedding. I thought she was married to Scott, I said. The friend said, 'Oh, that didn't work out. He flunked out of law school because all he wanted to do was sit around, watch television and spend money.' "

ABOUT THIS CASE STUDY

This is another example of how being involved with a "B" can quickly invade many areas of your life. Scott's attempts to pit Andrea against her boyfriend and her mother (as in the potato salad discussion) were antisocial "B" games. The lies Scott told in his law school interview were also games. Fortunately, Andrea and her boyfriend didn't engage with Scott's games. They refused to enter the "B's" nest with Scott, no matter how bizarre his behavior became. Lisa, on the other hand, did buy into Scott's rude game-playing behavior. Lisa admitted she had no boundaries in relation to Scott when she revealed that she would never ask a man to change. Lisa's thought that Scott was gifted likely made her feel special. This idealization created the perfect backdrop for her becoming his guard "B."

Andrea stepped into the "B's" nest the minute she gave honest feedback to Lisa about Scott. Although Lisa had observed Scott's devaluing behaviors toward Andrea and her boyfriend,

*she viewed Andrea as the persecutor. This explains why Lisa
became irate when Andrea noted her observations about Scott's
behaviors. Lisa's denial was an indication that she was guarding a "B." As a guard, Lisa placed Scott in the victim role with
Andrea as his persecutor and she went on full-force attack as
his rescuer. Andrea was shocked when Lisa refused to listen to
what she had to say but she was even more stunned when this
conversation ended their seemingly close friendship.*

Establishing Boundaries
with a Borderline "B"

BRUCE

"I had this friend, Jillian, who was also my coworker. My friends
warned me about Jillian but they weren't specific, so I just kept
our friendship going. They said it was a feeling they had about Jillian but I didn't want to believe them. A big reason for my denial was
because Jillian was so much fun. She would do just about anything on
the spur of the moment, and I liked that.

One of the first times Jillian's abusive nature surfaced was when I
helped her look for a condo. Jillian's allergy to cats flared while we were
inspecting one apartment and she verbally berated the realtor. I
thought Jillian's extreme reaction was inappropriate, so after she left
in a huff I apologized to the realtor. When Jillian called me to look again
the next day, I didn't want to go with her so I reminded her that her sister was a realtor and suggested that she ask her sister for help.

"When my partner suddenly broke up with me, I realized that Jillian's
lies about me had been responsible for the breakup. I confronted Jillian,

telling her she had manipulated me. After that, she gave me the cold shoulder at work. My hurt feelings grew when I realized that she and my ex-partner had become friends.

"After my friendship with Jillian ended, a coworker who had known Jillian since childhood shared specifics with me about her abusive behavior. I suspect this coworker didn't want to tell me while I was still under Jillian's spell because she thought I might tell Jillian and was afraid Jillian would retaliate against her.

"Occasionally during our friendship, Jillian would threaten to kill herself but I didn't know if she meant it. Within a week after our relationship soured, Jillian again threatened to kill herself. Kiley, another woman in the office, said she had dealt with Jillian's suicide threats by setting limits from the outset of their friendship. Jillian had accepted those limits and remained Kiley's friend.

"After our friendship ended, Jillian and I still shared tickets to a music festival, and I confronted her, saying I wouldn't go to the festival with her if she talked about killing herself. She left my office and released her ticket to me."

ABOUT THIS CASE STUDY

If this story makes you dizzy, it's because it's about the destruction caused by borderline "B" behaviors. In addition to threatening self-harm, Jillian was manipulative, unreasonable, impulsive and hostile, while also being dependent. Bruce initially saw her impulsiveness as fun and charming, until Jillian destroyed his relationship with his partner. Jillian likely lured in Bruce's partner by portraying herself as a victim. The coworker, who shared her experiences with Bruce only after his relationship with Jillian ended, also displayed the typical fear that borderline behavior can engender in those who observe it.

Kiley, who set firm boundaries at the outset of her interactions with Jillian, fared better than Bruce. By sticking to her boundaries, Kiley allowed Jillian to decide if she still wanted to be her friend. Bruce was not able to maintain a relationship with Jillian once he set limits because he had already entered Jillian's "B's" nest. When he finally set limits with the music festival tickets he changed the rules by leaving the "B's" nest. Jillian felt exposed, and that exposure threatened her sense of self. This example demonstrates the importance of establishing your personal boundaries early on in a relationship.

Hollow Friendships

ANASTASIA

"Sue and I had been friends for 15 years. In March of last year, Sue and I signed up for a cooking class. The class began in May and at the first class, Sue walked in, went to the other side of the room and ignored me. I went home and told my husband that things seemed strange with Sue. But she had a habit of being moody, so I assumed she was in one of her moods or perhaps it was my imagination. Sue's lukewarm behavior continued through all of the classes.

"On the last day of cooking class, I realized Sue had left early. I didn't see her leave, and she didn't say good-bye. I came home angry at first and then I felt worried. What if something bad happened? It seemed so strange that she wouldn't even acknowledge that she was leaving. My husband encouraged me to call and check in with her. I called Sue, and she informed me that I said something months before that had hurt her feelings. Feeling confident that I wouldn't intentionally hurt

Sue's feelings, I asked her what I said and I felt prepared to apologize. Sue said I had told her I liked one of my other friends better than I liked her. I couldn't remember saying anything like that and simply said I never meant to imply that I liked my other friend better than I liked her. Sue stated that she tried to get past her hurt feelings but she didn't think she was going to be able to.

"Nothing I said seemed to have any impact on her. She would respond by saying, 'Yeah, that was how I heard it.' She had no emotion in her reactions, and I felt completely blindsided. I realized that Sue's behavior at cooking class was intentional and that she was punishing me for something she thought I had done months before that she hadn't even spoken to me about. I felt angry at the way she was treating me, and it didn't fit with how I would define a close friendship.

"I got the sense that Sue needed to hear that she meant more to me than my other friend. The truth was, when I was with my other friend, my heart always felt full. Many times when I was with Sue it was like walking on eggshells. I was never completely at ease with Sue. Even after many years of friendship, things always felt better with us when we were buffered by husbands and kids. I told Sue that she meant more to me than the other friend. She replied nonchalantly, 'I feel better now, do you?' As I choked back my sobs, realizing our friendship was a farce, the phone clicked. She had another call and she took it. I realized that Sue felt nothing. Our phone call ended, and Sue didn't even call back to ask me how I was feeling though she knew I was crying. She never considered that her distrust of our friendship was painful for me.

"Not knowing quite what to do, I made the next move and invited Sue to a play. The three hours we were together, we barely uttered two words to each other, and it was extremely awkward. After that night we had no contact for months, until Sue sent me an email. I showed it to another friend, who read it and called it cruel. On the surface it looked like an apology, and I wanted to believe it was an apology. What was missing from Sue's email was any emotion about our friendship. There was no expression about feelings of loss, about the value of our friendship, about our love for each other as friends. Below the surface, it said, 'You are weak and neurotic. You make me angry. You owe me an apology.' I responded with an email. I expressed how confusing the situation was for me. The final straw came when Sue left me a hateful phone message in response to my email, saying that I needed to apologize to her.

"It seemed Sue's goal, consciously or unconsciously, was to have me build my life around her and abandon or decrease the significance of other friends in my life. Therefore, the 'fight' or 'argument' that ended our friendship was about my not choosing Sue over another friend but instead staying true to all of the friendships I cherish. When Sue realized that she would never achieve the goal of separating me from my friend, she took away her friendship and left me feeling like I had failed at one thing I take great pride in: my relationships with friends.

"As a casualty of this abandoned friendship, relationships that had grown from our friendship were lost. Our spouses were friends with each other and with each of us. Our sons were friends. Their extended families and our extended families were entwined in varying levels of relationships. The wake of destruction in the path of this failed friendship seemed overwhelming. Sometimes the sadness of losing all this made it seem worth swallowing my pride and my values regarding true friendship to give Sue what she needed to make this friendship work again. When I reflected on what that would mean, I couldn't begin to guess what would make things right with her. Every time I tried to take a step forward, she was on the other side, pushing back.

"When a friendship of this duration fails, you find yourself looking for clues to help understand how it can disappear overnight. You find yourself wondering if this friendship was ever real. When you start examining the history of the relationship and recognizing some of the patterns, you find yourself wondering, 'What is wrong with me that I would stay friends with someone like this for so long?'

"I remember once telling Sue about an argument I had with my mother. Her response was, 'Huh, I thought you were close to your mom.' Her reaction implied that one disagreement with someone negated all the love, affection and respect that developed over the years.

"I remember telling Sue after having my first baby that I had gone to a mom's group. She responded by saying, 'Huh, I never saw you as a mom's group type of person.' I couldn't understand what that was supposed to mean. It was as if she had a fixed idea of who she thought I should be and eventually, when she learned I didn't fit that mold, was disappointed. Sue didn't have close girlfriends. She had some friends through her husband but she always said negative things about them.

"If I had to do it over, I would've paid more attention not to what Sue said but to how she said it. Also, it's not what I said to Sue that mattered but how she heard it. Everything I said was subject to her skewed interpretation focused on her blaming me at some point, regardless of my actual intentions. I was always making excuses for Sue, convincing myself that she had good intentions deep down. I was always searching for commonalities, probably seeing them in places where they really didn't exist. This makes me think our relationship was doomed from the start."

ABOUT THIS CASE STUDY ————————————————

In this case the evidence needed to end this friendship was overwhelming. However, this is an example of how difficult it is to end a friendship that's entwined in many elements of your life. After Anastasia ended her friendship with Sue, it was much easier for her to see Sue's patterns of abuse. This is why it's so important to step back and observe the patterns in a friend's behaviors when you begin to feel uncomfortable. While it's good to look at your own patterns of behavior, it's more important to pay attention to how the friendship makes you feel. Sue played the role of victim, counting on Anastasia's propensity to feel guilty and look inward.

By playing the role of victim, Sue tried to make Anastasia the persecutor by implying Anastasia had hurt her feelings. When Sue openly accused Anastasia of being the persecutor, Anastasia made an attempt to rescue Sue. This switch caused Sue to quickly return to her real role as persecutor. Sue had Anastasia on the defensive from the start. She also used subtle intimidation with her aloof and indifferent attitude. This caused Anastasia to more vigorously pursue Sue's friendship. The more Anastasia tried to connect with Sue, the more unreachable Sue seemed to become. Once their relationship started to spiral downward, it finally became clear to Anastasia that there was no real basis to their friendship and it was built on false pretenses, created by Sue, to give the illusion of friendship. As soon as Anastasia abandoned her role as rescuer, however, Sue's game and the illusion of friendship were over.

JANELLE

"When I first met Karen, we were in college and moving into a house with three other women. I quickly noticed Karen was going to be needy and I consequently kept her at arm's length. I have a vivid memory of the first time Karen and I went running together. Karen asked me how far I run, how many calories I count and so forth, and I immediately felt she was competing with me. This was not a pleasant feeling, and I wasn't a willing participant in the competition. This friendship felt different than all my other friendships.

"My good friend Liz was also living in the house and was just getting to know Karen. Liz deduced right away that Karen wasn't someone she wanted to befriend. Karen had a habit of sharing extremely personal information with all the housemates about her relationship with her boyfriend. I remember feeling sorry for Karen's boyfriend, wondering how he would feel, knowing Karen was disclosing personal information about him. When Karen left the house, the roommates would discuss her inappropriate behavior.

"After college, I remained 'friends' with Karen because our lives took many parallel turns. I worked with Karen, and eventually we were neighbors. We had children at the same time, and our kids became best friends. We shared the same friends and simultaneously bought houses on the same cul-de-sac. We had the same hobbies and joined the same groups. Although Karen and I were together a lot, I always had some reservations about her. Our friendship never went below the surface. I tend to be an affectionate person and was puzzled about why we didn't have a stronger bond, given all we had been through. I noticed that Karen's other 'close' friends seemed to keep Karen at a distance, and mutual acquaintances with strong personalities expressed a dislike for her.

"The hardest times with Karen were when we were alone together. I always felt I was under Karen's microscope, and she was watching and judging me. One day I walked up to Karen's front door, and Karen commented about how I was wearing a new bra. I was dumbfounded that anyone would notice something so subtle. Another time I found out that Karen had commented to our friends that I wear my wedding rings wrong. I was hurt and confused about why something so innocuous would become idle gossip for her. When I talked with Karen, she always demanded my full attention. However, she didn't pay as much attention to what I was saying and was always peering over my shoulder, looking for the next person to come along. When I told Karen that my grandmother was dying, she took a call on her cell phone in the middle of our conversation. She also had a habit of coming to my parties a little bit late, always making a grand entrance and presenting me with a beautifully wrapped gift.

"People who got to know Karen on the surface described her as perfect. Karen also demanded perfection from the people in her life, and they always seemed to disappoint her. She used to tell our group of friends and me, 'My family let me down, my friends will never let me down.' Karen leaned on her friends and depended on them, expecting them to always include her. This got to be too much.

"After 16 years of friendship, I could feel myself trying to separate from her. I realized I didn't want to be identified by friends as one word: 'Karen-and-Janelle.' I felt guilty but our friendship had been exhausting me for years. I was one of the last in our group of friends to maintain a relationship with Karen.

"After a year of trying to distance myself from her, she approached me and said she wanted to talk to me about our relationship. The thought of meeting with her to discuss 'a problem' caused me great anxiety. I didn't want to discuss this with Karen for fear of how she might treat me. I reluctantly set up a meeting with her. After several cancellations, we met—and it was totally anticlimactic. We didn't discuss our relationship at all, and when I had to leave, Karen said, 'We'll have to meet again to talk about things.' I then realized there was a time when I thought we had to work things out to keep the peace, live in the same neighborhood, and have the same friends. But now I realized I didn't have the energy for Karen. My other friends told me they always wondered what hold she had on me. I kept questioning my responsibility, wondering what was wrong with me to cause this friend-ship to not work.

"The last several years our friendship sat in limbo. We co-existed when we were in common social situations, and I avoided places I knew Karen would go. I found out Karen was moving to a different state when I was out with a friend, and we ran into Karen. She didn't even look at me. She had a brief conversation with my friend and stated that she was moving in two days. I wished Karen luck and breathed a sigh of relief that this chapter in my life was finally over."

ABOUT THIS CASE STUDY

Many "B"s have loose boundaries, and try to get others to loosen their boundaries as well. Karen's extreme need to control every aspect of her life and the lives of others provides a great example of both narcissistic and histrionic behaviors. She used her loose boundaries and critical behaviors, by commenting on Janelle's bra and how she wore her wedding rings, to subtly demean Janelle and keep her in a one-down victim role. Karen expected attention from everyone but offered little in return. Her inability to value her friends showed through in her idle gossip, critiques and judgments. Karen set up her friends for the impossible while continually asking them to uncondition-ally meet all of her needs.

Those who saw her for what she was, or was not, could rec-ognize this quickly and not engage. Others, who gave Karen a chance by trying to develop a relationship with her, were left with emptiness, frustration and regret. Janelle distanced herself from Karen when she recognized her behaviors were abusive. Janelle's switch caused Karen to switch from the role of perse-cutor to victim, hoping Janelle would return to the rescuer/guard role. This would've allowed Karen to switch back to the persecutor, and Janelle to the victim. Instead, Janelle exited the "B's" nest, and the game was over.

The stories of Anastasia's and Janelle's one-sided friendships are similar not just for the content of the "B's" behaviors but also for the length of the friendships. One lesson we learn in these stories is that convenience and proximity are not necessarily good reasons to continue a friendship. The need for close relationships sometimes leads us to tolerate "B" behaviors we might not tolerate in different circumstances. Remember that high-functioning "B"s have an uncanny ability to assess our needs and use those needs to enhance their self-esteem. Once the "B" has you in the "B's" nest, he needs only to shift roles to keep you there.

Anastasia's and Janelle's desire to be warm and caring with their friends provided perfect targets for those with "B" behavior patterns. Both Sue and Karen counted on Anastasia's and Janelle's needs to make friendships work. Imagine friendship on a tightrope, in which one party is holding tight to one end while the other party is shaking the other end. These friendships were longstanding only because of Anastasia's and Janelle's steadfast desire to have true friends. Once Anastasia and Janelle matured and evolved in their own lives, they were able to step back and realize they were in empty relationships. The moment each of them started to assert themselves, the "B"s dropped their end of the tightrope because they knew the game was over and they were no longer in control.

SUMMARY

PEOPLE HAVE FRIENDSHIPS FOR MANY REASONS. This chapter revealed that true friendships are based on mutual trust. When a "B" is one of the partners in a friendship, however, it's difficult to know if the trust is real or one-sided, or if it exists at all.

Establishing a true friendship is risky and requires hard work. When you suspect that all of the effort to sustain a friendship is one-sided, you need to question whether you have a true friendship and whether it's worth your effort. Some people realize, many years into a friendship, that a friendship is not genuine. They then realize the extended relationships created by the friendship make the friendship difficult to dissolve.

Opening up to a "B" takes its toll, and when you steel yourself to end such a friendship, the slightest crack in your armor invites the "B" to buzz through, looking for new ways to sting you. The old saying, "With friends like these, who needs enemies?" was tailor-made for "B"s. Even a true friend can be lured away by a jealous "B."

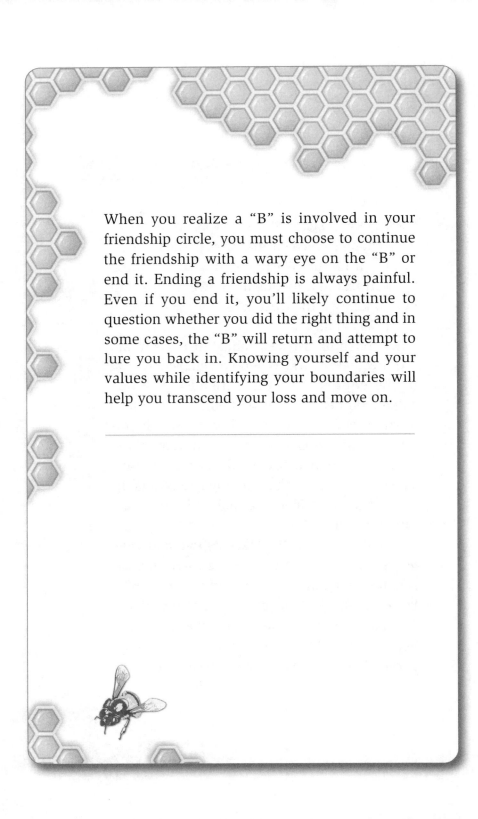

When you realize a "B" is involved in your friendship circle, you must choose to continue the friendship with a wary eye on the "B" or end it. Ending a friendship is always painful. Even if you end it, you'll likely continue to question whether you did the right thing and in some cases, the "B" will return and attempt to lure you back in. Knowing yourself and your values while identifying your boundaries will help you transcend your loss and move on.

Family, Spouses and Lovers

*"So, like a forgotten fire, a childhood can
always flare up again within us."*

GASTON BACHELARD

When we are young, we look to our families for guidance and support, love and kindness. It's a general assumption that family members support one another through good times and bad. You accept your family members with their quirks and foibles, just because they are family. Despite these common assumptions, you don't choose your family members, and because of that, you might share few commonalities. Family relationships often evolve without much question and without jointly establishing firm boundaries. Sometimes family members take advantage of you. When you feel like family members are repeatedly stinging you, it is likely that "B"s are in the nest.

It is one thing to be stung by a stranger or a friend. It is altogether different to be stung by a family member, a spouse or a lover. The difference lies in the complexity and dependency of the relationship and the fact that with family members, spouses and lovers, we not only share physical space but we have intimate physical involvement with them. These people become part of us and they know us at our weakest and most vulnerable moments.

129

Parents' values don't always reflect what their kids would like to value in their own lives. Siblings don't always see eye to eye. Spouses and lovers become part of our family, bringing "B" behaviors and tolerance for "B" behaviors with them. It's not always acceptable to have open discussions about family behaviors, especially when the behaviors are maladaptive and manipulative. This absence of conversation results in feelings of confusion, resentment and pain. Extended families also have layers of complexity wrought with opportunities for misunderstandings and hurt feelings. When a stranger "B" stings you, it can be painful and annoying but it doesn't typically turn your life upside down. When a family member stings you, it's like an infected wound. You have to tend to it diligently or it may never completely heal. When "B"s are part of a family structure, there can be a lifetime of cumulative stings. Real or surrogate parents have a great deal to do with how our relationships develop with our family and with our love interests.

Nuclear Families

Although most people crave love, trying to squeeze empathy and love from a "B" can be like trying to get honey from a wasp. We don't always recognize these patterns when we are young and dependent on our parents. We might even grow up thinking the behavior of a "B" is normal, and it's not until we engage with someone who is not a "B" that we realize that some past family behaviors were bizarre.

BECKY

"Before I met my husband, I think most guys I dated were a male version of my mom. She never asked me what I wanted to do. Instead, she would always force me to do whatever she wanted me to do. My whole childhood was learning to deal with situations I didn't want to be in. I kept a notebook of quotes—quotes that gave me the comfort of knowing I would survive. I was desperately searching for a haven in my mind, a refuge. I would cry myself to sleep because I felt overwhelmed thinking I would have to please everybody the next day, and needed rest. Starting in first grade I remember being anxious and looking for words of comfort, and I found them in books.

"I always thought that my father and I got along because he and I had similar personalities. However, he didn't stand up to my mother. Things were to be a certain way and you didn't question it. Then there was my sister, who was a lot like Mom. Her teasing could be hurtful. Whenever I would complain to Mom, she would say that it was my sister's way of showing affection. As an adult, I worked through these issues with therapists and friends, and they allowed me to extract myself from this destructive pattern through awareness and a lot of hard work."

FRANK

"As I grew up and became more independent, I realized that my father is selfish and totally self-absorbed. I have three kids now and we live close to my father, but he only sees his grandkids and comes around to visit on his terms. It is typical for him to come into my home unannounced, pick up the beer I'm drinking, drink from it

himself and then keep it. He always wants a hug from me but it's completely one sided. What about when I want a hug from him sometimes
and he isn't around? He is never around for me."

JULIANA

"My father owned a general store. From the time I was 13, I
worked for him at the store. He didn't pay me but promised the
time I put in would translate into college tuition. One day I was
talking to my father, and out of the blue he said that when I come to
the store he's always so embarrassed about my yellow teeth. He asked
me to please brush my teeth. I didn't know what he was talking about
since I always brushed my teeth and didn't think they were yellow.

"One day at home I caught a glimpse of my father out of the corner
of my eye just as I was going to brush my teeth. I purposely left the
bathroom door ajar so he could see me. With great flourish I put the
toothpaste on the brush but then my father suddenly burst in and
yelled at me for using too much toothpaste. Recently my brother told
me that our father had told him how ashamed he was to see him down
at the store because of his acne."

LIONEL

"In my family the message was, 'Be nice to people no matter
what.' The most important thing was to be liked. Dad talked about
our neighbors as though their lives were perfect. He was so
focused on how great everyone else was but never on the strengths
within our family."

ABOUT THESE CASE STUDIES

In these vignettes it's easy to see how parental "B's" who strive for perfection and who need to control their children can take a toll on their children, even when their children are adults. Parents who are "B's" usually have few if any boundaries. If children do not establish independent, personal boundaries early on, the "B" parent might draw them in as if they were part of the parent's own persona. Often it's only after children move away from home or establish a relationship with someone who doesn't exhibit these controlling behaviors that they finally can start to see patterns of "B" behaviors and realize they were in a "B's" nest.

Where Did You Get That Need to Please?

VIOLET

"My grandmother once took me aside at a family gathering and told me that I was her favorite grandchild and that I always have been. I have a sister, and we are close. I was upset by my grandmother's behavior because it made me feel guilty and also sneaky, because I never wanted my sister to find out what my grandmother had said. I thought it would hurt my sister's feelings. I felt I had to act extra nice so I wouldn't fall from my grandmother's good graces. Even though I didn't necessarily believe what she said was true, I also felt somehow indebted to my grandmother after she said it."

ABOUT THIS CASE STUDY────────────────────

It wouldn't be surprising if Violet's grandmother had also told Violet's sister that she was her favorite. Because of their incredible ability to weave in and out of the truth and play one person against another, it's often difficult to pin down the lies that "B"s utter. The desire to believe what someone says also enhances the "B's" ability to deceive.

JUDITH

"I dearly love my grandmother, but she can be a bit difficult. Shortly after earning my doctorate, I planned my wedding day. Knowing that I was including in the wedding ceremony many of the traditions that my grandmother treasured, I thought the wedding would please her. During the wedding and the reception, however, she sat with her arms crossed and with a disapproving look on her face.

"Two weeks after the wedding, my husband and I drove to Texas to visit my grandmother and her husband in an attempt to smooth things over. During dinner her vitriol surfaced. She made a point of saying her friends' grandchildren were much more accomplished than I was because they had graduated from college in only four years. I reminded her that I had earned a doctorate and it took longer because it was a higher degree. She retorted that I wasn't a real doctor.

"She proceeded to talk about my wedding, saying she didn't like the band even though she had recommended that type of band. She was upset that she wasn't invited to the rehearsal dinner. We had only invited the wedding party because of limited funds, but she didn't like that answer. She was also upset because she wasn't in any of the professional photographs. She had wanted the photographer to take some shots of just her, alone. Even though I started to cry and her husband started to cry, she didn't alter her behavior or show any compassion. My husband and I were supposed to stay for four days but we left the next day."

ABOUT THIS CASE STUDY

It is common for "B"s to have a need to show their best side to the world, and many "B"s are extremely talented. It would be common for children or grandchildren to look up to such "B"s and think of them as special. Since "B"s have a distorted sense of self, they are always looking for others to fill their constant need for admiration, approval and acceptance. They try to erode other people's boundaries so others will reflect back to them the image they are seeking to portray. When you are a child or a grandchild of such a "B," you have little wiggle room to express yourself and your desires. You might be in awe of them, however, and not notice their lack of attention to your needs. Thus, when it is your turn to seek approval from such a "B," you may be disappointed.

You will never be good enough to please someone with narcissistic "B" behaviors, especially when, like Judith, you are more accomplished than the "B." Judith's grandmother, with little subtlety, pulled several "B" tricks out of her book. She tried to place Judith in a double bind when she gave her these simultaneous but contradictory messages: "The reason you went to college was to be the best but you didn't do it in four years," implying that her accomplishments didn't count. When Judith called her grandmother on that insult, the grandmother devalued Judith by saying Judith wasn't a "real doctor."

Inability to Self-Reflect

GINA

"I have a brother who is selfish, egotistical, and has no ability to self-reflect. He is 62 years old, single, never married, no children, and has not had a job for the past two years. He is someone who's still trying to figure out what he wants to be when he grows up. Our parents were notorious for telling us how special we were when we were children. I feel my brother believed all the praise they bestowed on him and he was never able to recreate this adulation in the 'real world.' I also used to believe my parents when they told me I was special. I started to question it when I was starting out in my career and people would give me constructive feedback regarding my faults. I stopped believing my parents and learned that I needed to work harder to improve my skills.

"My brother and I used to be close but our relationship deteriorated when I completed graduate school and earned a higher degree than he did. He never acknowledges my son, his only nephew, on his birthday or on holidays. Our father recently passed away, and my brother was barely involved in any of the long-term planning for our parents during our father's illness. He is now in a fight with our 95-year-old mother, and they are no longer on speaking terms."

ABOUT THIS CASE STUDY

While it is healthy for parents to praise their children for a good effort or for accomplishing something after applying focused, hard work, parents do their children no favors when they tell them they are special for no reason at all. Such children might grow up exhibiting "B" behaviors, believing they are special and resenting those who work harder and accomplish more than they do.

They Give and Take Away

ELENA

"My aunt married a man who wanted to start a butcher shop. My father lent them money to start the business. My aunt was very happy that my father had lent them the money. But the business moved into the red, stayed there and finally, threatened with bankruptcy, my father bailed out the business and took it over. My aunt divorced her husband, blaming my father for her failed marriage. Then she came to live with us. I worshipped her because she was lively, pretty and a classy dresser. She was always angry with my father, but he just let her criticisms roll off his back. My father cheated on my mother, so I always had some doubts about his character.

"In later years I spent a lot of time caring for my aunt, even though she never seemed to appreciate the things I did for her. As my aunt was dying, long after my father had died, I found a letter she'd written to my brother and me about what a terrible man my father was. It was very unsettling, and I destroyed the letter because I didn't want any part of it."

ABOUT THIS CASE STUDY

It is very common for "B"s to blame others for their misfortunes. Borderline "B"s will turn on a dime to bite the hand that feeds them and then might turn again to be nice to that person and repeat the cycle. Elena's story highlights the way someone with

"B" behaviors might lure you into thinking she is an extraordinary person, and how it's easy to feel obligated to help such a "B," especially when the "B" also adopts the role of martyr. It's likely that Elena went out of her way to help her aunt because her father's womanizing had planted the seed of doubt in Elena's mind about her aunt's manipulative behaviors.

ZEKE

"My friend Mike was in a rocky marriage and when he was diagnosed with a serious illness, his marriage fell apart. In the ensuing months after he and his wife, Kitty, split up, Mike confided in me, saying that he was afraid of Kitty. He kept notes on his almost-daily encounters with her. An example:

Kitty called five times after 9 p.m. On the first call, we had a long discussion. The second call I couldn't answer, and she got the answering machine. The third call, Kitty said she wanted out of the marriage and that she wanted her old name back. The fourth call, Kitty wanted me to take her out for dinner on Sunday. I told her I would not. Kitty taunted me, saying that I couldn't take her but could take my sons to dinner. She again said that she wanted a divorce immediately and her old name back. On the fifth call, Kitty said she wanted me to tell her to have a good night and to tell her I love her.

138

ABOUT THIS CASE STUDY

These passages typify Mike's 70 pages of notes. Kitty's unstable and paranoid behaviors, along with how quickly she switched from persecutor to victim and occasionally to rescuer exemplify borderline behaviors. Rather than staying in either of the behavior patterns for long, Kitty kept changing. A review of Mike's notes revealed, unfortunately, that he readily fell into the rescuer role. The fact that Mike occasionally called Kitty and even asked her to dinner gave her intermittent positive reinforcement. This reinforcement only served to increase Kitty's maladaptive and often-stinging behaviors. By answering his phone, by engaging Kitty in conversation, and by succumbing to her invitation to socialize, Mike assured himself a place in the "B's" nest.

Our Internet Family

With the advent of blogs, Facebook and Twitter, the Internet has become a surrogate family for those in need. These devices enable "B"s, who have no boundaries, to push your boundaries. The Internet is full of the diatribes of "B"s and also of the forlorn cries of "B"s who have been stung by other "B"s. People who email nude pictures of themself to someone else, thinking the emailed pictures are forever going to be isolated to the recipient's inbox, have no boundaries.

We encountered a blog written by someone whose father had just died. The blogger had little good to say about her father and went on to express that as a child, she had received her father's undivided attention. In fact, she said her father had taught her not to trust anyone but him. She was not allowed to have friends because everyone she liked had something about them that her father disliked. It was the blogger's job to entertain her father, cheer him up, and even keep her father's secrets when he was unfaithful to her mother. According to the blogger, her father was a constant liar and seemed to lie about everything for no reason. She acknowledged that her father had taught her many things but when she surpassed her father's abilities in those areas, her father withdrew any approval he had previously given her.

It's easy to be drawn into such a story and to feel sorry for the blogger. However, as we examine her story, we're left to wonder if her story is true and whether she has assumed some of her father's traits. We're forced to question why someone would be writing about such personal issues in such an impersonal blogosphere. Surely some of her friends will read her story, but it's also open to the world to read. This situation causes us to question whether the blogger wanted readers to feel sorry for her by portraying herself as a victim. Perhaps the real victims in this situation are those who regularly read such blogs.

Children in the Age of Technology

PAULA

"When my daughter, Rae, started high school, she was a straight-A student and an athlete. Rae was immediately accepted as part of the popular crowd. Boys from the senior class started calling and texting. While this attention was flattering, Rae was a bit overwhelmed by all it entailed. Although Rae was a beautiful, kind and caring girl, she often struggled with low self-esteem and concerns that she was not good enough. She was quick to apologize for any conflict or wrongdoing, whether or not it was her fault. At the end of the first semester of her freshman year, Rae became involved with an older boy.

"One day at home, I noticed Rae was on the phone looking white as a ghost and crying. After much probing, she explained that something horrible had happened. Once I ruled out heroin addiction and pregnancy, Rae was able to tell me she had 'fooled around' with a senior boy. He was extremely charming and kind and had told her she was smart and beautiful and that he cared about her. But Rae later found out that the boy, whom she was still dating, was also dating a junior girl at their high school.

"She was mortified, and sought counsel from a 'friend' on how to best handle the situation. Should she confront the boy? Should she inform the girlfriend? Rae took her friend's advice and decided to break things off with the boy. Rae's friend then decided it would advance her own social standing and help her get in the favor of the older high school students if she told the junior girlfriend that Rae had been fooling around with her boyfriend. When Rae found out about her friend's plan to share the information, she was unsure how to handle the situation. The senior boy contacted Rae and told her to lie and to deny the whole thing. Between texting and Facebook, the rumors and hateful comments spread like wildfire. There were statements about Rae being a 'slut' all over Facebook.

"I saw my daughter's reputation destroyed in one click of a button. Parents of some of the high school students would approach me and say things like, 'It's too bad about what Rae did.' No one even knew the real story. I feared for my daughter, who internalized problems and blamed herself. I knew that when Rae was elevated so fast to the in-crowd, it was a dangerous place to be. She makes a perfect target because of her innocence and her need to please people. It was a very hard lesson for her to learn and it was sad to see her struggle. Although she had a best friend who lived outside of our community, Rae did not even tell her what she had been through because she felt embarrassed and ashamed, and she blamed herself."

ABOUT THIS CASE STUDY ───────────────────────

As painful as this lesson was for Rae, it also presents an opportunity for Rae's mother to teach Rae about "B" behaviors. There are so many cruel stories from our teenage years, and budding "B"s are often the perpetrators. While the technology may have changed, Rae's story has many of the same characteristics as the stories in chapter two. Unfortunately, because of advanced technology, the speed with which a sting can occur has intensified. This means it's more critical for parents to begin discussing "B" behaviors with their children at a very early age.

Partners and Significant Others

ERIKA

"Early in my relationship with Ed, we went to his niece's baptismal ceremony, where I met many of his friends and extended family for the first time. At the reception, Ed introduced me to lots of people. Then he pointed out a woman who was an old friend of his sister-in-law, and he told me that she was really nice. While he was leading me over to meet her, I asked Ed for a little background information and he told me some things about her. He introduced me and left me to talk to her.

"As I brought up some of the things he had mentioned, I found out very quickly that they weren't true. I looked over at Ed, and he was watching me with some other people and laughing. The thing that struck me most at the time was that the 'joke' wasn't even funny. I don't take offense very easily. I appreciate humor, even at my expense, but this joke was just stupid. And then it struck me that taking an opportunity for a joke (and getting credit for it—he told these other people what was going on as they watched me) was more important to him than any awkwardness I might have felt.

"I was quieter than usual on the drive home. Ed asked if I was offended but he didn't seem too concerned. He didn't apologize but only explained to me that I shouldn't be hurt or think it was a big deal. I was baffled because the joke was juvenile and I didn't understand why he would put me in that position on an occasion when I was trying to make a good impression. What a guy! It's like he was stuck as a 14-year-old boy. He liked to have fun and always had the newest toys. He was always trying to find himself, buying spiritual self-help books and searching for something to fill a void."

ABOUT THIS CASE STUDY

This story highlights the lack of compassion in "B"s who try to devalue you. When you associate with a "B" who seems to need the stimulation from practical jokes in order to feel animated, it's wise to be suspicious that you might be dealing with an anti-social "B." In such a situation, it is essential to set strict boundaries and continue to enforce them when the "B" engages in manipulative behavior. In this situation, Erika needed to describe Ed's behavior, tell him she would not tolerate such behavior in the future, and let him know what the consequences would be if he tried to embarrass her again in public. The last and most important point is that Erika would need to follow through with the consequences if Ed repeated his behavior.

DELORES

"My boyfriend, Stan, and I enjoyed doing exciting and interesting things together. Stan lived at home with his parents, who had a very strained relationship. At times, I had the feeling that Stan was a substitute for his father, who was physically and emotionally unavailable to his mother. In a way, it was as though Stan put his mother on a pedestal and she ultimately had control over him. His mother was attractive, athletic and bright. Stan would talk about her with pride.

"I never felt accepted by his mother, even though Stan and I dated for years. Once, we went on a picnic with Stan's parents, the only time in our relationship that I really saw his parents socializing together. His mother saw me drinking out of a soda can and said, 'Perhaps you could use a cup and be civilized.' That same day, Stan and I were goofing off and I was tickling him in the back of the car. His mom got out of the driver's seat, walked to the back of the car and told me to stop picking on Stan.

"Stan never stuck up for me when his mom was on the attack. Although Stan always talked about wanting to marry me, he remained living at home, not going to school or having any major life aspirations. I was finishing college and applying to graduate schools. I had plenty of friends, while Stan started to have fewer and fewer friends. His world seemed to be consumed by his time with his mother.

"As Stan became more isolated from the world around us, I wondered if he was depressed. I finally told him that his lack of involvement in his life and his dependence on me was becoming a burden. I explained that I cared about him and suggested that he might benefit from seeing a therapist. Stan went home and contacted me the next day. He simply said, 'I talked to my mom, and she doesn't think I have a problem.'

"We stopped dating shortly after that, and I tried to maintain some semblance of a friendship. I remember talking to him on the phone and gently trying to break it to him that I had started dating someone else. Stan replied by saying, 'I already knew you were dating Jon. My mom told me, and I think she actually got some pleasure out of telling me that.' He told me he was happy I had found a nice guy.

ABOUT THIS CASE STUDY

Stan is the perfect receptor for his mother's controlling behaviors. No one will ever be good enough for her son, and she'll be there to assure that he doesn't find anyone who will threaten her control over her son's life. Breaking into a relationship like the one Stan had with his mother is fraught with danger, and is a good reason to pay close attention to family dynamics during the dating process.

EMILEE

"I met Rupert when he prepared my taxes. He pursued me after that, and we married shortly afterward. We ended up having three children. Rupert mostly stayed home with the children and never worked much after our marriage, even though he had a college education. He was fired from several jobs, and other jobs he kept for only a short time and quit for various reasons. So I have been the primary breadwinner for most of our married lives. Rupert inherited some money a few years ago. Managing that money has become Rupert's full-time job. He doesn't help with the housework or cooking or anything else around the house. He served several terms on the town board, a very part-time job, and now he has decided to run for town chairman. Rupert likes being in charge and acting like a big shot."

ABOUT THIS CASE STUDY

This story presents an interesting version of narcissistic behaviors. No job is ever good enough for a narcissistic "B," and as long as he can find someone who will support him, he can stay in a non-work or limited-work role forever. William Glasser described this type of personality as the "workless."[35] It has many of the characteristics of a narcissistic "B." Remember, someone cannot survive in this role unless he can lure a worker bee into the "B's" nest, enabling him to live the lifestyle he thinks he deserves.

[35] Glasser, *Choice Theory*.

Exciting "B"s

CAROL

"Andrew was a guy who made me lose all my sensibilities. I was standing outside the hospital where I was working and saw this guy riding by on something that didn't look like a bicycle. It didn't look like anything I had ever seen before. The next day I saw him again and I said, 'Hey, did you make that?' From there on, I fell head over heels for this guy. He was very handsome and had this incredible sexual appeal. He was also extremely intelligent. He had a Ph.D. in physics, had been a professional soccer player, had done whale research in South America, and had worked in a research station in Alaska. He also had his pilot's license and co-owned an airplane. When I met him, he was working on a project at the university on alternative energy.

"I thought it odd that Andrew never wanted to watch soccer. One day I started thinking his list of accomplishments seemed unbelievable, so I called the professional soccer team he said he had played for and learned that indeed he had played for them. I later confessed to Andrew that I had called the team. He was furious that I had doubted him. That was the first time I ever saw his anger. I had also checked on his other accomplishments and discovered they were real. He remained a friend of the woman who was doing whale research and he showed me a journal in which she was featured and he was mentioned.

"But once Andrew had me snared in, he changed. I was living alone and had a king-size bed. One side of the bed was filled with magazines. Out of the blue, he said, 'Look at you. You can't focus. Look at all the books you have.' After that, everything was fair game for his ridicule. I discovered that Andrew had been married and quickly divorced to three very young girls. It never occurred to me that Andrew was a drug addict and an alcoholic. He was always drinking and asking to see if someone had Ritalin or alcohol. It was no coincidence that all of his close friends were young physicians.

"One day Andrew was driving erratically, like he was angry. He cut someone off in traffic, and the guy motioned to Andrew to roll down his window. The guy told Andrew he was driving like a madman. Andrew rolled up his window and blamed it on me, saying I'd made him do that. He was always blaming others for making him do poorly.

"His birthday was the same day as my daughter's birthday. I told him I couldn't do anything with him for his birthday because my daughter was turning eighteen and I was going to spend her birthday with her. Andrew couldn't understand why I would put my daughter before him.

"I remember one time when he came over and helped paint a room. He would call out to me, 'Carol, I need help painting.' I think he just wanted me to watch him. Also, he would tell me weird stories. He made comments about the police always chasing him when he was living in another state. One day I was talking about Aaron, my former boyfriend, saying he had done something that bugged me, and Andrew said, 'Seriously, do you want me to kill him?' That sent chills down my spine. He would tell me I was being abusive to him and would make a gesture of self-protection. When I finally met Andrew's parents, I felt sorry for him because his mother was so self-absorbed. She talked nonstop about her accomplishments. She had just had her eyes done, and they looked like they would pop out of her head. Andrew's father ridiculed him, saying he was a 'soccer has-been.'

"At dinner parties, Andrew would monopolize the conversation with talk and subjects no one could understand. I was seeing a therapist, who said Andrew sounded like he had narcissistic tendencies. The therapist directed me to watch the movie Surviving Picasso. I then collected as much information as I could on narcissism and left Andrew what I had printed out, naively thinking it would help him deal with his problem. Needless to say, Andrew didn't see it that way at all.

"Andrew had a former girlfriend who broke up with him. She was getting her Ph.D., and I emailed her, mentioning the things I had noticed in Andrew and asking her if she had seen the same things. She emailed back and agreed with everything I had said and indicated that she was still trying to heal from her relationship with him. When Andrew and I were sorting out our relationship, he started seeing another woman.

"Andrew was selfish, and I found myself always paying for everything because he never had any money. The last night I saw him, I had just moved into a new condo. He proceeded to drink one and a half bottles of wine. He kept calling a physician friend of his because he was desperate to get some pot and he knew his friend had some. We went to a lakefront bar to watch fireworks. He was inside so long getting beer that he missed the fireworks. On the way home, he wanted to go to a bar to smoke a cigarette. I had never seen him smoke a cigarette. When they wouldn't allow smoking in the bar, we went to my place and he said, 'I guess I can smoke here.' I said no, and we had a huge fight.

"I took Andrew back to his place and on the way home I yelled to myself, 'That's it!!!' And that is the last time I saw him. Andrew had made me a metal sculpture portraying how the stars were aligned when we met. I was so angry at how everything had turned out that when I saw it sitting in the garage, I took a hammer and hit it. I hit it again and kept whacking it, and it felt so good. I never spoke to Andrew again. I spoke with one of Andrew's physician friends after our breakup and the friend admitted Andrew had drug-seeking behavior. I had dated some peculiar people but they didn't have the magnetic attraction

Andrew had. Although I never lived with Andrew, the physical attraction kept me with him for a year and a half. Other guys, I could just drop when they got weird. I probably wouldn't have been attracted to my current husband if I hadn't had these experiences that helped me realize that I didn't want someone who was so self-absorbed."

ABOUT THIS CASE STUDY

In many of the books on personality disorders, a narcissist is described as someone who holds himself in higher esteem than he deserves. The story of Andrew is a great example of how a "B" can indeed have incredible talents. While Carol was wise to check on Andrew's credentials, it was Andrew's behavior after he discovered what she had done that should have worried her. There were many danger signs in Andrew's behavior indicating that if the right buttons were pushed, he could become very aggressive. Andrew's rage, along with his blaming demeanor, addictive behaviors, love of excitement, game playing, and his suggestions of violence all point to an antisocial "B." This story demonstrates again how "B"s are unable to recognize their bad behaviors. Andrew's case would be a job for a very skillful therapist who could direct a "B" to focus on his behaviors and to understand their inevitable consequences. Getting a "B" like Andrew to the point where he was serious about seeing a therapist would have to involve a major crisis of losing what was most important to him: money, power, status or his freedom.

SABRINA

"On a trip to a South Pacific island, I met and fell for Paul, who was attractive, intelligent, witty, exciting and an entrepreneur. He owned and operated an island resort. Soon after, I moved to the island to be with him. I immediately stepped in to help with his business and I quickly became the manager of the kitchen and reservations. I am a strong swimmer, and during the first year I became an expert in snorkeling and scuba diving and helped with the lessons we offered the tourists.

During that year, things began to change between Paul and me. He would do strange things and I suspected he was intentionally trying to hurt my feelings. I also suspected he might be running around with other women. Sometimes I felt he was playing mind games with me but I was never sure. Finally, I threatened to leave him unless he married me. He chose marriage.

"Paul was a real wheeler-dealer. He was always trading this for that, buying things he couldn't afford, and trying to find innovative ways to keep the creditors off his back. I discovered that he had purchased a plane almost totally on credit. One day we were out in the surf and there was quite a rip current. We were diving, and I was paired with Paul. The current started to pull me, so I reached out to Paul. He looked at me and just let the current take me out. Thank heavens I knew how to save myself, but I ended up totally exhausted. I never trusted Paul after that.

"We had been married about six years when Paul suddenly asked for a divorce. I soon discovered he had a serious relationship with a wealthy woman on the mainland. I had learned my lesson about Paul so I returned to the island when I knew he wasn't there. I secretly documented all of the business records so I would have an equal hand when we went to divorce court."

ABOUT THESE CASE STUDIES

The stories of Carol and Sabrina are perfect examples of why charm and excitement are not the best indicators of a good candidate for a long-term relationship. Extraordinary charm is often the first clue a "B" is in your midst. Charming behavior and offers of excitement alone do not define a "B." However, they are often some of the first clues to "B" behavior and raise a red flag that you should be on the lookout for other behaviors indicative of a "B." Lies, cruelty toward animals or people, insensitivity toward your feelings, or indications that someone has no true feelings are all further clues. Although a "B" can turn on charm, a "B" has difficulty sustaining the charm. Look for instances in which someone is charming toward you but not toward others, or vice versa. Look for cracks in the charm armor and don't fill the cracks with excuses.

Charm with a Price

VICTORIA

"When I was in high school, there was a student in my class, Brad, who was rumored to have a crush on me. He was a bit goofy and a little nerdy and wasn't someone I would've noticed in a room full of people and thought, 'I'm attracted to him.' Nothing would have come of his crush if not for his friends, who were persistent in trying to convince me to give him a chance. They wore me down, and I decided I'd go out with him as much to get them off my back as anything else.

"I was a very good student and very responsible. Brad was outside of the norm for me. He was spontaneous and a free spirit. He would urge me to have a picnic on the side of a highway, in the middle of a farmer's field. He was very flattering, and he showered me with expensive gifts. This was not something I was used to in my previous relationships. Eventually, I started to see a certain charm in Brad. I felt that as I got to know him, he could be a lot of fun. I think I accepted his intensity because it was my senior year and it was time to start breaking away from the rules of my youth. Brad was not a serious student and although everyone in our large high school knew who he was, which made him seem popular, he was probably also seen as a character.

"Brad quickly annoyed my family. He called incessantly at a time before voicemail and caller ID. He often called during meal times and this drove my father crazy. My family would complain about Brad monopolizing my time. Once, I had just returned from summer camp and my family was throwing me a welcome-home party. I had gone out with Brad prior to the party, and he was able to manipulate me into staying with him much longer than I should have, so I ended up being quite late for my own party. My mother was furious.

"In hindsight, I feel like I knew on some level that I was being manipulated but I didn't know how to extract myself from Brad's grasp. My sisters questioned Brad's sincerity from the beginning of my relationship. During an intense conversation, Brad told my oldest sister he was going to marry me. Brad's statement seemed extremely presumptuous and she walked away. He gave her the creeps. On my birthday, my parents had planned a night of celebration. Suddenly, Brad showed up wanting to take me bowling. My parents said he was welcome to stay and join us but bowling was not in the plans for the night. Brad stayed but since he didn't get his way, he acted like an ass and basically ruined my birthday.

"Brad was constantly pulling me into his mind games. For example, while Brad and I were still dating, he told me that he liked another girl in our class. He told lies, and every lie he told seemed to fade as he moved on to the next lie. I don't recall ever confronting him in person about the lies and honestly can't recall our ultimate breakup.

By my freshman year in college, Brad and I were no longer dating but he continued to call me and stop by my dorm room. It felt like he had become a stalker. I learned over time to stop being emotional around him and to not engage with him. He would go away for a while but he would always return. The last time he called was my senior year in college. My current boyfriend took the phone from me and threatened to harm Brad if he didn't leave me alone.

"Even though Brad was out of my life, it was difficult to leave him behind me. I still had nightmares and found myself troubled by thoughts of him. I went to a therapist and told her my story. I cried and vented my frustrations. She recognized his type right away and commended me on getting away from him. She recommended that I put my memories and feelings about Brad in a figurative box to put away forever on a shelf. The therapist validated what I'd been through and this really helped me move on.

"The nightmares recur occasionally but I certainly have learned a great lesson from my interactions with Brad. I feel as though I would recognize someone with characteristics like this much more quickly. If anyone describes someone to me as charming, that's always a warning sign for trouble. I've also learned to trust my instincts."

ABOUT THIS CASE STUDY ───────────────────────────

Brad is the nightmare of every teenager's parent. With his charm, perpetual lying, and stalking behaviors, Brad had the behaviors of an antisocial "B." Victoria was used to feeling special by virtue of her academic prowess. But Brad approached Victoria from another angle, by being charmingly disarming and putting her on a pedestal. In dating Brad, Victoria gave in to pressure from her peers. She didn't listen to her family's concerns and didn't initially heed her sisters' warnings. This story highlights the need to listen to and trust your instincts. It also demonstrates how someone can have lasting effects that mimic post-traumatic stress disorder from something as simple as a teenage romance.

The Lure of Status

PHYLLIS

"For a short time, I dated a physician who turned out to be a very angry man. One time he had put ground beef out to thaw during the day and when he returned from work, he was furious to find that his cat had gotten into it. It was January, with sub-freezing temperatures. He dipped the cat in water and tossed him onto the balcony. I came over and asked him where the cat was, and he told me what had happened. After rescuing the cat, I called the friend who had given him the cat and said he needed to come and reclaim the cat. This physician would call me to have phone sex and he'd always say he was wearing some piece of female clothing. One day he told me he didn't want to see me any more."

ABOUT THIS CASE STUDY ——————————————————

The story Phyllis tells is a frightening example of a professional whose job is to help people yet has been frightfully cruel to animals. It also offers the lesson that just because someone portrays himself as an upstanding citizen doesn't mean this is the case. Phyllis should consider herself lucky that this man broke off their relationship.

Hoping for Change

LACY

"Liam had been in a ten-year live-in relationship when I met him. When his girlfriend moved out, he said he had been unhappy because his girlfriend had a lot of anger-management issues. Now I see in him all of the issues he accused her of having. Also, he said that his ex-girlfriend was unhappy because he didn't want children with her because of her anger problems. I was immediately attracted to Liam and I felt he left her for me. He made me feel really special and I thought, this is it; we're going to get married and have kids. I see now that what happened with him and his prior girlfriend is very similar to what happened between him and me.

"Liam didn't always remember things I said. If we had a conversation about something we had already talked about, I would always drop a few details to remind him. On the other hand, Liam expected me to remember everything he told me. If I didn't remember, he would just leave gaps and when I couldn't fill in the gaps, he'd get angry and give me the silent treatment. When I converse with my friends, I always acknowledge in some way that I am listening and hearing what they're saying. When I did this with Liam, he'd say, 'Stop interrupting me.' I can best describe Liam as both exhausting and addictive.

"A few years into our relationship, my attention shifted. I had started law school and experienced the birth of my first nephew. As I devoted myself to my studies and made time for my nephew, my relationship with Liam developed big problems. Liam thought I was neglecting him. He felt I spent more time with my family than with him. I had always gone to his family gatherings but he rarely came with me to see my family. He was increasingly giving me the silent treatment. I would ask what was wrong and he'd respond, 'We never see each other anymore.' He'd never try to understand my perspective. It was all about him.

"Liam spent a lot of money buying me gifts. I told him it made me feel bad because law school made me strapped for money. He continued to do it. He wasn't giving me verbal affection but he was substituting it with monetary items. Liam often tried to make me feel dumb and he tried to shame me. The part of me that is the vulnerable little kid would come out. Sometimes he would want me to be intelligent and then he'd switch and put me down for it. He would agree with me on something, and when I brought it up later, he denied having agreed with me. I think he wanted me to break up with him.

"I can't remember one time when Liam apologized from the heart. It was like a child being petulant. It was never genuine. I always had to get him to say it. He was so high maintenance. I was constantly apologizing because his feelings could be hurt so easily, which was ironic. I was walking on eggshells. I knew I wasn't doing what he wanted me to do, focusing totally on him."

LACY, AS A YOUNG GIRL

"My family used to take long vacations in the family station wagon, and I was by myself nestled into the far back of the car since I was the youngest and smallest. My brother would inevitably beckon me to come to the back seat by offering to scratch my back if I would scratch his. I would climb over all the luggage and coolers and scratch my brother's back for longer than he had even requested. When it was my turn to get my back scratched, he'd simply say, 'No, I'm not doing it.' This was not a one-time occurrence. I guess I was stupid because I trusted him again and again."

ABOUT THIS CASE STUDY

Lacy's story as an adult is eerily similar to her experiences with her brother in the car as a child. Perhaps Lacy's experience with her brother set her up to hope for someone's behavior to change. There seems to be a pattern of repeatedly trusting someone who takes advantage of her. Lacy was concerned that Liam didn't love her but was too lazy to end the relationship. Liam, however, was likely incapable of loving anyone the way we would define a loving relationship. Liam's overt sense of superiority belied his fears about his own inadequacy. In addition to Liam's lying and game playing, there were other "B" behaviors. Liam demonstrated a lack of empathy, extreme arrogance, and the black-and-white thinking that typifies many "B"s. Making Liam happy would entrap Lacy as the rescuer, fitting neatly between Liam's roles of persecutor and victim. Lacy also demonstrated a sense of inadequacy that kept her in the cycle of abuse.

Extended Family

ZACK

"Barry was my sister's live-in boyfriend. At a family Christmas celebration, Barry started a political argument at the table with my son, Sean. As Barry viciously attacked Sean for his political views, everyone else quietly left the table. Sean's wife decided to stay and support Sean. Barry was monopolizing the conversation and not letting either Sean or his wife get in any rebuttals. Sean finally left the table, and Barry stormed into another room. After that, Barry visibly ignored Sean and his wife for the rest of the evening. However, I noticed how quickly Barry turned on his charm and engaged in an active discussion with my son-in-law. Barry was trying to show that he was not the problem; rather, he was the very epitome of social grace. Sean and his wife decided that they didn't want to attend any more family gatherings if Barry was going to be present."

ABOUT THIS CASE STUDY

It's interesting how "B"s will cut some people to the quick and then turn around and just as quickly ingratiate themselves to others. It seems as though they are trying to prove to themselves that they're still worthy of being liked. Barry presents a good example of how a "B" can turn charm off and on like a faucet. If you are seen as important to a "B"s agenda, the charm will pour forth. If you are seen as a threat, the charm will end and you might be the recipient of the "B"s favorite weapon: shunning you. Barry's behavior also highlights the tendency of "B"s to engage in black-or-white thinking. If you don't show agree-

ment, then no amount of logic will penetrate the barrier they erect against you.

AUBREY

"I dread family functions because my sister-in-law, Monica, insists on directing every aspect. I feel I can do nothing right. Last Christmas, Monica, who always dresses suggestively, wore a very revealing neckline. I usually refuse to put up with Monica's behavior by being direct with her, and have suffered by ending up on Monica's blacklist. I've become the focus of much of Monica's malicious behaviors.

"Monica has power of attorney (POA) for finances for her father, Simon. My husband, Simon's son, and I have POA for healthcare. I'm a healthcare provider and understand medicines, so during Simon's recent hospitalization I sorted his medications and put the current ones in his medicine chest. Monica subsequently threw all of Simon's medicines away and then blamed me because they weren't there. When I discovered that Monica had thrown away hundreds of dollars worth of medicines I asked her why, and she replied that all of those medicines were not good for her father."

ABOUT THIS CASE STUDY

This story highlights some of the behaviors of histrionic "B"s. They often use sexual seductiveness to get attention from others. When that doesn't work, they'll move to catastrophic thinking to dramatize situations as a way of keeping the attention focused on them, whether or not the attention is positive. They are always vague in their explanations of wrongdoing. It didn't matter that Monica's father was the one who needed care. Monica would not relinquish the spotlight.

The Death of My Mother

WENDY

"I was home alone the night I learned of my mother's terminal diagnosis. My on-again, off-again boyfriend, Carl, asked to come over, presumably to give me comfort. I was hesitant, given Carl's habit of redirecting attention to him. It took my mother's terminal illness and watching Carl's cold response to my grief to make me realize that Carl would never change. Carl came over and brought loads of negativity with him. I was trying to process the information I had just received when Carl started complaining about politics and everything he could think of that was irritating him. He spent the night drawing attention to himself. He acted like a kid jealous of the attention I needed to give to my own family.

"I needed Carl to be sympathetic with me because I was mourning my impending loss. This is what it took for me to realize he could never give me what I needed from a relationship. I broke up with him right after this. I had struggled with this relationship for years. Carl was always promising me a chance of children and holding it over my head. He would say that there was a sliver of a chance that he would want children. He knew if he told me there was no chance of having children, I would break up with him. He would shine this small glimmer of hope so he could maintain control over me. My reaction to my mother's illness and my breakup with Carl has given me clarity. I now grieve for my mother. I have lost Carl and feel a burden has been lifted."

ABOUT THIS CASE STUDY ——————————————

The ongoing contradictory messages from a "B" can be subtle and easy to overlook. Oftentimes it takes a crisis of some kind to get people to clearly see the true colors of the "B." Wendy was frustrated by Carl's mixed messages. On one hand, he gave the impression that he wanted to come over to support her in her time of need, but on the other hand, he couldn't get beyond his own needs and therefore wound up interfering with Wendy's ability to take care of her needs. Carl was vying with Wendy for the victim role in the "B's" nest. Unfortunately, a time of crisis is also a time when we have limited energy to confront the "B."

Dead "B"s and Gifts that Keep On Giving

◇◇◇◇◇◇◇◇ **NANETTE** ◇◇◇◇◇◇◇◇

"My mother-in-law treated me well during the first years I dated her only son. But she became progressively cooler toward me during the years approaching our marriage. I didn't know much about Faye's background but somehow I always felt inferior to her. Faye dressed well and was intelligent. After the wedding, I felt my husband pulling me away from my family and also from the siblings I felt closest to. We also moved away from the friends I knew, and I found myself in an environment where I felt isolated and lonely. We would never visit my parents, only Faye.

"During the years I knew Faye, she changed personas multiple times and I was never sure who the real Faye was. I discovered Faye had a daughter out of wedlock and was forced to marry the father of her child. Faye quickly divorced her husband and put her daughter up for adoption. This allowed her the freedom to work and date men in the evenings. Faye began seeing a wealthy married man. When he finally divorced, she married him, quit work and became a local socialite. She also had a son (my husband) by that marriage. When her second husband had an affair and divorced her, Faye returned to work, retaining some of the status she had achieved in the community. After the divorce, Faye looked to her young son as the man of the family.

"Faye dated another man for fifteen years and suddenly married him a week before I married her son. During Faye's third marriage, her party-girl persona emerged. She would host parties for friends who drank until everyone passed out on every flat surface in the house.

"After a few years, Faye divorced her third husband and married again. During this marriage, Faye morphed back into a previous persona of a respectable woman who attended church regularly. During her drinking binges, Faye made scathing comments about my family and me. Faye was always really high on some special person she had just met. Then at a later date she would suddenly despise that person and say nasty things about them. Or she would be very friendly to someone's face only to denigrate that person when they were gone.

"Faye reconnected with the daughter she had given up for adoption and decided to drive across the country to visit her. Her daughter's husband became angry with Faye because Faye was argumentative and played loud music all night. The noise kept Faye's granddaughter up on the night before she was to take the SAT. Faye's son-in-law was so angry he made Faye leave early the next day. Faye never contacted her daughter again.

"In like manner, Faye blamed me when I divorced her son. I didn't see Faye again. Despite this, I would hear from my son some of the scathing comments Faye still made about me. I had achieved some level of contentment since my marriage ended. However, I had been having occasional nightmares and although unsure of their details, I was sure at least some of them related to my former marriage. I would wake up in a cold sweat with that familiar feeling of dread like something awful was about to happen. It was during the time I was having nightmares that Faye died. I didn't know why I had to go to the funeral but I felt compelled. I rationalized it was to support my son, who lost his grandmother. I did want to make him feel better but the real reason was buried deep down where those things go that we never want to or expect to face.

"During and after the funeral, as I reconnected with some of the people who had crossed paths with Faye, I was able to piece together many of the answers to questions I had carried with me for years. The funeral was a cathartic experience. For the first time, I was able to put Faye's life into a broader context. It helped me to better understand her, to understand why my first marriage had failed, and to realize how I had become complicit in the patterns of behavior that were repeated over so many years. After the funeral, I never had another nightmare connected to those early experiences with Faye and her son."

KRISTA

"It was the summer after my sophomore year of college. I was wearing a short dress with black tights, standing behind a sofa, when I saw Charlie. He was very charming, and we started dating immediately. On the first date he said he loved me. He swept me off my feet with charm and attention. He wanted to be serious right away but wasn't really the man I'd envisioned for a husband.

"He had just been discharged from the army. He told me it was a medical discharge but much later I found out it had been a dishonorable discharge. Charlie told me he was the same age as I was but he turned out to be a year younger. Among my standards for a man to marry were that he had to be a college graduate, non-smoker, non-drinker, and didn't swear. Charlie was not the man I wanted to be involved with in a serious way. However, I was also very lonely. I wanted a boyfriend. I had been in love with a man for four years who met my standards but didn't reciprocate my feelings. So Charlie filled a void with his attention, proclaimed love, and the promise that he would go to college and quit drinking and smoking. Those promises allowed me to let my heart give it a chance.

"When it became obvious that Charlie wasn't going to meet my expectations, I broke it off. I was enrolled in a four-year college out of town, and when I broke up with Charlie I really missed him. He repeated his promises again, so we got back together but I still didn't agree to marry him. One problem was that Charlie wanted to have sex, but I was committed to finishing college and remaining a virgin until I married. One night, on a deserted beach, Charlie raped me and I became pregnant. I was mortified, and when my parents found out they urged me to get an abortion. I was very torn between having the baby and giving up my dream of finishing school or having the abortion. I knew I didn't want to marry Charlie.

"My parents convinced me to have an abortion out of the country, and we were on the first leg of our trip when Charlie showed up and begged me to go with him — just so so we could talk. I went with him and he took me to his married sister's house where he tried to convince me to marry him. When I refused, he forced me. He told me if I didn't marry him he would take a knife and carve up my face so no one would ever want to look at me, let alone marry me. He also threatened to harm my family. He forced me to go to Las Vegas with him, watched me whenever I had contact with anyone else, and even listened in on any phone calls until after the marriage was performed. We returned to his mother's house after the marriage, and the first night the bullying continued because I was now his wife. I told him I had never wanted to marry him. Enraged, he hit me across the face. Through my tears and bleeding lip, I told him that if he ever hit me again, I'd figure out a way to get away from him.

"Months later, Charlie was having a temper tantrum and picked up my little kitten and threw it across the room. I realized he was jealous of the love I had for the kitten. For the first time in my life, I felt red-rage anger and I stood up to him. Charlie swung his arm back and wound up to hit me. But then he stopped, remembering what I had said—I could see it in his eyes. He stormed out the door and raced away in his car. I stood there shaking, thinking that the kitten could have been the baby. I knew it was just a matter of time before Charlie couldn't control his anger. As long as we were with him, my unborn baby and I would both be in danger. I knew then that despite his threats, it was much more dangerous to stay than to try to escape.

"Hoping Charlie would stay away long enough, I called my father and told him to come and get me RIGHT NOW! He came immediately, armed with a pistol, and took me home and locked all the doors and windows. My father and brother went over later to get my things. Charlie came to my house many times to apologize and beg me to come back, but I never opened the door to him.

"I delivered a baby girl and was terrified that Charlie would abuse her if he had contact with her, so with great difficulty I gave my daughter up for adoption. It was the hardest thing I ever did. I also had to get over Charlie. I still loved him in spite of all he had done.

"I returned to college, had a great time, had lots of terrific boyfriends, got a super education, graduated, and met and married a wonderful man, Larry. But when Larry and I were first married, I began having nightmares. I dreamt Charlie was coming back to get me. I would wake up crying and terrified. I think my subconscious associated the state of being married with being held prisoner. Larry would comfort me and hold me. Then Larry told me that the next time I dreamt Charlie was coming to get me, to dream Larry into my dream and he would beat Charlie up. I did, and it worked.

"Many years later, when my daughter reached adulthood, she and I sought each other out and reunited. We have a special relationship. Her adoptive parents loved and cared for her and raised her to be a very sweet and kind person but she also has many of her father's tendencies, which she has to fight. Eventually she tried to find her birthfather, something I discouraged because I still feared for her safety. But it turned out that Charlie had committed suicide when he was 30. My daughter also found that Charlie had married another woman and abused her, even breaking her jaw. His wife told my daughter to send her thanks to me. She said, 'The abuse would have been much worse if your mother hadn't stood up to him and left. He remembered that.'"

ABOUT THESE CASE STUDIES

Nanette and Krista's stories demonstrate how past relationships with "B"s can continue to haunt us. Some of the most painful "B"s are dead ones, voices from our past. All of the "shoulda, coulda, wouldas" that dance in our heads can set us up for a lifetime of post-traumatic stress. Post-traumatic stress can trigger nightmares about people who have stung us in the past. Others who respond to us with similar "B" behaviors can trigger memories of past stings. We can be reminded by simply hearing the name of the person who stung us. We can even be reminded by seeing someone who looks like the person who stung us. It is easy to see how powerful some of the "B" behaviors can be.

Faye's ability to devalue people who were not in her favor left an indelible mark on Nanette. Both Charlie and Faye exhibited a typical "B" behavior of expressing charm early in their relationships with others. Later, their charms morphed into attempts at bending those relationships to their wills. Although Nanette and Krista made their escapes in different ways, they were both able to remove themselves from the "B's" nest. In both cases, escape came at a cost.

The first step in fighting back is to understand ourselves, why we link up with certain people and why we are taken in by certain "B"s. Funerals can be conduits to re-discovering our past and placing our memories in perspective. It might take time to recognize the paths and patterns that "B"s create. However, when you finally recognize these patterns, it is important to establish your boundaries and regain control.

Nanette learned an important lesson in dealing with "B"s: You shouldn't let them separate you from your loved ones or your support system. If you are in a relationship in which someone devalues your loved ones, you must immediately establish boundaries. While you might acknowledge your family members' flaws, make it very clear to the "B" that they will remain a part of your life and you won't tolerate behavior that undermines your relationships.

SUMMARY

IN WHATEVER THEIR FORM, FOR BETTER OR WORSE, extended families have a profound effect on how we define ourselves. Our childhood families shape the way we interact with our future families, how we deal with conflict, and also our tolerance for "B" behaviors. People who were raised by or with "Bs" might have a higher tolerance for being manipulated than those who were not raised by or with "B"s, and need to be extra cautious to prevent falling into another "B's" nest.

CHAPTER SIX

Coworkers

*"Man is the only animal that can remain on friendly terms
with the victims he intends to eat until he eats them."*

SAMUEL BUTLER

Work is any physical or mental activity you engage in to achieve
a purpose or result, and coworkers are people you engage with to
accomplish your work. We spend much of our time working,
whether at a designated place or in cyberspace. In some instances,
coworkers can become a second family.

The assumptions that everyone comes to work to do their job,
that group members work toward a common goal, that you can
change a worker's behavior by telling him to change, and that
workers respond to the logic of their supervisors are all myths. In
truth, the world of work is often full of "B"s.

The rules governing workers often support "B" behaviors,
and these rules present unique challenges when you attempt to
avoid the "B's" nest. Coworkers come in all shapes and skill
levels. A coworker can be your boss, your peer, someone you
occasionally work with in cyberspace, or someone you supervise. As a worker or supervisor who might be the recipient of
"B" behaviors, it is important to be aware of the patterns
encountered between coworkers.

In many cases, "B"s, especially those who are extraverted and charming, have an advantage during the hiring process. Some types of businesses, like investment banking, high-rise contracting, real estate, and entertainment might value "B" behaviors such as expressed self-confidence, charm, risk taking, and a need to be the center of attention. Some businesses are tolerant of some "B" behaviors and not tolerant of others. Also, if those who do the hiring in a company exhibit "B" behaviors, they might be inclined to hire others who are like them.

The "B's" Need for Control

JANIE

"I believe our interim dean is possessed by the devil. Needless to say, I thought everyone like her had retired or was dead. I was even wondering if an exorcist would help. One faculty member stated that the dean's need for total control and her authoritarian style are disguised as a democratic style. She captured it perfectly. We functioned all last year without a dean, and our department was better off than it is now. I've given up on women who have power because it seems so many of them don't know how to handle it. Maybe the next generation will do a much better job."

BEN

"As a researcher, I've been researching a particular topic for many years and in 2007, I published an article in a scientific journal.

After the article was published, I received an email from another researcher who does work in this area. In his email he asserted that he had first recognized the phenomenon in 2005. I guess I didn't have much of a sense of humor that day because I quickly sent him a paper from 2003 in which I had identified the phenomenon. His emails seemed a little less strident after that."

ABOUT THESE CASE STUDIES

Remember, one of the hallmarks of "B"s is the need to control everyone and everything in their path. Unfortunately, females are commonly judged more harshly than males for their narcissistic behaviors. Narcissistic "B"s, whether male or female, must always be first, right, and better than anyone else, especially anyone they perceive as a threat. At work, it is important for narcissistic "B"s to make most decisions without incorporating or acknowledging input from others. If a narcissistic "B" can demonstrate an idea was his, he will accept input from others. If you're on the same organizational level as a narcissistic "B," you might get away with giving direct feedback. If the "B" holds a position higher than yours, however, it's wise to tread lightly.

The Awakening

OLIVER

"I was a tenured professor in the English department of a university and had just been diagnosed with stage three colon cancer. I knew I would be in for a difficult time because I had a rough schedule of chemotherapy and it was to start in the middle of a semester. Despite my concern, I was determined to lead as normal a life as I could and I also knew my friends in the department would help me through the tough times. I planned for my chemotherapy treatments to occur after I had lectured for the week and was able to attend to most of my teaching duties. There were a few very rough weeks, however, when other faculty had to fill in for me.

"A new adjunct professor in the department knew about my cancer and was apparently upset that other faculty were covering for me. He mounted an email campaign against me, sending emails to faculty members questioning my ability to do my job. At one point I emailed him, saying I was doing my job. I was so upset because I was counting on all of my friends on the faculty to support me. I went to talk to the department chairman to ask him to put a stop to the emails but he was not supportive, and the emails continued. Unfortunately, the chairman had the power to shut down the emails and he chose not to. Finally, I met with the equal opportunity counselor and the emails stopped. I also received a lot of support from my other colleagues during this time.

"During the following year, the chairman suffered a bowel obstruction that almost took his life. At the end of that year, the chairman and I were sitting in a room alone, and I told him that he had disappointed me because he did nothing when I had asked him for help. He said he

I was going to be as a professional. It also made me stronger. I thought if people were going to treat you badly when you did something right, it wasn't going to stop me."

NOREEN, AS A TEENAGER

"I was 17 and needed money for school. I had been babysitting for three boys who were holy terrors. However, their father and mother were well-respected pillars of the church my family attended. I saw it as a steady-paying job, and had babysat for them for a long time. Since I did not drive, the boys' father would give me a ride home.

"One night he stopped the car and started kissing me. I was horrified. I told him to stop it, and he did. I felt guilty afterward, so I didn't tell anyone. I never babysat for them again, and my family couldn't figure out what was going on. They never asked, however, and I never shared the reason I had quit that job. I had to go to church every Sunday morning and see this guy up front in the church being a perfect gentleman.

"This incident taught me that nothing is what it seems. It also made me somewhat suspicious of other people. On the other hand, because the father stopped when I asked him to, I think it boosted my confidence in terms of influencing the situation. It taught me that I was really a strong person."

ALLEN

"When I was a college professor, a student came to me concerned that another professor was telling sexist jokes at the beginning of each class. I asked her for examples, and she produced transcripts of all of the jokes he had told. I subsequently went to the dean with my concerns over a potential lawsuit. The dean invited the professor in question to a meeting and asked the professor to bring copies of his jokes. The professor gave the dean a watered down version of his jokes. Using the student's transcriptions as evidence, the dean reprimanded the professor. The professor was very angry at me for telling the dean about this situation."

ABOUT THESE CASE STUDIES

One of the most important things to learn as a professional is how to establish boundaries. Although young and relatively inexperienced, Gretta and Noreen had already developed a sense of their professional boundaries. A young Noreen had learned that she could set her boundaries with an adult who tried to kiss her and she was aware of her boundaries as a nurse. Gretta immediately recognized that the surgeon was trying to control her by asking her to do something that was not part of her job. If she had done what he had asked, he might have tried other controlling tactics. The surgeon was asking Gretta to rescue him, but she refused to step into the "B's" nest and become the victim. Sometimes there is a fine line between going out of your way to help someone on your team who is in difficult circumstances and violating your professional boundaries.

Allen had been a professor long enough to know that not defining your boundaries can come back to haunt you in the form of a lawsuit. These encounters with "B" behaviors have likely become part of the fabric of the careers of these three individuals, and part of the learning experience that defines a competent professional.

The Histrionic "B" in the Workplace

KIERA

"Lisa came to our office party dressed in a very sexy outfit. She approached my husband and told him that if she were married to him, she would treat him a lot better than I do. Later on during the party, Lisa told all of the women in the office that she could have any of their husbands anytime she wanted them. After that, all of the women in the office were wary of Lisa and kept their distance."

SAMMY

"I supervised an employee whose emails and other communications had little content and his analyses of problems had no depth. In employee counseling sessions he seemed to listen to what he had to work on and he made it sound like he would work on the items we discussed. However, I would soon receive feedback from other members of his team about his lack of specifics. I also had trouble getting him to give specifics on what he would do to improve. Sometimes he would chastise other employees for reporting his behaviors even though all counseling sessions are private, and employees are not supposed to share the nature or details of their employee counseling sessions.

"The other odd thing about this employee is the way he dressed. He had long, gray hair and although he was quite young, he dressed like an old man. His dress prompted younger employees to look to him for advice, and he would counsel them on issues he was not trained to address."

ABOUT THESE CASE STUDIES ————————————————

The image of someone with histrionic "B" behaviors is a woman who dresses provocatively and is sexually suggestive like Lisa. However, as in the case of Sammy, histrionic "B"s can take other forms. The histrionic "B" needs to be the center of attention, so he or she will dress or act in a manner that accomplishes that goal. As a coworker it's important to hold such a "B" accountable for specifics when he or she becomes overly dramatic and attempts to communicate in a vague and superficial manner.

Co-existing with a Narcissistic "B"

APRIL

"As a computer systems analyst, I had very little contact with my boss, Malorie, because she was not particularly helpful to me in my job. Malorie was condescending and demeaning if she perceived you as having something she wanted. What she seemed to want was something in your personal life that she didn't already have. She could be friendly when she felt her life was on track. But if anyone attained any of 'Malorie's wants' before she did, she would reward them with cold indifference.

"I dealt with Malorie by keeping my distance and attempting not to disclose personal information that would make her feel inferior. I asked her questions about her personal life when I knew she had something exciting to share, and then expressed great excitement over her many accomplishments. When I needed her help to complete my job, I showed tremendous gratitude for her expertise."

ABOUT THIS CASE STUDY

April is correctly reading Malorie's constant need for success, perfection and admiration. Malorie appears to have a severe case of jealous entitlement. April has wisely chosen to stay out of the "B's" nest by not sharing any personal information with Malorie, although she occasionally strokes Malorie's ego. This is a situation in which you need to set your boundaries early and maintain them.

JAN

"I am an occupational therapy supervisor, and recently my boss made a decision to transfer his supervisory authority to Fiona, another occupational therapist who had been hired and trained by me. I was disappointed by this decision because Fiona has proven herself to be untrustworthy and manipulative, and is not respected by others in my program. Unfortunately, my boss promoted Fiona and, therefore, he would view any negative feedback from me as extremely threatening.

"Instead of telling him my concerns about Fiona as a boss, I told him how much I would miss my meetings with him because he provides me with information that is invaluable for me in my position, and he's the only one who can accomplish this for me. After hearing my plea, my boss offered to continue to meet with me on a regular basis to give me whatever information I needed."

ABOUT THIS CASE STUDY ──────────────────────────

Jan capitalized on her boss's narcissistic need for admiration and his need to rescue in order to protect herself from her new manipulative supervisor. Jan will need to establish strict boundaries if she accepts Fiona as her supervisor, while viewing her former boss as a source of support and information.

Blinded By Talent

WHITNEY

"As a mental health professional I was discouraged from diagnosing my coworkers. However, as I gained experience, I noticed lesser-trained staff members could, and did, identify manipulative coworkers by saying things like, 'Watch your back' or 'Keep your distance.' I had worked with Dr. Jones for many years and had only recently recognized him as very needy of attention. I heard a nurse describe Dr. Jones by saying, 'Oh, him, he would knife you in the back any chance he gets. Don't trust him.' How could this nurse be so perceptive when it had taken me so many years to see Dr. Jones's true colors? In fact, Dr. Jones had deceived me numerous times, and I had refused to acknowledge it.

"Several times Dr. Jones had said he would support me for a new position when, behind my back, he was actually supporting someone else. As I moved up the ladder, he began to turn coworkers against me. I made excuses for his behavior by saying things such as, 'He didn't really mean it,' 'The person who told me this information is lying,' or 'I must be losing my mind.' Consequently, I did nothing to confront Dr. Jones. He was very talented and I admired him, erroneously thinking he was trustworthy.

"It should have been a clue to me when, on his first day of work, Dr. Jones made several major decisions without consulting other more senior members on the administrative team. It should have been a clue when he expressed a definite lack of compassion for physicians struggling to learn under his tutelage. It should have been a clue when he promised to help me with a promotion and then did not. It should have been a clue when he got all excited and conscientious about his own projects but sloppily breezed through the administrative details for my projects.

"My admiration of his extraordinary talents caused me to loosen my personal boundaries for respectful equality. When I finally allowed myself to respond to Dr. Jones's manipulative behaviors, his "B" behaviors escalated. I told him I would no longer tolerate his abuse and reestablished my boundaries; but it was too late to change the course of events."

ABOUT THIS CASE STUDY ────────────────────

The amazing ability of a talented narcissistic coworker "B" to zero in on your needs and tell you what you want to hear is what often sets you up to enter the "B's" nest. You will feel honored to be able to work with such a talented "B," thinking you're helping each other to achieve common goals. Over time, talented "B"s will use you up and spit you out when they don't need your services anymore. Whitney should have recognized the signs of a "B," but was too engrossed in her own goals to realize that she was not being treated fairly and with respect.

The Power of Administrative Assistants

BRIDGET

"For several years, Alexa had dated a widowed banker who was physically impaired with probable mild dementia. When the banker died, he left his money to Alexa, making his own children very angry by leaving them out of his will. Shortly afterward, Alexa became an administrative assistant for our office. One day Alexa told me that another administrative assistant was selling beauty products from her desk, indicating that I should go and see them. I went down to that administrative assistant's office and saw she had an abundance of beauty products on her desk. When Alexa asked if I had seen the products, I said yes, and that it was against work rules to be selling anything at work. Alexa then went down to the other administrative assistant's office and told her I had said she was violating work rules, thereby making that administrative assistant angry with me.

"Another time, Alexa invited everyone in the office except me and another worker to a special luncheon she had prepared. After that I stopped using her as an administrative assistant even though she remained in our office for the next five years. From our office, she went to be the administrative assistant for another employee that she gushed over, calling him 'Henry the Great.' Henry was later fired for violating work rules."

ABOUT THIS CASE STUDY

Alexa exhibited classic borderline "B" behaviors. Borderline "B"s love creating chaos like Alexa did by creating conflict between Bridget and another administrative assistant and by accepting all of the money from the impaired banker she dated, leaving his children with nothing. Since borderline "B"s can be totally alluring, it would be expected that Alexa would use her charm to attract the banker. Although Bridget's avoidance of Alexa kept her from being overtly stung again, it didn't prevent Alexa from covertly stinging Bridget. Bridget's avoidance allowed Alexa to remain in the role of persecutor and Bridget to remain the victim since she wouldn't use Alexa's administrative services.

JERRY

"Jennifer was one of the best administrative assistants we have ever had. Jennifer was extremely intelligent and she cheerfully accomplished whatever task she was asked to perform, despite being in pain from arthritis. Since Jennifer got along with everyone, I was concerned when she explained to me that Gavin, another administrative assistant, was not treating her well. Jennifer mentioned that Gavin didn't seem to understand when she explained things to him, so she was concerned, thinking it was all her fault.

"Because of the tension in the office, Jennifer left the company. Gavin was given the task of processing the time cards. Although Gavin was very bright, he had an ability to pit workers against each other and also to make you doubt yourself. It was the week before Gavin's probation was to expire when I discovered he had, for reasons known only to him, altered my time card and forged my initials on it. On his last day of probation I was forced to fire Gavin, knowing I would sustain the ire of one of the other managers who had been praising Gavin and doing favors for him so that Gavin would give priority to his work. I knew this manager would blame me for firing his favorite administrative assistant. Because the manager was out of the office and I was unable to warn him in advance, he never forgave me. I was left wondering what Gavin's motivation was for changing my time card and, for a time, I doubted my own sanity."

ABOUT THIS CASE STUDY

Gavin's behavior toward Jennifer and his ability to make others doubt themselves and to pit workers against each other were clues pointing toward Gavin's potential destructiveness. But in a workplace, we are often forging ahead at great speeds and not always taking the time to put the pieces together to expose "B" behaviors. Clearly, Gavin knew how to play the game, drawing in the people he felt were important in raising his status. Although the aftermath of his firing was painful for Jerry, it was a much better outcome than if Gavin had stayed and had continued to play his detrimental games.

ADRIAN

"I was a sales agent for a large chemical supplier. Karla, our new administrative assistant, arrived at work on time, dressed to the nines. Karla was a bright, fast learner and immediately took charge of the office, gravitating toward the agents she thought were most important. A few of those agents would stop and chat with Karla and would bring her presents whenever they went on a trip. One of the agents inundated Karla with her work to the point that Karla would delay jobs for others in the department.

"Oddly, Karla seemed to be extremely dull and distant whenever the administrative manager tried to teach her anything, or when a staff member who wasn't in Karla's favorite circle asked her to do a task. One of the lower-ranking agents in the department asked me, 'What's wrong with Karla? Whenever I ask her to do something for me, she acts like she's as dumb as a post. I finally stopped asking her.' She exhibited similar behavior toward me. Although I complained to the departmental director about Karla's behavior, he never intervened. I suspected the few agents who she did work for had convinced the departmental director that she was wonderful.

"The chaos in the office had increased exponentially since Karla had entered the picture. We lost some of our best agents during this time, and I don't think the boss ever realized the probable source of their leaving."

ABOUT THIS CASE STUDY

Support workers wield tremendous power in organizations. It is extremely important to provide them with sound guidance and consistent monitoring. If one or more of them exhibit "B" behaviors and there is no clear authority or there are inconsistent boundaries, a "B" can destroy a work group or team in a matter of weeks.

Surprising a Boss "B"

IVY

"A flood occurred in a nearby town, and numerous people were displaced. The facility in which I worked provided meal tickets for some of the displaced people. Because of red tape, writing up the tickets was a time-consuming task. Three weeks after the disaster, the crisis had diminished and residents were preparing to return home the following day.

"I was at work late that night and noticed a light under my boss's door. Knowing that my boss, Logan, never worked at night, I opened the door, intending to turn off the light. There was Logan, busily filling out free meal tickets like the ones that displaced citizens had been using to get food, even though he knew there was no longer a need for them. Several weeks later, Logan went on vacation and extended his leave using the overtime hours he had put in filling out useless meal tickets for people who were already back in their homes. Several months earlier, Logan had denied my request to use overtime hours to extend my vacation.

"I considered reporting Logan but the word was that he was sleeping with the director of the agency, and I needed my job. As time went on, I realized I had become Logan's target. All of Logan's favors were directed at others in the department and as he continued to pass me over for promotions, I finally moved on to another job."

IVY, AS A YOUNG GIRL

"My birthday is on New Year's Eve, and it was common for my mother to either forget it or ignore it. She would often invite relatives over around Christmastime, but not to celebrate my birthday. My mother did remember one of my birthdays but since there were cookies left from Christmas, she said she wouldn't make me a birthday cake. I thought this was very unjust because my mother always made birthday cakes for my siblings."

ABOUT THIS CASE STUDY

Logan's deception was an affront to his employer and to his employees, who were evaluated on their honesty. Ivy's experience with her mother not celebrating her birthday as a girl made her attuned to the theme of injustice. Accumulating overtime by doing unnecessary work, when you deny overtime to your employees, is an unjust act. When you catch a "B" in an unjust or illegal act, you become the mirror that reflects to them what they never want to see.

It is one thing when a coworker peer exhibits "B" behaviors at work, but deceit reaches a new level when someone who's in a leadership position gives the message that deceit is okay for the boss. Such situations put an employee in a bind. An employee who witnesses an illegal act by her boss is confronted with the dilemma of reporting it to a higher authority. Ivy felt that she had to choose between what was right and keeping her job. Because a surprised "B" is often the most dangerous "B," Ivy was lucky to leave her job with her reputation intact.

Power Plays by Coworker "B"s

BRENT

(CONTINUED FROM CHAPTER TWO)

"I was frustrated with my job and was trying to be supportive of other employees who were realizing the significance of the organization's problems. Our human resources (HR) director gained my confidence to the point that I shared some of my thoughts about the CEO that I probably shouldn't have shared. After I did a couple of things the HR director wasn't supportive of, she found ways to get back at me.

"The HR director had worked herself up in the organization, and her power source was the confidence that the CEO had in her. Since the CEO was part-time, the HR director assumed a lot more power than someone in her position should have. She would get information about people in seemingly innocent ways, and if they criticized her at some point, she would invoke revenge on them. I actually did verbal battle with her, and she wanted to take me out.

"The HR director brought in an outside HR consultant. The outside consultant assured me of confidentiality, telling me she had been called in to get a sense of how the organization was functioning. I said that the organization lacked leadership. This got back to the CEO, and he confronted me. To the dismay of the HR director, the CEO and I eventually worked through our disagreement.

"Shortly afterward, there was an opening on my staff for a key management position. The HR director tried to control every step of the selection process, including the panel and the second interviews. She built a case for a candidate who I didn't think was suitable for the job. The HR director drew my boss (the CEO) into the battle by telling him that I was making it hard and that I was a friend of the person I wanted to hire. The CEO forced me to hire someone who wasn't qualified. The HR director knew this incident would trigger me to look outside the organization for another position. I did leave, and within two years I found out that this mistaken hire had already left, because my successor recognized he couldn't do the job.

"My successor told me last year of some very similar incidents that had occurred after I left. He said that because he was challenging something the HR director wanted, the HR director was ignoring him. The HR director knew how to influence and manipulate the CEO without him knowing it. The CEO was narcissistic, and the HR director played to that narcissism.

"I ran into a similar situation in a previous position in which a lower-ranked woman was able to manipulate the director. Other workers tried to expose her manipulative behaviors, but she would undermine them. They would either leave or she would set them up and they'd be fired. There were parallels that were just too obvious. Both organizations were relatively small, 300 or so employees. People who had been there a long time and had worked their way up had every reason to try to protect their power. But when someone appeared to gain influence that exceeded theirs, they would try to bring that person down.

"After that incident, I decided I wasn't going to fight that kind of crusade, because it wasn't productive for me or my career. You become so preoccupied with the battle that it affects you, and you become as much of a liability to the company as the person who is creating the problem. You either have to find ways to work around the manipulators or find a different job."

ABOUT THIS CASE STUDY

As told in chapter two, Brent had a similar experience of being stung by his best friend when he was a young boy. At this point in Brent's life, however, the stakes were higher. Brent certainly recognized the "B" behaviors of his HR director and the CEO, and the destruction that can be caused when two "B"s band together. While Brent made the mistake of trusting the HR director, he also came to realize the importance of staying out of the "B" hive by avoiding the roles of victim, persecutor and rescuer. Fortunately, Brent had both the education and the skills to find another suitable job. Perhaps experiences of being stung, like the one Brent had as a boy, propelled him to excel in his work. Brent's education and experience allowed him to speak his mind and escape future stings.

SEBASTIAN

"As a counselor for a residential housing facility for the disabled, I planned a Mardi Gras for the residents. On the night of the Mardi Gras, many of the facility's staff members were there to help out. The CEO, however, who usually crowned the king and queen, was nowhere to be seen. When the CEO arrived, he appeared to be inebriated. He proceeded to inappropriately touch some of the staff members. The queen was a woman in a wheelchair, and when the CEO bent over to crown her, he kissed her on the lips before she could turn her head. The staff members let out an audible gasp.

"I felt obligated to let the CEO know that his behavior had crossed the line, so I confronted him in his office the following Monday. Another staff member must have reported the CEO's behavior to the corporate office, because they sent a representative to conduct mandatory training on respect, and the CEO was forced to attend. The CEO was also told to apologize to the facility staff for his behavior. An outside advocate was asked to meet with the queen. The queen did not want to speak to anyone about the incident because she was afraid she would be asked to leave the facility. For the next year, I was both harassed and ignored by the CEO and those who were his close advisors. One day I looked up, and the director of human resources was standing over my desk. He told me that I was fired and escorted me to the door."

ABOUT THIS CASE STUDY

When a coworker "B" has power over your position, he can make conditions at your workplace miserable for you. This makes it very difficult to stay out of the "B's" nest by becoming first a victim and then a persecutor as you try to fight back. Some people belong to unions, and when drawn into a "B's" nest, can use powerful forces to defend against the "B." Some people use whistleblower hotlines to report "B" behavior that is harming the company or harming others. However, any method you choose to deal with the stings of a coworker "B" can hamper your career. If you choose to address "B" behaviors within the workplace, you must stick to the facts, keep your message clear, provide documentation and witnesses if possible, and always have an exit strategy.

Remember, "B"s by their nature do not like to be surprised by being shown their faults. They will immediately try to sting the messenger. But if the "B" perceives that it's not safe to sting the messenger, he'll look for a surrogate to sting. Even if Sebastian had not directly confronted the CEO, someone did report him to the corporate office, and the CEO would likely have singled out Sebastian whether he was involved or not. Like Brent, one of Sebastian's most effective strategies was having an edu-

cation and a wealth of experience that he could fall back on to find a new position.

Leadership from the Inside Out

ANNE

"In my first job out of school, I worked at a religious goods store. My supervisor was second in command to the owner of the store. For some reason unknown to me, she seemed to be threatened by me. I was becoming proficient in keypunching, which got the attention of the store's owner and consequently he gave me some complex tasks to keypunch in. As soon as I got started with his assignment, my supervisor would come over and assign me to check in new orders. For a while I tried to do both jobs. But one day the owner came over and noticed I wasn't working on his keypunch assignment, so I switched back to doing that task. My supervisor then came over and told me to check in orders. This went back and forth about four times, and finally I stood up and threw down the punch cards, told them to figure out who was the boss, and walked out. A few days later I received a call asking me to return, but I never did. After I quit, I heard that the supervisor had accused the owner of poisoning her. He dismissed her with the understanding that she would not return without a doctor's notice that she was well."

ABOUT THIS CASE STUDY

Repeated "B" stings can have a numbing effect on some people, and after a while the victims seem not to notice them. Despite her youth, this did not happen to Anne. She was strong enough to recognize a "B" was stinging her at her work-place. Anne resigned because she felt she didn't have the power to stop the "B's" behavior toward her. When given the opportunity, Anne refused to return because she knew the "B" was still there, and nothing was likely to change. While any-one can establish personal boundaries, it takes power to establish work boundaries against a "B's" behaviors, and Anne felt she didn't have that power.

The Interview: To "B" or Not to "B"

If you are lucky, you're in control of those whom you choose to hire. If you are watchful, you can choose not to hire a "B." One of the first principles of interviewing is to make sure that you do not interview someone all by yourself.

FERN

"Kelly and I were jointly interviewing a candidate for a mid-man-agement position. I came in a few minutes late and immediately felt out of the loop, and started to question myself. It became clear that the candidate had aligned herself with Kelly, and she was positioning herself between Kelly and me. I was never able to engage the interviewee because the candidate was only responding to Kelly.

"After the interview we compared notes. I said that when I walked into the room, I thought, 'What's wrong with me? I feel warmth coming from Kelly toward this candidate, but I don't like this candidate at all.' I tried to figure out the source of my negative feelings and concluded that I should pay attention to them. The candidate was very confident and self-assured, which can be a good quality, but the behavior was pushing my buttons because the candidate seemed so full of herself. Her lack of humility also raised a red flag.

"Kelly said she liked the candidate's spunk. The candidate was able to easily draw people in because she was extraverted, fun and likeable, with a cool personality. Everything on the outside seemed okay about her from a thinking point of view, but the positive thoughts Kelly was having about the candidate didn't coincide with the negative feelings I was having. My strong reaction to the candidate made Kelly and me realize that the candidate might have been playing us against each other.

"Needless to say, the candidate did not get the job. If both Kelly and I had not been in the interview, the candidate's personable demeanor might have convinced Kelly to hire her. It wasn't until I showed up that the candidate's demeanor felt awkward. It felt like the candidate and Kelly had inside jokes, and I was intruding."

ABOUT THIS CASE STUDY ⎯⎯⎯⎯⎯⎯⎯⎯⎯⎯⎯⎯⎯⎯⎯⎯⎯⎯⎯

The tactic of playing one person against another is a favorite of many "B"s. This behavior is often unconscious. Theoretically, the more hiring you do, the better you should become at spotting "B" potential. It's a good strategy to have two interviewers in the room when you interview anyone for a job, because some "B"s have the habit of triangulating people. Three in a room is a great number because the person being interviewed will inevitably leave one of the interviewers out of the conversation. The more you make the candidate talk, the greater the chance she will reveal her "B" traits. Also, sometimes it's wise to listen to your gut feeling rather than your rational mind.

Secondary Infections from a "B" Sting

MAYA

"I have a master's degree in nursing and was working in a hospital at a job I loved. I was getting vibes from the director of nursing that left me with the impression that she was somehow threatened by me. She always surrounded herself with the same few nurses. One day I was laid off with no warning, and the director gave my hours to her friends.

"I subsequently got a job as case manager in a psychiatric hospital, and one day the head nurse asked me if I wanted to apply for a nursing director position. I was caring for my invalid mother and decided I couldn't assume more responsibility at that point in my life, so I declined her offer. Several weeks later, I found out they had hired the same nurse who had let me go from my previous job, and that she would be my supervisor. I was in total shock. That evening when I went to care for my mother, I must have been in a daze, and fell down my mother's porch steps. I suffered permanent neurological damage, and was never able to return to work."

ABOUT THIS CASE STUDY ─────────────

Maya's story highlights some of the dangers of finding yourself in a coworker "B's" nest and the long-term effects of having been stung. Our work is one of the most important aspects of our lives, and we have difficulty shutting off the effects of the "B" stings just by leaving work because the pain follows us. Although extreme, Maya's experience highlights the level of distraction that can occur when we are embroiled in conflict in an important area of our life. It is important to be able to confide in someone we trust who is outside of our workplace, and talk through the events leading up to the sting. By taking this step we can learn from our experience and, hopefully, avoid getting stung in the future. More importantly, the act of discussing our experiences can help us to take steps to reclaim our self-esteem and re-establish our boundaries, so we aren't haunted forever by our past experiences with "B"s.

SUMMARY

RECOGNIZING "B" BEHAVIORS IN A COWORKER WHO IS a peer or someone you supervise is one thing. When your boss is a "B," however, your difficulties can multiply quickly. "B"s who are in charge might hire controlling narcissists to do their dirty work. But they are just as likely to hire employees who will function as guard "B"s, to protect and rescue them when their "B" behaviors get them into trouble.

Thinking that organizations are like machines and that coworkers always operate above board without hidden agendas is one of the biggest mistakes a supervisor or coworker can make. Those hidden agendas can destroy departments and ultimately devastate organizations. Understanding some of the subtle clues given off by "B"s can help you make better decisions when you interact with current and potential coworkers.

CHAPTER SEVEN

The Group Effect: Our Responsibility to the Collective

"It's the group sound that's important, even when you're playing a solo."

OSCAR PETERSON

Being Part of a Group

Because we are social creatures, being part of a group is important. Historically, group activity has been key to the survival of our species. Whether at work or play, it's very difficult to go against the direction of the group. We have a strong need to belong to the group, even when we disagree with the direction the group is moving. Because we want to belong or not be embarrassed in front of the group, we sometimes just go along with the direction we think the group wants to go. If the group happens to contain one or more "B"s, things can get dicey very quickly.

A large body of literature on group psychology demonstrates this. According to Irving Janis, members of groups who unconditionally go along with the group engage in the mental process called groupthink.[36] They believe in the rightness and morality of their cause; they view any outside groups in a negative light (us versus the enemy); they pressure members not to argue with other members of the group; and they protect the group, especially the leader, from information that might be contradictory.

It's easy to see how a charming, deceitful, opportunistic, anti-social "B" could encourage a group to take excessive risks and threaten non-group members who try to sway the group in another direction. It's not difficult to see how a smart narcissistic "B" could convince a group to shun someone who the "B" sees as a threat to his power over the group. It's not hard to see how a charming borderline "B" could engage the members of the group by portraying himself as a sympathetic character and keeping others out of the group by portraying them as non-caring. It's equally easy to see how an attractive and talented histrionic "B" could make the group exclusionary by portraying it as the "in" place to be and to exclude other "lesser types" from joining.

A group that has members with prominent "B" characteristics will be less likely to allow true discussion and freedom of dissent. Such a group will make inferior decisions compared to the decisions of a group or team that has worked to value individual creativity and has developed and maintained an atmosphere of interest in new ideas. A group or team with little training and no ground rules is ripe fruit for a stinging "B." It would also be interesting to speculate how individuals who had been repeatedly stung when they were young functioned in groups later in their lives.

In this chapter, the group effect refers to the collective influence of "B"s on a group. Groups can be very complex, and there can be groups within groups. An example of the complexity of the group effect was the Jonestown Massacre. The cult leader, Jim

[36] Janis, *Victims of Groupthink*, and *Groupthink: Psychological Studies.*

Jones, and his inner circle of confidants masterminded the mass suicide of Jones' cult followers. Many followers did not die willingly, however. When some members saw children drinking the cyanide-laced drink, they tried to protest but were actually murdered by members of Jones' inner circle.[37]

This event demonstrated that group members can and do stand up to groupthink. But if Jones's followers had recognized the "B" behaviors in their leaders earlier, they might have chosen to join other groups.

The Effect of a Company's Policies on the Integrity of Its Workers

SANDRA

"I needed a cell phone for road emergencies and my travels, so while I was at a conference I signed a contract with a national cell phone company. But I was unable to use the phone because of poor service. During the process of canceling the contract, I started to wonder if all of the workers in the company were infected with some kind of evil virus that made them not care about their customers.

"I wrote a letter that stated the following:

I have to drive 40 miles east or 80 miles south of my home before I could pick up a signal. I realize your marketing people have lied to me. I've tried numerous times to call the company and ask for a remedy. I've been repeatedly placed on hold for long periods of time, and then after 30–45 minutes, would be disconnected before I could speak with anyone. In all, I've spent five hours on

[37] *Jonestown: The Life and Death of Peoples Temple.* PBS, 2009.

*hold waiting for someone to help me. When I finally found a per-
son to help me, I thought the problem was solved until I received
a bill for over $100 for service I've never received. It's become
obvious that no one has listened to me, and after all that effort,
nothing has been settled.*

"Months later, I received a letter from the company saying I was past
due on paying my bill. When I called to complain, it took another 45
minutes to find someone who said they would help me. That person
acknowledged that the contract had been cancelled and told me not
to pay the bill. Two months later, I received another letter from the company telling me I would be receiving a bill. There were no return
addresses on the statements or on the letters.

"One year later I received a phone call from a collection agency trying to collect the money that this company said I owed. The caller
threatened to destroy my credit rating if I didn't pay. After multiple
phone calls, I finally found a sympathetic person who settled the matter
for me. I had spent a total of 18 hours on the phone trying to resolve
this issue.

"Several months later, this company collapsed as a corporation. I
wonder about the people who worked there. Why did they engage in
such shoddy business practices, and who was directing them to
behave in this manner? Were they getting paid to act the way they did
toward customers? Did any of the employees object to what they were
doing? Were they just following the practices of those around them?
And who was the kind gentleman who finally helped to end my telephone hell? Why was he able to buck the system when no one else
seemed to care?"

ABOUT THIS CASE STUDY ——————————————————————

No matter the setting, a group can be a powerful force for good or evil. If the team is not fully formed and the formal leader is corrupt, the team members will likely not question the formal authority. The team needs unity and an understanding of how to discuss conflict if it's to question the behavior of any "B"s that might be part of the team. If the leaders in the company form a corrupt culture, the team members within that culture will likely follow the leader's path to corruption. If the culture of the group isn't strong enough to deal with a corrupt leader, the group will go the way of the strongest or most opportunistic leader, and too often the strongest leader will be a "B." Those in the group who decide they do not want to follow a "B" will likely be chastised, fired, or blatantly ignored until they leave.

"B" Creep

⬡⬡⬡⬡⬡⬡⬡⬡⬡⬡ BERYL ⬡⬡⬡⬡⬡⬡⬡⬡⬡⬡

"Gloria, a member of our historical society planning group, had a way of irritating others in the group. Although I have observed the group over a number of years, I find it difficult to pinpoint just exactly what she does that makes people feel manipulated.

"Gloria is married to Dave, a very powerful member of the group. She seems to hide behind Dave's opinions on every issue, never disagreeing with him. Both of them disagree with many suggestions members of the group make. However, other group members go along with them to avoid conflict. Fundraising had been Gloria's job until she began complaining that it was too much for her to handle alone. At a subcommittee meeting Gloria attended without Dave, a decision was made to handle the fundraising for the society in a more distributive way. Weeks later, when the entire group reassembled to discuss fundraising, Gloria presented her own plan for the fundraising and ignored what the subcommittee had decided. Gloria did it in such a way, intertwining it with other issues, that the members of the subcommittee didn't immediately recognize what she was doing. Gloria seems to delight in luring another person into presenting ideas she can subsequently attack. She will seldom give a clear answer to any question. Often, she answers one question by asking another.

"The planning group had scheduled a meeting to occur in the middle of the day. But Gloria's husband liked to meditate in the middle of the day, so Gloria called me, saying that Trudy and Sam had requested that the meeting be changed to an evening time. I thought it was strange that neither Trudy nor Sam would not call me directly but agreed that the meeting could be changed. Gloria then emailed all of the other committee members instructing them that the meeting had been changed.

"The next time I spoke with Trudy, I asked her why she had wanted the meeting changed. She said she did not want it changed and had nothing to do with the change. Trudy was angry because Gloria had used her as an excuse to get what she wanted. Trudy emailed Gloria, telling her that the next time she wanted to change a meeting, she should take responsibility and not blame the change on her and Sam. A few weeks later, Sam encountered Gloria at the historical society, and Sam repeated their conversation to me:

SAM: "Do you think there is a strain between us?"

GLORIA: "You mean between Trudy and me?"

SAM: "No, between you and Dave and Trudy and me."

GLORIA (attempting to put Sam on the defensive): "I had called Trudy asking if I could pick up some papers, and she seemed to not want me to come over."

SAM (avoiding the bait): "Trudy was just thinking of saving you a trip because I was going to see you at the historical society that same morning."

GLORIA (trying to bait him again): "I was confused about the email Trudy sent. I didn't understand it."

SAM: "I think we should sit down and talk."

GLORIA: "You, me and Trudy?"

SAM: "No, the four of us."

GLORIA: "Well, I'll think about that."

BERYL, AS A TEENAGER

"In junior high school, I had a bag of special pink wintergreen candies in my gym locker. After changing into my gym uniform, I didn't lock my locker before going into class. After class I had to use the bathroom and I saw one pink candy dissolving in each toilet. I remember my face turning red and being embarrassed and feeling sick to my stomach. I knew which "in" girls were last in the locker room and knew my friends would never do that. The thought of them going through my locker upset me for days, and I knew it was a put-down. I locked my locker every time after that and avoided them as much as possible. I have recently heard rumors that the ringleader isn't very happy, and I can't help but find vindication in that."

ABOUT THIS CASE STUDY

Beryl learned something by being harassed in the locker room as a teenager. Her gut reaction to Gloria's manipulation is notable because it brought back that memory, and it was clear that Gloria's behavior bothered her. Sam's responses to Gloria were swift and to the point. When you discover that you have been stung, it's important to quickly state your boundaries. In this story, Sam defended his wife's boundaries by deflecting Gloria's attempts to manipulate him and put him on the defensive. Sam, by his open-ended comments, was able to redirect Gloria's manipulative behaviors and avoid entering the "B's" nest without openly alienating Gloria.

The Candy Store

TOBY

"My friend John and I landed summer jobs at a candy store in a resort village. Our manager, Ethan, was in his thirties. After working several weeks into the summer, John, who worked a different shift, confronted me, asking why I was telling lies about him. As we compared notes, we realized that Ethan had been telling each of us lies about the other. Ethan also told the other boys who were working there to help themselves to candy, that the owners wouldn't mind at all. It was like Ethan enjoyed telling us to do unethical things while trying to convince us that it was okay."

ABOUT THIS CASE STUDY

It is important to stay true to your morals and ethics that tell you it's wrong to take things without paying. By doing what Ethan said was okay to do, the team members would have given him the upper hand and Ethan would've used the information against them. This story is an example of the importance of openness among members of a team.

In addition to personal boundaries, a team needs to define its boundaries, and it's up to the team's members to collectively establish those boundaries. Ethan exhibited antisocial behaviors with his unethical game playing. However, he didn't realize the team's members would compare notes. The team as a group needed to let Ethan know that they didn't want to hear tales about the other team members and if Ethan had anything to say, it should be said to the entire team. By establishing team boundaries, it's much easier to stay out of the "B's" nest.

The Group as Defender

VIOLA

"My husband had just died. The priest who was going to give the sermon at his funeral had been angry toward my husband because my husband had given the priest negative feedback about the way the church was being run. Before my husband died, the priest even refused to visit him in the hospital.

"At the funeral service the priest loudly praised my husband, even calling him a saint. I thought that it was very strange behavior considering his feud with my husband. A week later the priest disappeared, and the rumor was that he had absconded with a large sum of money. I never heard that story refuted by the church or by any priest who came after.

"Many years later, I was perusing a website that was a national database on pedophile priests, and this priest's name was on it. It appears he had been sent away for sexually abusing a child. I felt the church had lied and I wasn't sure if I was angrier at the church or the pedophile priest. I found it interesting that the church thought it was better to let the parishioners think a priest had stolen money than to reveal the truth, that he was a pedophile."

ABOUT THIS CASE STUDY ───────────────────────

This story illustrates how the priest ignored someone who reflected back to him what he didn't want to see in himself. However, he showed his good side to the attendees at the husband's funeral. The story also demonstrates how a guard "B" (the church) might use the pretext of "the greater good of an institution" to defend someone who persecutes others. The victim was not just the child who was abused; it was the entire congregation. This story suggests an undercurrent of manipulation and condescension on the part of the clergy, leading to a violation of trust with the parishioners.

Using the Power of the Group Against a Member

LEORA

"When I started a new job with a media group, the group seemed very exclusive. I soon realized my boss and two other women were the ringleaders. These three women were neither friendly nor welcoming. There were several other staff members in the group who tried to be kind, but they seemed torn between befriending me and staying loyal to the ringleaders.

"I discovered that the CEO had a reputation for promoting under-dogs who were not well-qualified for their positions. My boss had little education, and the CEO had put her on the fast track to become super-visor of the entire department in which I worked. I also discovered that the CEO had promoted others using this same formula.

"It all came to a head one week when the ringleaders privately arranged a party to celebrate inauguration of a new media campaign. I found out about the party when one of the ringleaders approached each of the cubicles except mine and loudly declared that it was party time. This was hurtful, but I was dealing with it by just focusing on my job and the work I needed to do. It's one thing to not include me but it's another to rub my face in it. I didn't even care about the party but no one should be treated that way, ever. A short time later I resigned because I felt I was unable to work in such a sick environment. A year later the entire group folded."

ABOUT THIS CASE STUDY

The group in which Leora worked was a classic example of how a "B" at the helm of a company can infect workgroups and eventually destroy the entire organization. The CEO was likely a less-than-competent narcissistic "B" who played out his insecurities through his promotion practices. In this case, the CEO hired someone who was not well qualified and made her a supervisor. This supervisor didn't pose a threat to the CEO, and he knew elevating her would make her feel special. This favor cemented her obligation to the CEO to become his guard "B." With gratitude for her admiration and the need to protect his own incompetence, the CEO protected her in return.

"The supervisor satisfied her need for further self-protection against her incompetence by surrounding herself with her own swarm of guard "B"s. The supervisor must have felt threatened by Leora, and by using intimidation, split her off from the rest of the group by ignoring and devaluing Leora. The supervisor's guard "B"s performed their guard roles well and went along with the supervisor's wishes. With no one to turn to for help, Leora made the right choice and resigned. We suspect this pattern was played out in other departments within the agency until the entire agency was turned into an imploding nest of incompetent "B"s.

The Spa

FAITH

"I owned a large spa in a major city. Melanie wasn't one of my best massage therapists but she was good with people, and over the years she became a close friend to my husband and me. My son took care of the books for the spa, but at one point Melanie told me I didn't need my son to run the spa, that she could run it with me. She kept saying that she had a lot of ideas for the spa and indicated that she wanted to go into business with me. I actually paid her a higher percentage than the other massage therapists for helping me with some managerial duties.

"One day, out of the blue, Melanie announced that she and six of my other massage therapists were leaving immediately for another spa. I was in a state of shock and wondered what I had done wrong. I remembered a goal-setting session where everyone said everything was great. It was after that session that the group of seven became more exclusionary of others in the spa. They would frequently whisper to one another. One of my loyal staff members told me that Melanie had agitated the massage therapists at a meeting they had. Melanie said they should be getting paid to attend staff meetings. The staff meetings were not mandatory and they were encouraged to attend but were not paid to attend them. Apparently Melanie used this issue to draw the other massage therapists in, and when an offer came from another spa, Melanie organized them enough so they all left together.

"Oddly, Melanie's brother had told my husband that Melanie wasn't who he thought she was. Melanie would tell me things about staff and swore me to secrecy. That should have been a clue that she was manipulative. Melanie's negativity about the spa she used to work in should have been another clue. Later on I found out some of the things Melanie had told me about the staff weren't true.

"This experience has left me less trusting. I believe questioning everything is a good model. After Melanie left the spa, my husband wanted to contact her but I said no. When someone violates my trust, it's done. My beloved mother had just passed away and I was grieving her death when, nine weeks later, I lost the seven employees. The worst thing was that I was totally surprised by Melanie's behavior. After they left, I heard many stories of things they had said about me that weren't true. Shortly afterward, I was diagnosed with a serious medical condition. What scares me the most is that one person telling lies about you can undo all of your good work. If anything good has come of this, it's that the spa feels calmer and the chaos is gone."

ABOUT THIS CASE STUDY

While Faith had witnessed clues to Melanie's impending coup, these clues were subtle. Melanie's "B" behaviors were covert and remained under Faith's radar. Melanie was actively searching for power, and when Faith rebuked Melanie's offer to take over the bookkeeping functions that Faith's son was performing, Melanie plotted her revenge. She knew that the way to plan a group coup was to endear yourself to your coworkers and attack something for which they had a common dislike.

This story reinforces the caveat that when you hear conflicting stories about someone, it's wise to check them out. Also, when someone repeatedly asks you to keep secrets that are detrimental to other members of the team, be suspicious. Someone with a good heart and a helpful spirit is wise to check for reciprocal giving. If you go out of your way to help someone and then notice they confer kind acts on others but seldom on you, you might be dealing with a "B."

A Power-Hungry "B's" Effect on the Group

CECILIA

"The director of social work for our agency has learned the language of leadership. She has read books on 'servant leaders' and professes she wants all of her staff to feel like they have the power to change things for the better. This director knows all of the catchy leadership terminology and uses those words continuously. She makes her staff read books on leadership and conducts training sessions on leadership. However, this social work director cannot give up any power. She makes all of her staff members consult her about minute details. She appears to trust no one but herself. When someone within the agency, whether a social worker or not, does something she doesn't like or makes a decision of which she disapproves, she chastises them in public.

"Given what I'm dealing with at work, I try really hard not to solve any problems. Sometimes I'm tempted because I think I know the answers to the problems, but I really try hard to hold back and not share my knowledge. Anyone who does share their knowledge risks being burned unless they can convince the director that the solution to the problem was her idea. This same director actually was elected president of a state organization, using the platform of promoting teamwork in the workplace. She must have a nice side that she only shows to people who she wants to impress."

CECILIA, AS A YOUNG GIRL

"In the fifth grade, I was swimming in the community pool with my friend, Kayla, who remained my best friend through high school. I don't remember how the subject came up, but Kayla revealed that a mutual friend had spoken ill of me behind my back. I felt especially wounded since I had just spent the night at this girl's house and thought we had a good time. This incident defined the phrase 'two-faced' for me, and I decided the girl would never be a close friend."

ABOUT THIS CASE STUDY

The lesson Cecilia learned about being two-faced has sharpened her observations of her coworkers. True leaders offer informed guidance. In our experience, pretending to believe in the principles of true leadership is a common game for narcissistic "B"s. In their minds they are the only ones smart enough to be the leader. Power-hungry "B"s must own every decision, except mistakes. They are control freaks and are skilled at destroying the spirit of a group or team by using the weapon of public devaluation.

It's particularly difficult for highly trained professionals to work with controlling "B"s because the professionals are often seen as threats to the "B's" ego. Because of this dynamic, many valuable employees become the focus of a controlling "B's" ire. Under the leadership of a narcissistic "B," the most talented group members tend to become the first casualties of a poorly functioning group and are often the first to leave. Those workers who choose to stay in a dysfunctional work group out of financial necessity may feel isolated, lose their dignity, and jeopardize their health. Anyone who chooses to remain in such a catch-22 needs to consider its potential negative effects on their health.

The Need for Witnesses

JENNA

"I had been working for a small federally funded program for the elderly. We had an excellent director and a very skilled, hard-working team. The director moved on to another job, and it quickly became apparent to the staff that the board had hired a new director who was totally incompetent. Apparently, the new director had interviewed well.

"In a very short time, he had alienated many within the county offices we worked with. This director relied on other people and then took full credit for their work. One of our team members quickly recognized the dire situation and went elsewhere. The remaining members of the team were reluctant to talk to the board. The team members all talked about the new director and were not sure what to do. We all felt particularly bad that the new director had moved his family across the country to take this job.

"One of my coworkers and I decided that we should get advice from the representative who ran the state agency that interfaced with our program. Everyone thought this representative was a good guy. My coworker and I didn't really want to report the behavior of our new director but felt obligated to tell the truth; and we felt the state office needed to know. We met with the state representative who agreed that our comments would be in confidence. The representative appeared very understanding and he advised us to go to the human resources (HR) committee of the board, because he felt we had enough information. He indicated that he understood our predicament, since we were reporting on our boss. The state representative reaffirmed that he would talk to no one about our conversation.

"The HR committee was composed of older retired gentlemen who were somewhat out of touch with current hiring practices and they were surprised when we reported on the shortcomings of our boss. However, they took our comments seriously and decided to meet with our boss. In the meantime, the state representative had reported to our boss that we had complained about his performance. When our boss met with the HR committee, he knew what was coming and was extremely aggressive with them and challenged them. Not being used to that kind of response, the committee members ended up doing nothing. After that, our boss had it in for all of us because he knew we had contacted the board. He even fabricated lies for our performance evaluations and essentially destroyed the team. It was such a mess that eventually the entire team left. The director, however, stayed in the position until he retired."

ABOUT THIS CASE STUDY

Although Jenna and her teammate used the proper procedure and played by the rules, the state representative stung them when they least expected it. The state representative turned out to be a shape-shifter, appearing to be considerate and professional, and then behaving unethically by breaking the confidence of Jenna and her teammate. These two teammates were performing a heroic task, but reporting the poor performance of a boss is always fraught with hazards. When someone who's in a superior position is performing poorly and dishonestly, consider that you might be dealing with a "B" and proceed cautiously. Since Jenna and her teammate observed their boss taking credit for someone else's work, they would have been wise to have a witness who was a trusted member of the board attend their meeting with the state representative.

The Executives

WARREN

"Ursula and I were two of four executives who were charged with building a new arm of a high-tech manufacturing company. I had worked closely with Ursula for many years as we built other divisions within the company. Ursula and I had worked hard to receive the backing to build this new division.

"Al was hired as senior executive for the new division, and Mitch was hired as marketing director. Al had a reputation as a charismatic leader who could pull people together. We all knew the task ahead would be difficult because the job involved creating a totally new structure that would be able to fit within the larger system. The three executives and I professed that we would work closely together. But it soon became apparent that Ursula, Al and Mitch were each going full speed ahead in separate directions.

"We had agreed on an initial approach to development and divided up the tasks according to the talents within the group. We had also agreed to meet several times a week to continue refining goals and to review our progress. Al, who was charged with keeping the executive team together, had many irons in the fire and began to miss the twice-weekly meetings. Mitch also started to miss meetings. Because Ursula and I had a history of working together, we charged ahead with the tasks and tried to work around Al's frequent absences.

"About six months into the new venture, I sensed Ursula's attitude toward me had changed. I soon found out that she was sending out memos in areas that had been assigned to me. Ursula also seemed to be avoiding me. Since we had worked together for a number of years, I felt comfortable confronting Ursula to ask what was going on, reiterating that I thought it was important to work closely with her on this new project. As I confronted Ursula, she was silent, not engaging in the conversation. I knew something was wrong and I couldn't figure out what was bothering her.

"As Mitch initiated his marketing plan, he ignored more and more of my suggestions and I felt a wall developing between all of the members of our group. I tried every way I knew to keep the four of us communicating and working together. But I began noticing that some of the other employees I had worked closely with in the past seemed to be ignoring me, and I found that to be very unnerving. By accident, I discovered Ursula had given another person credit for a report I had written. Another employee told me Ursula had claimed full credit for a project they had worked on together as equal partners. Another friend of mine in the company told me Ursula was actively trying to turn employees against me. I found myself engaging in behavior that could best be described as paranoid as I tried to protect my back.

"One of the other things that became increasingly obvious was the tight alliance that had formed between Ursula and Mitch, while Mitch was increasingly distancing himself from me. I discovered that Ursula and Mitch had been meeting regularly. My concern for the success of the new division was growing by the day.

"I desperately tried to engage Al in this dilemma and thought I was making progress, when Al suddenly transferred out of the division. Ursula and Mitch were moving in a direction that met their needs but not the needs of the company. I had considered talking to the CEO about the developing chaos but I wasn't sure where he stood, because the CEO's demeanor toward me had changed. I finally met with the CEO, and it was clear that Ursula had already regaled him with her version of what was happening in the new division. He made it clear that he believed Ursula.

"Despite the heavy investment I had in the new division, I decided it was time to move on. Within months, I was hired by another company but at a reduced pay. I discovered that Ursula left the division three months after I left. Several years later, while walking to my car, I noticed Ursula across a parking lot. She yelled at me and waved like nothing had happened between us. I was speechless and wondered if the outcome would've been different if Al had done his job of coordinating the new division."

ABOUT THIS CASE STUDY

Ursula and Mitch seemed to have no guilt about destroying Warren's career. However, if Al had provided leadership for the administrative team, the outcome might have been different. Al's behavior allowed and encouraged Ursula and Mitch to develop an entire swarm of guard "B"s that was counterproductive to the needs of the company and the welfare of its customers.

Never underestimate the power of "B"s to use lies and charm to sway those around them. Just because you have a conscience, you cannot expect the same from a "B." The rules of ethics you choose to live by are the same rules "B"s profess to believe in but don't. Another lesson in this story is, if you are not the boss, the higher you move up in an organization the more difficult it is to find someone who can help you change a bad situation. Having several high-ranking "B"s within a division can act like a virus, eventually infecting the entire operation.

Warren's story is similar to that of Johanna's, in that a trusted colleague turned on them and stung them when they least expected it. We tend to get caught up in our work from time to time and forget to review our boundaries and assess whether or not they are being violated. One of the boundaries you need to set early is defining how much and what kinds of abuse you are willing to accept. How far will you allow your coworkers to stray from the rules before you call them on their maladaptive behavior? One of the tactics of a swarm of "B"s is denying that there are any problems and then stinging you by deflecting your concerns back to you to indicate you might be the problem. The most important lessons in Warren's story are knowing when to cut and run and quickly pulling out the barb so it doesn't continue to infect you.

Rallying Around a Cause

MARITA

"While working for a large corporation, two high-level programs merged, and when combined, formed a fairly large management team that seemed divided along the lines of the two previously separate programs. In meetings and at lunch, staff from the original program would sit together and staff from the new program would cluster together. People didn't speak up much, and after a year of transition, the division between the old and new staff seemed to be deeper than ever.

"Frank then joined the team. At times he was assertive, bordering on abrasive. Staff members tried to welcome Frank, but often their attempts were met with strange reactions. A seemingly friendly exchange could later be thrown in your face as a demonstration of how this guy felt isolated and misunderstood. Frank tried to tell us at every meeting and interaction that his job was unique and more special than any one else's, suggesting we treat him accordingly. The tone of the meetings shifted, and they became a forum for this guy to chastise the rest of us for not welcoming him into our group.

"Frank talked about how none of us could understand what he was going through, even though he failed to realize that we weren't very cohesive, and all of us had been through the same thing when we entered the newly formed group a year before. Things started to spiral downward when Frank began feeding his discontent to the people he managed. Frank became possessive of the staff he managed, and even though the expectation was for all of us to collaborate as managers, he refused to share information about his staff.

"On the rare occasions when Frank did share information, he would paint a picture of chaos, stress and crisis. When members of the group would step up to help him, he would say that he had it under control or the problems were getting resolved. Frank implied that our involvement would make things worse because we couldn't possibly understand the complexities of the issues. In one staff meeting he was talking about feeling alienated, and I called him on it by offering to meet with him to hear his concerns and work out a solution. We set a meeting time but he never showed.

"It was amazing how this one member being added to our team brought the rest of us together because we all started to work toward a common goal of learning to manage Frank's behavior."

ABOUT THIS CASE STUDY

Occasionally "B" behaviors can create a healing function within a group that is split into factions. This is an opportunity for the group to openly establish clear group boundaries.

Infecting the Group

NAIA

"On a group trip, our leader, Anne, met us at the airport with a bus, and we all arrived together at the compound where we would be staying. Anne offered a friendly self-introduction to Sylvia, the woman who ran the compound. Sylvia coldly retorted, 'I assumed that (you were Anne).' This interaction set the stage for the next 12 days. Prior to the trip I had phoned Sylvia several times to clarify something on the trip instructions, and had found her answers to my questions to be short and overly condescending. At the time I had dismissed her tone, thinking I had caught her at a hurried moment.

"Three days before the trip began, my credit card company called to say they had put a stop on my credit card due to a breach in security. Because of an intervening holiday with no mail delivery, the company agreed to send my new card to the compound. I had immediately emailed Sylvia, asking her to watch for my new card, hoping it would arrive before I did. Upon our arrival, I asked Sylvia if my new card had arrived, and she said no. The next day my roommate, Mary, said she wanted to sleep in, and asked me if I would bring her just a bite of something from breakfast. As I ate breakfast, Sylvia noticed that Mary wasn't there and insisted on putting together an elaborate tray of food to take to her. I told her that Mary wanted to sleep, and requested a small bit of food for when she awoke. Sylvia insisted on bringing Mary the tray and wouldn't let me carry it. She entered our room in a flourish, awakening Mary from a sound sleep.

"At breakfast, Sylvia had informed the group that cocktail hour would be at seven o'clock and that everyone was expected to be there at 'exactly' seven o'clock. I noticed that she had been making various controlling comments to some of the group members about where not to put their suitcases or about where they could and could not relax, that one of the kitchens was off limits, and which chairs they could and could not move. During our walk into town, I began to notice childish behaviors by some of the group members.

"A woman who was hard of hearing complained that she couldn't hear but didn't move closer to the guide, nor did she ask the guide to speak louder. Two members of the group complained that the guide was giving misinformation. When I tried speaking to one of these two men, he growled at me, so I decided to keep my distance. A woman complained that we were walking too fast for her but didn't ask the guide to slow down. At one point during the walk, we encountered a huge spider crossing the road. One of the group members immediately pulled a rubber duck out of her pocket, threw it down next to the spider, and began taking pictures. As others gathered around her, I found myself dropping back to distance myself from all the strange behavior.

"As group members attempted to get their bearings in a new situation, little things were brought to the attention of Sylvia. In response to the mostly minor incursions, Sylvia seemed to have a vague answer for every question. She exhibited two expressions of emotion: one of shock and dismay, and the other a biting humor that left the recipients wondering if she was serious or just trying too hard to make them laugh. For example, I was looking for an item I had momentarily misplaced when Sylvia chided me, saying, 'I guess you are just another pretty face.'

"Most of the time, Sylvia's verbiage went over the edge of civility. Sylvia told one woman that she had the heater turned up too high in her room. The woman said she wasn't sure how to operate it. Sylvia said, 'Off means off in any language.' Early in our stay, Sylvia accompanied us on the bus for a daytrip. When it came time to board the bus, the front double seat was occupied, although there was a single seat in front of that. When Sylvia entered the bus, she told the women sitting in the first double seat to move because she wasn't sitting in the single seat. Later during our stay, Sylvia allowed someone to sit next to her in the front seat seemingly to convince us that she really was a nice person.

"Sylvia delivered a short lecture during the first cocktail hour. She said dinner was to be served at exactly eight o'clock and everyone was expected to be on time. Dinner was a bland affair. Sylvia mentioned some of the daytrips we could embark on and made a few sexually suggestive comments about the men whom we would meet at those sites. The comments seemed oddly out of place from the stilted demeanor Sylvia had been trying to project.

"On the second day of our stay we embarked on an excursion to market day in one of the regional cities. After our return, I waited until I was settled to ask Sylvia if my credit card had arrived, and she said no. Because a week had passed since the credit card company said they would mail my card, I expressed concern, asking her to help me get through to a number in which I could call the company collect. I asked Sylvia if she knew how to get an operator. She looked in the phone book and dialed five or six different sets of numbers. As she was dialing, I would ask her what the number was so I could write it down. She wouldn't give me the number. Finally, I wrote down the last set of numbers as she dialed them, and those were the numbers that went through to the toll-free operator.

"After half an hour on the phone with the credit card company, I discovered that my credit card had been delivered, and the person who received it had signed my name to the receipt slip. Expressing concern that fraud had been committed, they promptly cancelled my new card and said that they would mail a new one to my home. That left me, once again, with no credit card. Dejected, I reported my concern to Sylvia. She bombarded me with questions, and I told her the little I knew, which was that someone had signed my name when receiving my credit card.

"It was after seven o'clock when I finally walked over to cocktail hour. As I walked in, Sylvia waved an envelope at me, saying, 'Look what arrived.' In shock, I grabbed the envelope out of her hand and stormed out to make a hopeless attempt at reinstating the card that was now in my hand. While I was making the phone call, Sylvia reportedly gave a lecture about how unruly our group was. She said she felt like she was 'herding cats.' This comment angered most of the people in the room, and they became silent.

When I returned to cocktail hour, the tone was more subdued than it had been. My friends and roommate were sitting at the bridge table. It was almost eight o'clock and most everyone had left the room. After I listened to a recounting of Sylvia's lecture and of my friends' complaints, Sylvia made an appearance, saying, 'You will have to stop playing now. It is dinnertime.' As people started to clean up the cards, Sylvia said, 'From now on, there will be no bridge before four o'clock or after seven o'clock.'

"More strange behaviors began to emerge from the group. Lisa and Sarah, two longtime friends, fought over what time they should go to bed. Sarah complained that Lisa's slippers slapped the floor and woke her up. Sarah asked Lisa to wear socks instead, and that made Lisa cry. After that, they ignored each other. Sarah had confided to Lisa that she felt inferior because she was the only one in the group without a college degree, and she asked Lisa not to disclose that to anyone. Lisa announced the news at bridge and then went back and told Sarah she had told all of her bridge partners what Sarah had asked her not to reveal. The mindless chatter at meals diminished with only a few peo-ple dominating most of the conversations.

"On the third day of the trip, Anne was very concerned about Sylvia's condescending attitude and made an appointment to speak with her. At the onset of the meeting, Sylvia attacked Anne by first saying that this was unlike any group she had ever had. Anne informed Sylvia that during the 13 trips she had led, she had never had someone ask to go home on the second day. This stunned Sylvia and she temporarily acted contrite, asking Anne to apologize for her. Anne told Sylvia that she should assume a low profile for a day to let the group cool off.

"By this time, Sylvia was neither talking to me nor to Mary. However, in our presence she was exceptionally friendly with several other group members. When the group returned from a daytrip, Sylvia's ritual was to run around with keys while opening everyone's room. I always said a hearty hello to her and never got a response. There were two long tables in the eating area. On one of our days off from traveling, when I arrived for breakfast there were only four people congregated at one end of a table. I was surprised when Sylvia greeted me warmly and then promptly said, 'I don't suppose you want to sit at that table (point-ing to the empty table).' I said no. She then asked me what I would like to drink. I proceeded to gather my food at the buffet line, and when I sat down amidst the group already seated, I wondered where my orange juice and coffee were. Finally, I noticed them sitting at a place at the other end of the table.

"Early in the trip, Mary and I bought two cups. Sylvia had not pro-vided enough cups for everyone, so we could never find a cup to make tea. By late in the trip, we frequently had to seek out our own toilet paper and had found the hiding place for clean towels and toilet paper. One of the women speculated that Sylvia was trying to determine who was raiding the toilet paper supply by changing the color of the toilet paper.

"One of the group members told me about an interesting cave that her husband, Frank, had encountered during one of his runs, so I walked there with another woman. When we returned, I told Sylvia that we had walked to this cave and Sylvia exclaimed, 'Isn't it a lovely place?' She hadn't told us about it, however, even though it was a mere two and a half miles away. When other group members questioned Sylvia about the cave, she told them that she didn't take groups there because there was no bathroom. Her comments didn't make sense, since we were in a place where the locals regularly stopped by the side of the road and created their own facilities, and we had gone to other places without bathrooms.

"On one of our trips, most of the group was seated around a large table listening to a lecture. Sylvia didn't have a place at the table, and was seated several chairs away from the table at the far end, within direct eyeshot of Frank, one of the few men in the room. At one point, Mary nudged me to look in Sylvia's direction. Sylvia had on a long dress; she was sitting with her dress hiked up and with her right heel on her left knee, effectively giving Frank an eyeful of whatever was under her dress and between her legs.

"On the final morning of the trip, just before we boarded the bus, I asked Sylvia if she had an evaluation form I could fill out. She said no but she was sure that Anne had one. As I boarded the bus, I noticed Sylvia talking to Anne and I later asked Anne what Sylvia had to say. Anne said Sylvia had told her I was asking for an evaluation form. Anne had retorted that it would be nice to have one. Sylvia said, 'I agree, an evaluation would be a good idea but let's make it positive, like what did you like best about this town or that town.' Anne replied that she thought an evaluation should be for feedback that would enable Sylvia to improve the experience.

"Aside from the credit card incident, none of these singular occurrences would have been particularly notable, and most of them were rather subtle or would engender a laugh. By reflecting on them as a collective, however, a chill went down my spine. I also became somewhat angry as I thought about the impact Sylvia's behaviors had on a group just out to have a good time. I also wonder why the entire group wasn't up in arms about the verbal abuse, the bad food and the inconsistent service. In truth, some people liked enough of the food to be satisfied, and the bad service and abuse were selective. Sylvia seemed to target some and to endear herself to others. Those who seemed somewhat weak became targets, and those who appeared strong became targets. Mary and I were actively targeted early in our stay, but when that didn't work, we were given the cold shoulder.

"Sarah and Lisa, the longtime friends, were still not speaking. At the beginning the trip they had sat together on the plane, but on the return trip their seats were in different areas of the plane. In the airport, Lisa was telling stories that didn't make any sense. Lisa was not mentally impaired—she had played a masterful game of bridge. In the context of the group that had been agitated by Sylvia, Lisa seemed to become someone totally different from her prior persona. Every time Sylvia opened her mouth, she rattled your brain."

ABOUT THIS CASE STUDY

Be aware of your reactions to reading this story. Some people have told us it made them feel crazy. This is because this story mimics the effects one stinging "B" can have on a group of unsuspecting people. According to Naia, at least half of the 16 people on the trip developed strange behavior patterns. On the surface, these were successful and well-to-do individuals who presumably could function well on their own. Some of their strange behaviors might have been caused by the stress of living with a "B" for 12 days. Many of the travelers seemed to have been tipped over the edge when they found themselves thrust into this temporary "B's" nest.

SUMMARY

MANY OF THE "B"S WE WRITE ABOUT IN THIS CHAPTER demonstrated considerable talents in many areas. Certain fields invite specific "B" behaviors like risk-taking, feigned sincerity, showiness, searching for perfection, or exercising total control. "B"s can appear anywhere in any group. Once you recognize "B"s within your groups, the question becomes whether the advantage of keeping the "B"s around for their talents balances the destruction they can wreak on team or group cohesiveness.

Group members and managers need to stay tuned to "B" behaviors and continuously assess how much imminent and potential damage "B"s might be causing to the structure and function within and between groups.

Individuals who find themselves in a group "B"s nest should evaluate their situation and weigh the pros and the cons of staying in the group. Another important question to ask is whether the "B's" nest extends beyond the group to an entire organization.

CHAPTER EIGHT

Organizational Politics: When to Hold, Fight or Fold

"It is better to know some of the questions than all of the answers."

JAMES THURBER

The State of Our Organizations

This chapter is as much about organizational politics as it is about situations organizations have learned to accept as the "politics of doing business." We often hear people say, "You know how narcissistic doctors (or lawyers or educators or business people) are. I just try to work with them and survive." Or you frequently hear the phrase, "oh, that's just politics" or "politics as usual," like it's something that occurs every day and should be accepted. Another phrase we often hear people say is, "I just do my job and don't pay attention to what's going on in the office."

Although stress seems to precipitate "B" behaviors in interpersonal interactions, "B" behaviors may also increase during times of too little stress. Gregory Rodriguez discusses how in stable wealthy democracies we quell our need for excitement by taking sides in trumped-up controversies.[38]

---

[38] Rodriguez, "Haiti Quake Brings Dose of Reality," *Los Angeles Times*.

It seems that every day the 24/7 media document crises with victims who portray themselves as indignant and entitled. The latest words uttered by a prominent figure become fodder for scathing blogs, tirade television and talk radio shows. These tirades keep us locked in a virtual "B's" nest, alternating between the roles of victim, persecutor and rescuer. Because we become accustomed to living in a virtual "B's" nest, we feel that we're powerless to change the situation, and we accept life in this virtual cycle. Interestingly enough, it was in a period of relative prosperity the United States banking system choked the world with its lending practices.

While the presence of "B"s within organizations probably remains static, tolerance for and favoring of "B" behaviors seems to fluctuate. With the booming economy in the 1990s and early 2000s, organizations increasingly seemed to sanction and even prize the behavior of "B"s. The pervasiveness of "B"s in many organizations became legendary. Companies such as Enron, WorldCom, and Tyco became the poster children of "B" behaviors. The documentary *The Corporation* proposed that sociopathic corporations attract similarly disposed people.[39]

On the other hand, Michael Maccoby wrote about narcissistic leaders, indicating that companies *need* narcissists to meet the challenges in the world today.[40] He portrayed narcissists as being good for companies that seek vision and new directions. And although Maccoby saw the pitfalls of a corporate world led by narcissists, he presumed narcissists were capable of policing themselves, that they only needed someone they trusted to counterbalance and ground them to reality. Maccoby actually portrayed narcissists as being willing to seek counseling to triumph over their basic character failings. But the failing of banks and other corporations along with the dis-

[39] *The Corporation*, Big Picture Media Corporation, 2003.
[40] Maccoby, "Narcissistic leaders."

coveries of huge Ponzi schemes in 2008 and 2009 raise skepticism that narcissists can ever police themselves.

The business culture that evolved during the 20 years prior to 2008 welcomed those who exhibited "B" behaviors. This "B" culture assumed narcissists were optimally suited to be innovators and visionaries. Singing your own praises, whether true or not, was raised to a new art form. In truth, these assumptions of narcissists being good for corporations in the long run are not founded in research. Furthermore, we could find no research demonstrating that those who are *not* narcissists cannot be innovators and visionaries.

A common saying, "power is an aphrodisiac," indicates that power somehow charges us up and relaxes our inhibitions. A research paper by Keltner, Gruenfeld and Anderson shows that disinhibition is at the source of power.[41] Power doesn't make someone engage in bad or hurtful actions, it simply uncovers whatever traits the person already possesses. Power has the opposite effect on those who do not have it; they become more inhibited. If a person who is narcissistic and self-serving obtains power over others, he will expect others to praise him and to tell him only what he wants to hear. He will protect himself by refusing to listen to those who have opposing viewpoints. He will think that he is right and everyone else is wrong. He will not compromise, because he thinks that he is right and entitled. He will be a perfect target for people with money who play to his narcissism and use him to transmit their own agenda. This is a very important lesson for us to apply to our elected officials. It would be wonderful if we could see this side of them before they are elected, but with the power of money and the media, these things are not always evident.

[41] Keltner, Gruenfeld, & Anderson, "Power Approach and Inhibition."

Since "B"s have very little insight into their behaviors, their presence as leaders and administrators is doomed to fail if they aren't forced to take direction and advice from those who will give them honest feedback. As we have learned from our own experiences, it's common for "B"s to rise to the top during the hiring process. There is evidence that narcissistic "B"s interview better than those who are more inclined by anxiety to be less effusive about their accomplishments and most CEOs are hired based on their interviews.[42] It seems that interviewers notice the energetic, outgoing, self-confident, competitive, and achievement-oriented qualities of candidates and choose to ignore the signs of aggressive, exhibitionistic, egotistical, manipulative, and self-serving behaviors.

Organizational Leaders

A major factor in promoting "B" behaviors in organizations is the kind of leaders who are prominent during a given time. When organizational or political leaders exhibit "B" behaviors, ethical practices are obscured, and those who follow such leaders are more likely to assume behavior patterns similar to their leaders. Occasionally, someone uses the Internet to break out of the virtual "B"s nest. In early 2000, a series of emails—between a president of a large management organization and one of its members—either inadvertently or intentionally became public on the Internet. The discussion centered on the lack of ethics courses in the nation's business schools. Despite initial denials of the need for such courses, the public conversation greatly embarrassed faculty from colleges and universities all over the country. Within a few years of these discussions, almost all business schools were offering courses in ethics.

---

[42] Hogan, Raskin & Fazzini, "The Dark Side of Charisma," 352.

Unfortunately, including ethics courses in business schools doesn't confer a conscience on a "B" who doesn't have a conscience. The almost unbelievable breach of ethics by those in businesses from banking to housing to energy production to manufacturing and healthcare has become excruciatingly evident as this country suffered the financial meltdown of 2008–2010, including the 2010 environmental debacle in the Gulf of Mexico. The sources of these disasters will be hotly debated for years. The blatant denial of any wrongdoing and a denial of responsibility suggest an epidemic of "B" behaviors.

There Is No Greater Good than My Greed, and My Greed Has No Limits

The 2009 documentary *House of Cards* detailed the history of the worldwide banking failure. Many key players in this disaster were interviewed, but no one assumed responsibility. Each of the players denied guilt for the failed housing and banking industries. Housing lenders made large commissions by lending money to people who couldn't afford the houses they were buying. The investment bankers grouped mortgages into bonds that included bad loans. They then earned large sums by selling those bonds to large investors such as pension funds and other development projects throughout the world. The "B" behaviors needed to accomplish this scheme trickled down when bond raters just out of school, or those wanting to protect their jobs, rated these bonds as AAA, the highest quality.

People who knew they couldn't afford a house or a building project took advantage of easy money and entered the "B's" nest by denying reality. These actions hastened the collapse of banks, resulting in a worldwide financial meltdown. By bailing out some banks, the federal government came to the rescue of some of the persecutors. This unprecedented action didn't alter the behavior of these persecutors, for bankers from failed banks took huge bonuses. One bank that had taken money from the federal bailout was planning to reward workers with paid vacations to Puerto Rico before customers complained and went to the press.

Encouraging "B" Behaviors

It's difficult to encounter coworkers or teams that exhibit "B" behaviors. It can be unbearable to be embroiled in an organization that defines itself with "B" behaviors. When the individual "B"s and the group "B"s influence the culture of an entire organization, it raises the level of personal pain for those who do not wish to play the games prized by such an organization. When top management includes a number of "B"s, it becomes a powerful force for creating the culture of a "B" organization.

The reader might wonder how an entire organization becomes infected with "B"s. In fact, "B"s are often attracted to other "B"s. A high-functioning "B" who interviews for a job will readily demonstrate why special qualities make him the perfect choice. In the process, the "B" will quickly assess the interviewer's need for recognition. By keying in on subjects that are important to the interviewers or by praising them or their company, an interview candidate can easily make the interviewers feel special. This praise engages the interviewers' narcissism, causing them to think they would be fools if they didn't hire the "B." This interaction intensifies each time a "B" is hired, because soon an organization that has amassed a cadre of "B"s has "B"s hiring guard "B"s.

The Seductiveness of "B"s

The buzz of "B"s can be very seductive. Successful organizational "B"s have an uncanny ability to instantly assess your weak spots, subsequently finding effective phrases or questions to draw you into their drama. Since we all have a streak of narcissism, one of the most effective ways for an organizational "B" to draw you in is to propose tasks that seem important. Since we all want to get ahead and make a good impression, we want to associate with people who are good for us, or our careers. It becomes difficult to ignore the charms of the organizational "B." Some of our interviewees described hanging with a "B" as a "rush," "like a sugar high you get after eating cake," or "like getting high on drugs." If the "B" can give the impression he or she has power and is advancing in the organization, then we want to be a part of it—and another sycophant or toady is born.

How Sycophants and Extortionists Shape the Culture of Organizations

ADAM

"Joella, a mid-management employee, had been accused of embezzling a large sum of money from a nonprofit company where I worked. At the time of Joella's arrest, she'd been approved to take a class that would've made her eligible to apply for the chief financial officer's position. Joella had worked at this organization for more than 20 years, but the records that were investigated only went back eight years.

"Joella had always been exceptionally nasty to me and other employees she thought were beneath her. However, Joella was exceptionally nice to the organization's top management. Joella joined the country club and developed relationships with all the wealthy people in the community. After many months of legal wrangling, she pleaded guilty in front of the third judge assigned to her case. The first two had recused themselves because they had social connections with Joella. On the day of sentencing, the courtroom was filled with Joella's supporters—businessmen and friends—who were sitting on one side of the room. There were a few non-supporters seated on the other side of the room.

"Joella's minister testified at the hearing, saying he had known her for 12 years, and he believed Joella to be contrite for the situation she was in. 'God has given her many talents, and she will continue to be an asset to our society.' The minister said he had seen a change in her since this happened. 'I see a more spiritual side, a Joella who thinks about what she can be and about what honesty is about. I believe she is dealing with her weaknesses in a healthy way, and if she isn't sent to prison, she can be a valuable asset to our society.' But parishioners of that church said Joella didn't regularly attend church until she was caught.

"Someone from her workplace testified, saying that initially he was shocked and saddened but was impressed with Joella's talents. He also said his own son had gone astray and was put in prison, but it didn't help him.

"A retired probation and parole officer was engaged by the defense to conduct a pre-sentence investigation. He said he was allowed to look into the case further than anyone else, but upon cross-examination, he acknowledged that he failed to do so. Instead, he performed a risk assessment by investigating Joella's personality. He was impressed that Joella didn't rationalize or justify her behavior, which was rare, and he was sure she wouldn't re-offend. On cross-examination, the prosecuting attorney asked the parole officer if he'd interviewed anyone from work about Joella. The parole officer replied, 'No, I didn't know there was someone there I could talk to.' Perhaps he really didn't want to find out the truth.

"The prosecuting attorney summarized letters that had been sent. All but one letter supported Joella. The authors of the letters of support made excuses for her behavior, i.e., a high stress level, she had had surgery and was in a lot of pain, her work wasn't appreciated by her supervisors, and her medicines were bothering her.

"The prosecuting attorney reiterated that a lot of other people have had those problems but they didn't steal $400,000. The prosecutor mentioned that Joella's household income was approximately $100,000, she had no drug abuse or gambling addiction, and that she could've stopped at any time. She only stopped after she was confronted. The prosecutor questioned the impact on the victims who couldn't speak for themselves.

"Suddenly, one of Joella's attorneys said he was thrilled to report, 'At 10 o'clock that morning, Joella received a cash offer of $395,000 for her house,' meaning Joella could now pay back most of what she had stolen. One of Joella's real estate friends had apparently purchased her house. Joella had two attorneys, and the second one then quoted the bible about forgiveness and he said Joella was remorseful, repentant and cooperative. He said she had talent and had done a good job at work. He went on to say prison was no answer for her.

"I was flabbergasted when he said, 'Not being able to work with people she has grown to love was enough punishment for Joella.' None of the people who testified on her behalf had any real evidence to support what they were saying. Even some of those who had been directly swindled by Joella were there to support her.

"Next, Joella spoke. She apologized and also quoted the bible. She said she wasn't sure how her behavior started but that she went to buy something for work and didn't return the change. A pattern was established. She said it started after she had two serious surgeries. She stated that she should've resigned when she couldn't stand the pain. She said she stopped drinking after she was arrested.

"The prosecuting attorney asked for a two-year prison sentence. The judge gave a long lecture about the seriousness of the crime and sentenced Joella to a year in jail with Huber privileges. I was angry and disappointed that she didn't get more time in jail, and I was even angrier toward the people who testified in support of Joella."

ABOUT THIS CASE STUDY

This story demonstrates how an organization's boundaries can extend beyond its walls. The story is notable for the sheer number of prominent community members who were charmed by this antisocial "B." It was evident that people in the organization who had been swindled continued to support Joella and even showed their affection for her. This is a common phenomenon among those who guard "B"s, and typifies the intoxication of a "B's charm.

Deciding to Hold and Pay a Physical Price

THOMAS

"I was working as an assistant superintendent of schools as director of instruction while I was getting my Ph.D. Five of us ran the office, and I was in charge of the content and staff development for teachers and administration. A man was appointed to the school board as a replacement in the middle of an election cycle and was then elected for the following term. He was popular in the blue-collar community and was known for hanging out at the local bars. Staff members referred to him as 'Allmouth.' There were two other board members who aligned with him along an anti-intellectual vendetta, and my Ph.D. was part of it.

"Allmouth was miffed because we had wanted extra pay for excellence, and he was even angrier that the superintendent was given the task of granting the bonuses. Only two bonuses were granted, and I got one of them in the second year. This became a target on my back. I was always neatly attired but he didn't approve of the way I dressed. He said people were making comments about my language—he said the common man couldn't understand my language—and I was asked to dumb it down. Those three board members were picking apart just about everything I was doing.

"These three board members were anti-change, and they influenced the board to cut my pay by three percent. I worked five more years until the next election. After the next election, the board became anti-change by a five-to-two margin. I was promoting a whole-language approach to learning but they wanted only phonics. All of the other teachers preferred the whole-language approach, because they knew it worked better than just teaching phonics. There was only one board member who was very supportive of my approach to teaching but she couldn't contend with the rapid-fire speech pattern of Allmouth.

"The superintendent didn't stand in the way of the conservative board, but I had completed my Ph.D. so he raised my salary. He then resigned because he knew he couldn't work with the board. The next superintendent was someone whom I had worked shoulder to shoulder with but he wouldn't support me against the board. He should've been a Ph.D. but had never finished his dissertation. He might have just been insecure around the board and thought he could deal with them by schmoozing. I was finally fired because no one would take on Allmouth.

"I worked my last four years before retirement as a kindergarten teacher, taking a $30,000 pay cut. When I retired, at a faculty assembly the superintendent started to say a few words about my career when 500 faculty members stood up and cheered. This really gave me a lift. I can't begin to describe the deep level of depression that enveloped me when the school board fiasco occurred. I had TMJ [temporo-mandibular joint disorder] so badly that my jaw bulged out. The only thing that kept me sane was running. After I retired, my TMJ disappeared and never returned."

ABOUT THIS CASE STUDY

Thomas's story is a painful example of how "B"s resist change because they need to feel in control of a situation. Narcissistic "B"s are desperate to have you reflect back to them the comfortable image they have established for themselves. They become afraid if you reflect something that is foreign to them. They will use whatever power sources they can muster—race, education, socioeconomic status, organizational membership, religious affiliation, or even appearance—to sting you and make you appear unworthy to be in their circle of "B"s. This "B" board member successfully used rapid-fire speech patterns, often used by "B"s, to intimidate others.

This "B" board member succeeded in destroying Thomas's career because the superintendent was unwilling to stand up to him. Research has shown that workers suffer ill effects from working with those who exhibit "B" behaviors.[43] Thomas suffered serious physical problems that were likely caused by this experience. He was lucky to get out in time to recover his health.

---

[43] Kivimaki et al., "Bullied Workers Take More Sick Leave," 656–660.

Learning to Fight Back:
Yin and Yang of Organizational "B"s

ARNIE

"I was a nurse supported by a grant that trained healthcare students. The faculty team was based in a private hospital near the university. The hospital's chief of staff made it very clear that he didn't want the grant in 'his' hospital, but that's where we were assigned to work.

"Despite my nursing degree, I had never worked as a staff nurse in a hospital. I was desperate to get up to speed, so I asked the hospital's director of nursing if I could accompany members of her staff to their respective units to obtain a clearer picture of nurses' roles on each unit. One of the nurses showed me around the neurology unit, and the following day I found a note from her in my mailbox that said, 'What are you doing taking over my patients?' I was both stunned and perplexed. I knew the hospital staff was wary of the grant's faculty, and some staff felt threatened by them. But this behavior was so out of line that I decided I must act on it.

"I reported the incident to the nursing director, but she didn't appear to take the matter seriously. At the departmental meeting the following week, the nurse that had left the note in my mailbox made a disparaging remark about the grant, and I decided to respond by detailing what had happened when I accompanied her to the unit, and I mentioned her note. I stated that I wouldn't tolerate such behavior, and if anything like that happened again I would make it public. To this day, I'm not sure why I chose that response and don't know what trained me for it, but that nurse never bothered me again.

"Our grant director was a powerful physician in the hospital where we worked. Since he had little time for his grant duties, he often sent me to national meetings as his representative. Although I felt out of place at these meetings being the only non-physician, I learned the behind-the-scene behaviors that enabled someone to protect a program from people who had their own organizational agendas.

"The grant director had received funding for a second training grant that involved training for physicians who wanted to receive certification in oncology. During the second year of the physician-training grant, the grant director recruited several new physician trainees who entered the program specifically because of his excellent reputation. Unfortunately, the month they arrived, he left to assume a new position. Although our replacement grant director was a physician, he didn't have the grant-writing abilities or the research credentials of his predecessor. The new physician trainees were furious, and one in particular decided to take his fury out on the team. He assumed that being a physician placed him as head of the team. And since I had been the person who had led the team meetings, I became the target of his ire.

"The new physician quickly realized that all of the team members wanted to do a good job, were afraid of making mistakes, and saw themselves as ethical professionals. But this physician felt he could control the team by selectively telling team members he thought their behaviors were unethical or their suggestions were immoral. He did this often and vociferously in team meetings. In a very short time, team members were afraid to speak up, essentially crowning him king. Team members who had worked closely together for several years, mutually respecting each other as colleagues and friends, withdrew into their own disciplines. The team members literally stopped talking to me and to each other.

"During this time I gave a lecture that referenced new research on a topic that the new physician trainee didn't believe in. He entered the room ten minutes into my lecture and proceeded to whisper loudly throughout my talk. Several days later, I found out he had asked our director to fire me. After collecting information from my colleagues, the director decided he had no grounds to fire me. Subsequently, I avoided this physician as much as possible and only spoke up to him when he threatened my students or me.

"Tiring of the cat-and-mouse game with the disruptive physician trainee and not wanting the team held hostage, another physician and I contracted with an outside consultant to intervene. Through a confidential solicitation of letters, the consultant formulated a list of the team's problems. The most pressing problem turned out to be the manipulative physician trainee who had shut down the team's internal communication. Openly exposing this physician's manipulative behaviors released the team from its culture of avoidance, allowing team members to voice their concerns about problems within the team.

"When the disruptive physician finished his training, he used the skills he had gained from the training program to start an oncology department at a nearby hospital. During the last year of the grant, the granting agency discovered that our university wasn't willing to fund our program. However, the granting agency also recognized our training program's successes, and they called me to Washington to convince me to write a program proposal for continuation of our program within the hospital currently housing our program. The grant representatives said they wanted me to direct the new program. Thanks to my political training in the previous five years, I was willing to write the new program proposal. In response, they decided to perform a site visit.

"I helped set the agenda for the site visit. I knew that the former physician trainee, who had been so disruptive, would need to be a part of our revised program proposal as a source of community support. He was placed second to last on the agenda, and the site visitors were to close their interviews with me. The site visit went well until the former physician trainee's interview exceeded the time limit. I had received word from a friend at the university that this physician wanted a friend of his, not me, to be the director of the new program. As I paced outside the room, fully aware our program was being hijacked, I tried to think of a strategy to use with the site visitors.

"As the door opened, the visitors announced they had no time to meet with me and that they'd have an exit interview with the hospital director. I quickly offered them a ride back to their hotel after their exit interview. On the way to the hotel, I asked how the day had gone, and they said fine. I said everyone they had interviewed was a supporter of the team program, except one person. They quickly shot to attention and asked who wasn't supportive. I simply said, 'Invite me in for a drink, and I'll tell you.' Over that drink I relayed the history of the program and the problems with the physician who had been so disruptive as a trainee. By the end of the conversation, they re-invited me to write the proposal and said they would support me as the program director.

"A few months after I assumed the program directorship, the hospital director asked me to take the lead on writing a proposal for a new program grant. He said the request for proposal (RFP) was unique to each hospital, required considerable work with chart reviews, and when we received the RFP he would direct it to me. I waited for the RFP, and weeks later, when I ran into the hospital director, he asked if I was done writing the proposal. In shock, I said I had never received it, and he just mumbled that he had given it to the chief of staff for review (the same chief of staff who didn't want us in 'his hospital'). The hospital director stopped short and said he would get me the RFP. When he discovered that the chief of staff had destroyed it, the director surreptitiously sent someone to Washington to get another copy. The team banded together and was awarded the program with the highest score of all the hospitals that had applied.

"I spent many years trying to expand the program while maintaining what we had already built. I relied on team members and coworkers to let me know when someone was trying to steal our positions or eliminate our program. During those years, the hospital had many different directors, and depending on the number of manipulators in the hierarchy, protecting our programs often became my full-time job."

ABOUT THIS CASE STUDY

In the world of organizational politics and organizational "B"s, Arnie's story is not unusual. From the chief of staff who wielded tremendous power, to the nurse who tried to derail Arnie's first days on the job, to the problem physician trainee who used stinging words and suggestions to manipulate the vulnerabilities of the team members, there were many lessons to be learned. If the manipulative physician trainee had been shrewder, he might have made 'friends' with each of the team members and manipulated them to openly support him as the team's leader. However, many "B"s don't have the patience to use such a methodical approach to their manipulative goals.

Although success is never guaranteed, it's important to respond to coercion quickly and with equal force. Don't underestimate your personal power whether it lies in technical knowledge, knowledge of the company, your reputation as a dedicated worker, or relationships with your coworkers. Assess your power, and when you feel a sting, use that power to establish your boundaries, letting the persecutor know you will sting back. By stating the behavior that you will not tolerate and the potential consequences if the behavior continues, you're avoiding the "B's nest. For this approach to be effective, you must follow up on any threats you make. Being willing to speak out in the correct forum is essential when you have limited power like Arnie did when he met with the nursing staff early in his tenure. Arnie was clever in enlisting a sympathetic physician in responding to the physician trainee's attempt to coerce the team. Arnie later applied this same principle when enlisting the site visitors to block the former physician trainee from inserting his friend into the position of new program director.

Learning the inner workings of the organization will give you informal power. Many high-functioning "B"s innately know this tactic, and it's in your best interest to make it part of your repertoire. Arnie and others also brought the unspoken actions of "B"s to the table for discussion. Organizational "B"s flourish on stinging workers into silence. If an organization equates speaking up with negativity or disloyalty, a "B's" nest will thrive.

High-functioning "B"s will cement their positions by "making friends" with people whom they need to accomplish their goals. It's equally important for you to solicit powerful allies. Although Arnie had to contend with many "B"s during his tenure, he made alliances with other powerful players within the hospital and used those allies to fend off "B" stings. Because alliances constantly shift as staff members move on, it's essential to replenish your allies as necessary. And never turn your back on "B"s.

The Power of the Group

AUGUSTUS

"My first job out of college was for a small but growing health-service firm. Liza, the chief executive officer, was personable but also a bit arrogant. As the company grew, Liza brought in a chief operations officer, Marty, a handsome man with limited experience. It was rumored that Liza and Marty were intimately involved. In the process of bringing Marty on board, some staff changes were made. Two managers, who had been with the company's largest and most visible program since its inception, were demoted. This action placed Marty in charge of an expanding, complex program, and the two people who knew the intricate inner workings of the program were placed in positions with no authority over the day-to-day operations.

"Marty was very insecure, and he began making big changes that didn't seem logical to the program staff. Marty sent memos stating that people had been fired and positions were eliminated 'effective immediately.' Marty very quickly created an atmosphere of fear and frustration. Staff also suspected Liza was using Marty as her puppet to do her dirty work. Liza would call meetings and go on about how she could still look at herself in the mirror, despite the changes they were making. Staff felt so powerless that no one even bothered to challenge Liza on the lies she told during these meetings. Staff bonded together, for the sake of salvaging what was left of the program.

"As conditions at the company deteriorated, I began emailing one of my mentors to ask for advice. My mentor told me it was important to make my complaints known to management. He also said I should start at the lowest level possible and progress to the next level if I didn't achieve any satisfaction. After meeting with some of the lower-level supervisors to voice my complaints and to formulate plans for collective action, I was disappointed with their lack of response. I next brought my complaints to the human resources department to ask for advice, and was told nothing was wrong. I then met with Marty to no avail, and finally met with Liza, who brushed off the complaints. I emailed my mentor with the news of my impending resignation and was surprised when he wrote back, saying I hadn't finished my job. He said I had one more level to address, and that was the board.

"I hadn't considered going to the board with these problems but thought it was worth a try. I called the staff members together and asked for volunteers to write down examples of either Marty or Liza interfering with client care. Twelve people came forward with their stories. I then asked for volunteers to accompany me in presenting the stories to the board. We practiced our presentation, making sure that it would be just the facts, without emotion. Subsequently we met with the entire board. The board members appeared to take our concerns seriously, and the board chair asked for more information.

"When Liza and Marty found out that some of the staff had met with the board, they increased their manipulative behaviors. Liza and Marty chastised the staff for going to the board, calling it a 'work freeze that had jeopardized our clients.' When we asked for specific examples of how we put our clients at risk, they were at a loss to provide any details.

"The board discovered that Liza had told the staff the board was angry. One of the board members later told a staff member he was 'sickened by executive management's ability to lie to the staff members who had taken the risk of coming forward with their concerns about their clients.' When the board asked to meet with Liza, she sent Marty. Liza must have known Marty wouldn't do well with the board but he'd stay loyal to her. Shortly after Marty met with the board, it became evident that Marty and Liza were no longer getting along.

"There was even more strange behavior. At a staff meeting led by Marty, he referred to someone named Joan. Liza, who was sitting across the room, interrupted loudly by saying, 'No one knows Joan. Is Joan your cousin?' Marty was dumbfounded and obviously humiliated by Liza's tone. There was an awkward 30 seconds of silence, broken by Marty giving a forced laugh and telling Liza to 'shut up.' Six weeks after the staff first met with the board, Marty was fired. Three months after staff first met with the board, Liza's contract was up for renewal but wasn't renewed. Fortunately for the staff and the clients, the board had done a thorough investigation."

ABOUT THIS CASE STUDY

The leaders in this organization used intimidation to accomplish their purposes and were totally out of touch with the needs of the employees. Multiple lies and staff manipulation were two clues that the top managers were "B"s. This story exemplifies the tremendous toll "B"s can take on an organization when they are unchecked, even for relatively short periods of time. Distrust in leaders causes turnover. Staff turnover in organizations is expensive in terms of money, morale and time. In situations like this, it's important for staff members to become quickly unified and to be willing to confront unreasonable requests. Many of the staff members chose to leave. If Augustus and his colleagues had not decided to fight back, it's likely that turnover in this organization would've been close to 100 percent.

Deciding to Fold:
The End of a Long Struggle

JOE

"Before retirement I worked for a large consulting firm. The way to succeed in the firm was by growing business by expanding current contracts or attaining new contracts. Our success was based on maintaining good relations with our clients and the business community at large. Although many of our clients placed heavy demands on us, it was the chaos that was created in one assignment that nearly drove me over the edge.

"For a year I had been working with my consulting team on a five-year contract in the home office of a multi-site manufacturing company. My firm had a long history with this client, and I had developed a good relationship with all of the major players in the company. If something went wrong, I would've lost one of our firm's biggest contracts.

"When our client hired Hayden to lead their research division, he appeared soft-spoken and very friendly, and came with years of experience in another highly rated company. Hayden emphasized that he wanted to do great things for the company. And after meeting with Hayden several times, I was convinced that he was capable of growing the company.

"Since the research division was quite large, I was surprised that Hayden arrived by himself without negotiating his contract to include support staff. When I asked how he was going to implement the changes he wanted, he said that he'd hire top-notch people within two months. I knew how difficult it would be to get highly skilled people to move across country with their families to a relatively small city, and I certainly didn't think it was possible in Hayden's timeframe. Within two months, however, he had hired 18 of the best people in the country. When I saw how quickly Hayden hired top people, I thought it was incredible that he had such a following.

"Initially, working with Hayden seemed pleasant, although he often communicated by sending me terse emails of three or four words, forcing me to read between the lines to figure out what he wanted. And he'd get angry when I didn't understand his emails.

"Shortly after Hayden was hired, he said he had conducted a survey across all the business owners at the company, which revealed extremely negative attitudes toward our consulting firm. Hayden said that the company wasn't happy about the direction our firm was taking it. I was shocked, because we had developed such a good working relationship with this company. I started to suspect that the quality of the survey was bad, and after talking to people in other divisions who said they hadn't taken Hayden's survey, I realized that it was a scam. Meanwhile, Hayden visited the company's other sites and used the fake survey results to change the perceptions of the employees and to redirect their focus to his plan.

"I realized that it was all about Hayden. He sent out a file titled, 'Who Am I?' It was a document about an article that had been written about him and what he believed in. I had to find ways to work with Hayden and discovered that if I could get him published in the industry, it would be the biggest button I could push for him. It was never about the quality of the work but about whether he could get press. I also discovered that Hayden developed loyalty through money. Hayden's father was extremely wealthy, and whenever Hayden needed money his father would provide it. I realized that the way Hayden acquired such a skilled group was to pay them off. Hayden created loyalty by giving people money under the table, and those people would follow him anywhere.

His overt attitude was, 'You scratch my back and I'll scratch yours,' but at the same time he was negotiating with a third party, to give his business to them.

"Less than a year after Hayden had enticed his staff to come and work with him, the manufacturing company decided not to pay year-end bonuses. One of Hayden's staff told me that Hayden assembled his staff of 18, and he handed them each a brown envelope with $50,000 in it. Fifty grand that you don't have to claim for taxes can be a powerful incentive to stay. Nine of the 18 people that Hayden enticed constituted his inner circle. They were smart and worked very hard. It was fascinating because each of the nine had some oddity. It was as if Hayden picked people with defects so they wouldn't challenge his self-image.

"Derek was Hayden's right-hand man, and I had to go through him to get to Hayden. Derek had worked for Hayden four other times. He was slick and a fast talker, everything that Hayden wasn't. They went everywhere together. Derek needed to be the center of attention all the time. Even at important meetings, Derek would try to draw attention away from the speaker. The first time I was introduced to Derek, he told me a long, sad, drawn-out story about how sick he had been. I asked him why he came, and he said it was because he believed in Hayden. He also said his wife was dying of cancer. Later I discovered these were both lies. I heard these lies played out over and over as Derek used them on contacts with other companies to gain sympathy and gather information.

"Many times Derek would take me aside and say, 'Hayden is upset because your competition spends a lot more money on other customers.' If we didn't do some of the things he asked us to do, they'd threaten to take the business away. Occasionally, Derek would say to me, 'There are times I need to get my wife a gift just to keep things going.' Derek seemed to have no boundaries regarding work versus personal life. Often he would call in the middle of the night or when I was busy with my family and he'd talk for hours.

"During this time, a competing consulting firm was trying to commandeer our contract with the company. It was clear to me that Derek was using it as a threat. A woman from the competing firm would show up in the dead of winter wearing the shortest mini skirts. If our consulting firm didn't have a strong working relationship with this entire company, Derek would have succeeded at ending our contract.

"There was a summit meeting for thousands of people in the industry. The company was going to send 20 people. Derek called me to ask for a penthouse room at the hotel and told me he expected there to be presents and toys for his wife and kids so they would be entertained. I had to say no.

"Derek was overt but Hayden was the puppeteer behind him. As Derek's behavior escalated, I tried to get my management to understand the chaos and how it was causing my team distress. My boss confronted Hayden, saying, 'We have this problem with Derek, help me understand.' Hayden said he would deal with it, and my management came away from the meeting saying that Hayden was a true partner and that we needed to do more. I saw the reality but my bosses didn't.

"Hayden brought both Derek and me into his office and told us we needed to improve this and that. Hayden didn't single either of us out to our face but he wrote me a 10-page letter that was like a diary about my team and me. You could tell that he had written it over many days, because it went on and on. He wrote that he was frustrated about work not getting done and he sent the letter directly to me. Once the letter was written I realized that he could take it to my management, so I immediately wrote a response to the letter. When my boss met a second time with Hayden, he told my boss that he might want to ask me about the letter he'd written me. Although I knew that getting myself out was a major risk for my staff, I immediately applied for a job in another area of the firm.

"I was angry and frustrated because my bosses didn't believe me. I didn't leave my firm because I knew that it was going to be acquired by a new owner, and the CEO would be gone. I was more intent on getting attached to something in the firm that was challenging. I began working in another area of the firm where I was separated from the manufacturing company.

"As I reflect back on this experience, I realize that when you acknowledge the stories of people like Hayden and Derek and flatter them and don't call them on their absurdities, it gets you nowhere. All of my time was spent trying to keep these guys in check. I was proud of some of the work we did, but most of it was about keeping the contract alive and managing Derek and Hayden. It took an immense amount of energy. I also realize how isolating this experience was for me. I went to my boss, and he was unable or unwilling to help me. I really couldn't talk to anyone about it.

"The worst part was what it did to the people who worked for me. They were looking to me to achieve some control over this insanity. They knew how bad it was. They all supported me. Derek tried to coerce two of my people to come over and work for him. They would come to me to talk about it. None of my people went to the other side. When our firm's five-year contract expired, however, every one of my team members left the company. Hayden often sent me emails telling me that these people were 'the most stupid people he ever knew in his life.' However, each one of them landed jobs at top-notch companies.

"Some people aren't as affected by people like Derek and Hayden. The guy who succeeded me seemed to have a higher tolerance for their manipulative behaviors. He would go closer to the line than I would. However, even he called me after three months in the job, acknowledging what a frightening situation he was in. He met their families and was playing the game, but ultimately the game got him, and the firm fired him.

"Hayden's wealthy father was indicted for racketeering, and Hayden went on to work for another company. I wondered whether Hayden would be indicted as well. I had learned why I needed to keep work and family life separate. A new owner took over the firm. When I started growing close with my new boss at the firm because of work we did on a large account, I knew to keep my distance, realizing that we were not friends. Later, when I discovered that he was friends with Hayden's wealthy father, I decided to retire."

ABOUT THIS CASE STUDY

Joe transferred to another area within the firm when he saw that Hayden had him in a bind. Joe did not want to jeopardize his firm's largest contract. Joe learned that he needed firm boundaries separating work from family and friends. Ultimately, Joe and his entire team decided that it wasn't worth sacrificing their wellbeing by continuing to work in a "B's" nest. Whenever you work in a large organization, you can expect to encounter "B"s from time to time. If the "B" sees you as helpful, or at least doesn't find you threatening, he might be willing to work with you. However, if a "B" sees you as interfering with his self-image, you'll enter his radar screen. If a "B" fears that you might claim some of his power or threaten his goals, you're in for a rough time. It's important to know your strengths and your goals within the organization and keep your boundaries firm.

This story packs a punch because it contains antisocial, narcissistic, borderline and histrionic behaviors that are approaching the center of the "B" severity diagram presented in chapter two. Someone like Joe who is surrounded by this many "B" behaviors with so much at stake is at high risk for lasting effects such as post-traumatic stress disorder or burnout. Luckily, Joe finally got out and moved on.

Falling into Your Own "B's" Nest

JASON

"I had briefly worked in the same university department as Morris, another researcher. Morris was friendly but arrogant. When I transferred to a new research center on campus, Morris's demeanor changed, and he became quite cool toward me. Morris's wife, Avery, was a senior professor at a prestigious institute within the same university. She had refused to work with my research center on several projects. Because Avery brought millions of dollars of research money to her institute and to the university, she was a valuable commodity. It was well known that whenever Avery didn't get what she wanted from administration, she would threaten to leave for another university. It was also known that whenever Morris wanted something from his dean, he would tell Avery and she would threaten to leave unless her husband got whatever he wanted.

"Six months after moving to the new research center, I applied for a very large research grant. One of the requirements of the grant was the ability to work together with other resources in the university and beyond. It was critical to the grant process that we include a letter of support from both Morris and Avery. Morris refused to write the letter of support. Avery went a step further than her husband by writing a memo to the faculty members within her institute, forbidding them to collaborate with us. But Avery seemed to forget that one of her faculty members was married to the director of the research center where I now worked. That faculty member gave her husband, my boss, a copy of Avery's letter and sent it to the dean of the university. Needless to say, our grant wasn't funded. The next time Avery threatened her dean with leaving for another university, however, the dean told her to go. Six months later, Morris and Avery left the university."

ABOUT THIS CASE STUDY

It's not uncommon for even smart narcissistic "B"s to wall themselves off in their own exploitive "B's" nest. Sometimes patience is its own reward. Occasionally you get lucky, and if you wait long enough, "B"s might sting themselves. That's what happened in this case.

SUMMARY

ONE OF THE MOST DESTRUCTIVE THINGS ORGANIZA-tional leaders can do is to deny the existence of "B"s in their organization. Executives give many reasons for not addressing the destructiveness of "B" behaviors. Perhaps they are "B"s themselves and don't want to look in the mirror. Perhaps they think the "B"s are too valuable and they don't want to rock the boat. Perhaps leaders don't believe that people can be so manipulative. Perhaps they blame it on a bad day or on the stress the employee is suffering. Perhaps leaders think you should just get over it. Whatever their reason for not addressing "B" behaviors, it doesn't excuse their failure to look at the good of the organization and positively address the manipulative behaviors.

CHAPTER NINE

The Dance of Denial

"When a man suspects any wrong, it sometimes happens that if he be already involved in the matter, he insensibly strives to cover up his suspicions even from himself."

CYRIL CONNOLLY

A Domino Metaphor

WENDY

"I had been contemplating the little piece of concrete in my new sunroom. It had oozed out of the form when they poured the floor and hardened into a lump in the corner. When I discovered it, I talked to the men from the different trades. The concrete contractor said, 'That isn't my job.' The carpenter said, 'It was the concrete guy's job to chisel that out. I didn't see it. You know, we're carpenters and we work with wood.' The flooring contractor said, 'They think I do glass and concrete and stone. Anything that didn't work out, they leave for me. They don't talk to me. They just assume I know what they're thinking.'

"Later, the carpenter returned to say he had fixed it. When I looked, I found a tiny wooden box the carpenter had built to cover the tiny piece of concrete sticking out of the corner of my sunroom. I took a picture of the final product and told the contractor that I was going to take an ad out and publish it in the paper."

ABOUT THIS CASE STUDY ─────────────────────

This situation is simply a metaphor for what happens when people either don't see or don't want to see the "B" behaviors that ooze out at the seams and affect everyone they touch. By ignoring "B" behaviors, we often magnify the damage "B"s can cause.

The Progression of Denial

This chapter is about people who encounter "B" behaviors and quietly deny their existence. It's easy to identify these people by their comments. The tenor of the comments changes as the situation gets worse. The first round of comments tends to defend our denial. The second round of comments seems to defend the "B."

First round of comments:
- "He is really a good boy deep inside."
- "He is such a quiet man, he could never do that."
- "He seems like such a nice person."
- "He always says hello when I pass him in the hall."
- "She is a volunteer at church."
- "He was a Boy Scout leader."
- "She gives so much to charity."
- "He has such a nice smile."
- "My child is innocent. He would never do something like that."
- "Just do your own job and don't worry about him."

Second round of comments:
- "He had such a tough childhood."
- "Let's not forget all the good things she's done."

- "Who hasn't done bad things?"
- "He didn't mean it."
- "I felt sorry for her so, I didn't press charges."
- "She admitted doing wrong and is sorry."
- "She seems contrite."
- "He is very unlikely to re-offend."
- "He has apologized to all those that he offended."
- "She is going to pay the money back and that's punishment enough."
- "He is going to church and professing his sorrow."
- "He is a changed person."

In July 2009 Daniel Boyd, a 39-year-old drywall contractor, was arrested for masterminding a plot to kidnap, torture and kill people. He and a group of friends had been secretly buying guns and training for jihad. Boyd's neighbors refused to believe he was capable of such heinous actions. Associated Press reporters Adam Goldman and Mike Baker quoted a neighbor of Boyd's as saying, "If he's a terrorist, he's the nicest terrorist I ever met in my life. I don't think he is."[44] Apparently Boyd had made certain to leave a good impression on his neighbors as a way of avoiding suspicion. And they complied by dropping their guard and trusting him. It turned out Boyd had been convicted of bank robbery in Pakistan. And even though Boyd's two adult sons were complicit with him, Boyd's wife chose to ignore the behavior that was going on around her, saying she didn't believe it and people shouldn't rush to judgment.

A documentary on the history of Bonnie and Clyde, two murderers who went on a killing spree in the 1930s, was equally fascinating. One of the men interviewed in the documentary described Bonnie and Clyde as "just a love story of two kids who happened to fall off the wrong side of the fence."[45] When people

[44] Goldman & Baker, "Brother Defends Accused Terror Head," *NewsBreak*.
[45] *Love and Death: The Story of Bonnie and Clyde*, A & E Home Video, 2000.

frame the actions of "B"s this way, it's easy to dismiss their aberrant behaviors as "just an accident," implying that it wasn't their fault. Both Bonnie and Clyde grew up poor, just like many other people who weren't serial killers. There's no way Bonnie and Clyde's life histories could justify their antisocial behaviors.

It's difficult to know when people become aware of "B" behaviors and then choose to deny their existence. When you don't recognize "B" behaviors and eventually get stung, it can be devastating. On the other hand, when someone needs you, is nice to you and only shows you their good side, it's easy to be blinded and deny that they might act differently toward others. A person like this can be stepping on and crushing everyone else in his or her path but you might not see the destruction unless you look for it.

There are situations in which the power differential is so great that ignoring or denying a person's "B" behaviors acts as a survival mechanism. This is true in many parent-child relationships, or in a situation where someone is kidnapped. However, even in these situations, the victim might find ways to fight back. Ultimately, denying or ignoring a "B's" manipulative, cruel or destructive behaviors provides a tacit license to continue that behavior.

Too Close for Clarity

The closeness of real and surrogate family members often initiates denial, preventing us from confronting a family member who commits an illegal, malicious or manipulative act. Those who grow up with "B"s in their families or who spend a lot of time with "B"s might become emotionally numb to "B" behaviors. When we are exposed to unchecked "B" behaviors in our youth, we learn to see these behaviors as normal. In some families, the stories of family members who engage in "B" behaviors have become legends and can actually become a source of reverence.

GENE

"I was curious about a priest I served mass for while I was in grade school. In those days a priest was regarded as part of your family. As an adult I discovered that the priest had been accused of molesting young boys. Representatives of the archdiocese were holding a meeting to discuss the allegations. Although the priest had died a number of years earlier, credible allegations from more than thirty victims had surfaced. What struck me most about this meeting was the number of people who came to defend the priest. Given the number of credible allegations, I simply couldn't understand why so many people were speaking out in his defense."

PETE

"My brother was the world's biggest practical jokester. We used to laugh at his antics but now that I think about it, many of the things he did were cruel. Once, when we were visiting a friend of his, he reached into his friend's freezer as we were leaving, grabbed a package of fish and put it under the guy's mattress. His friend looked for months for the source of the odor. He cleaned out his entire apartment and threw many things away and still couldn't get rid of the smell. I don't know if he ever figured out what had happened."

MILT

"I remember my father telling me about the time my grandpa called to ask him if he'd bring over his trailer so they could haul some junk. My dad complied, and my grandpa directed my dad to a corner downtown where a car had smashed into a telephone booth. After loading the remains of the booth into the trailer, my dad asked my grandpa who had given him permission to take the booth. My grandpa replied, 'No one.' My dad didn't confront my grandpa to tell him he was stealing. He just silently refused to ever run an errand for him again."

TILLY

"After my father died, I was visiting with my siblings and we were reflecting on my father's abuse of us as children. My brother remembered a day that was seared into his mind, asking which of us our father was beating that day. I answered that it was me who was beaten. I had refused to wash the dishes because I didn't think it was fair—it had been my sister's turn to wash and she'd skipped out of the house right after supper.

When I refused, my dad started beating me. The more he struck me, the more staunchly I refused. The beating and words that went with it were loud and continued for a long time. I asked my brother where he was during my beating, and he said he was hiding under his bed.

"Many years after this discussion, I realized my brother was the one who had moved farthest away from the family. My brother couldn't remember having been beaten by our father, but he remembered being ignored by him. My oldest sibling didn't remember being mistreated at all by our father. It's like she grew up in a different house than the rest of us. She was the firstborn and was feminine like girls were supposed to be. She married and moved a few miles out of town.

"My middle sister and I sustained most of the physical abuse in our family. She was the one our father beat for wetting the bed. Sometimes she put comic books in her pants and laughed in his face. Finally, my parents discovered she had a serious kidney disorder, which landed her in the hospital for several weeks. She joined the military shortly after she graduated from college, ending up in Africa for two years. It was pretty hard to get farther than that from our parents and the town where we grew up. She said she hated my father for what he did to her. She disclosed that when she was alone with him on his deathbed, she had asked him in vain for an apology.

"I was the stoic, taking my beatings quietly. I remember afterward glaring at my father, thinking, 'Kill me mother-fucker, go ahead and kill me.' I spent the majority of my childhood thinking of legitimate ways to run away from home so I could avoid his verbal and physical abuse. One evening I was standing behind the garage with a cousin and her boyfriend. I said I wanted to know how a kiss felt, so she told her boyfriend he could kiss me. My father saw this happen and he berated me every night at dinner for the rest of the summer.

"When our father abused us, my mother didn't intervene. Although my father berated my mother, he never beat her because she wouldn't allow it. I remember my mother telling my sisters and me to never allow our husbands to hit us. But for some reason, my mother allowed my father to beat us. Somehow, it was okay coming from him, but not from our husbands. I grew up knowing nothing about emotional abuse, only that I should never allow my husband to beat me.

"When I graduated from high school, my father told me I had to live at home unless I got married. So I entered a marriage doomed to fail because it was a way to break free of my father's abuse. Although my marriage was devoid of physical abuse, it repeated the same patterns of emotional abuse that I was trying to avoid by running away from home.

"As I reflected more on my situation, I realized that I'd been focusing on the physical abuse when what bothered me the most was the lack of respect I felt from my family members who didn't help to defend me against my father. I now realize that each of them had been using different forms of denial and avoidance, just to survive.

"Even when my father was dying, I was still looking for a shred of remorse from him, so I naively asked him if there was anything he wanted to say to me. He said, 'No, I just want a blond nurse to bring me a hamburger.'"

ABOUT THESE CASE STUDIES

Tilly's story demonstrates that denying the existence or denying the effects of "B" behavior can lead you into future relationships that are similar or worse than what you had originally experienced. Also, it's often the more subtle "B" behaviors that can do the most damage to our psyches. The previous stories reflect the different reactions of parishioners, a brother, a son-in law, and four siblings to the "B" behaviors of someone they saw as a member of their family. The reasons people choose to deny the existence of "B" behaviors or to avoid confronting a "B" are many. Their styles of denial are equally as varied. Different personalities might experience and react to similar situations very differently. Everyone seems to have their own personal style of denying or avoiding a situation they cannot face.

Tilly's story reminds us how an aggressive "B" might treat his children differently by selectively abusing only some of them. It also teaches us that direct affronts by family members might not bother us as much as surprise affronts. It's the element of surprise that plants the "B's" barb firmly and squarely right in our backs. In addition, people with similar experiences may interpret and remember them differently. If all of the members of a group suffer a common abuse but some group members deny or fail to recognize the abuse, it's very difficult for the other group members to bring their experiences to people's attention for conscious discussion. This is one reason abusive behavior proliferates within a family or other group. Collectively denying the detrimental effects of a "B's" behaviors allows the "B" to justify his actions and assures that the "B's" nest will continue to thrive.

The Military

There have been numerous reports of sexual misconduct in the military.[46] A reporter for the Associated Press wrote that in one year there were 100 reported attacks by recruiters.[47] This misconduct included harassment and sexual attacks by males against females and males against males.

Fear of retaliation prevents attacks from being reported. Fears of recrimination are real, for the abusers often verbally attack those who report abuse. If the abuser's story sounds credible, it's the abused that might be discharged from service, while the perpetrator remains. Men fear being accused of being gay if they report being attacked by another male. The published reports usually

---

[46]*The Source On Women's Issues In Congress*, "House Subcommittee Examines Sexual Assault in the Military."
[47] Mendoza, "Sexual Conduct Mars Military Recruiting, *Associate Press*.

include several quotes from someone who denies any evidence of such behavior. When people say they've never noticed a behavior or when they deny seeing something they've never looked for, it makes it more difficult for those who are trying to speak the truth.

Babe in the Woods

KATHRYN

"My internship in graduate school became my introduction to the world of manipulative behaviors. However, it wasn't the behavior of clients but the behavior of coworkers that taught me the most important lessons of "B"s.

Toward the end of academic preparation, especially in graduate school, internships became the preferred training method. In graduate school I was placed with a board under the tutelage of its executive director. The purpose of the board was to lobby the state legislature and rule-making bodies to improve the plight of a disabled population. The executive director, although competent, was preoccupied with his personal affairs and also with an incident in which the chairman of the board had allegedly made a pass at his wife. I naively stepped into this conflict and for the next four months watched these people deny their mutual disdain.

"Despite this elephant in the room, I moved forward, learning how to write press releases and how to understand the ins and outs of lobbying for a cause. I also observed some of the backslapping and disingenuous banter that went on between politicians and lobbyists.

"A powerful member of the board felt strongly that a certain medical condition led to dire consequences for the health of our constituents, and convinced the chairman to pursue this issue. The executive director asked me to gather data and write a report to demonstrate that we should produce an initiative that would ward off this health condition. I decided to take this problem on for my master's research project and subsequently spent considerable time constructing a meta-analysis, reviewing and categorizing every piece of research that had been written on the topic. Toward the end of my research, I realized the results of my review weren't what the chairman and board members wanted. In fact, I found the opposite of what the powerful board member believed. But I was happy that my research had produced some useful knowledge that I thought would save the board from going down a dead end.

"When the chairman of the board realized my results were inconsistent with what the board had wanted, he banned me from attending further meetings and wouldn't release my report to the board. Although I complained to my supervisor, the executive director, he ignored my pleas and refused to intervene. I felt like I had been stung twice. This was my first professional encounter with manipulative behavior. It was also my first real learning experience related to the politics of the organization and politics in general. I made the mistake of thinking this sort of occurrence was an anomaly and never reported it to my academic supervisor.

"The board continued to pursue their interests and wasted their resources when they could've been pursuing some more important problem that would've made a difference for their constituents. As a student I didn't feel I had free access to board members and thought I had to go through the board's executive director. I later realized if I had approached each board member individually and explained my position, I would've had a much better chance of them being exposed to the results of my study. And even if the board had subsequently rejected my report, I would've willingly moved on, knowing I had done everything I possibly could have done. Because I was uncertain of my power, I allowed myself to feel powerless."

ABOUT THIS CASE STUDY ─────────────────────────

It's interesting that the executive director in this case assumed the role of guard "B" for the chairman's role of persecutor. This happened despite the fact that they were feuding. Perhaps the executive director had another battle to fight and didn't want to take on this one. It's much easier to ignore a "B's" behavior if you aren't the one who has been directly stung.

As a student, Kathryn was in a difficult situation and might have benefited from having the backing of her academic supervisor. It's difficult to know if she would've experienced any success by lobbying individual board members. It might have raised the ire of the executive director who controlled her grade for the internship. On the other hand, if you have never been encouraged to speak up or to make your views known, it's relatively easy to fall into the trap of believing you don't have much power in a situation. Kathryn's denial that the board's decision could be reversed left her powerless, and she readily assumed the role of victim. The feeling of powerlessness that denial generates is something an arrogant and interpersonally exploitive "B" relies on to retain a sense of control over others and to keep you in the role of victim.

Breaking Through a Wall of Denial

The following story illustrates how far we might go to deny that a "B" is trying to harm us.

BROOKE

"Cleo was a former neighbor who was fascinated with human behavior. She had a special gift for figuring out why people behaved the way they did. Cleo was driven to understand any behavioral problem that presented itself to her. She would think and think until she could grasp the meaning of a perplexing situation. After I moved away, Cleo and I occasionally spoke on the phone. Cleo had an adult daughter by her first marriage. Cleo's current husband, Ralph, was always very cordial, but I always had the sense he wanted Cleo to stay away from me.

"One October day Cleo called to tell me Ralph had left her. He walked out with no explanation, other than to say he didn't love her. Cleo and I talked for a long time. I was worried about her because the last time I had seen her, Cleo had lost a lot of weight. She was not forthcoming with any information on her health.

"In November, Cleo called again and told me she had received an initial diagnosis of viral hepatitis. A week later I spoke again with Cleo, who had discovered she had severe liver failure that was likely terminal. Cleo said her husband had talked to as many physicians as he could before she even received her final diagnosis. After discovering the seriousness of her condition, Ralph quickly moved back into Cleo's house, telling her he wanted to take care of her. Cleo reluctantly allowed him back in, knowing she would need help. However, she also desperately wanted to believe Ralph still loved her.

"Ralph apologized for leaving and told Cleo he had been depressed and had been planning to kill himself. He promised Cleo he would see a therapist. I later discovered that Ralph had told a friend he had initially left because Cleo was always nagging him.

In January I visited Cleo at home and asked her how things were going with Ralph. She started to cry, saying he was drinking heavily at night and she didn't feel safe. I asked whether she would rather he left home if he continued to drink. Because Cleo said yes, I decided to wait for Ralph to return home so I could speak with him. While she slept, I waited three hours for Ralph to arrive. When he finally came home, I mentioned Cleo's concern about feeling safe and asked him if he could give up drinking at home while Cleo was alive. He said he could do anything he set his mind to, and if she and I wanted him to stop, he would stop. He also said that at Cleo's request, he would see a therapist.

"The next day I returned for another visit and was told by Don, a friend of Cleo's daughter Elsa, that Cleo wanted me to witness her life insurance policy beneficiary form. When I discussed the insurance with Cleo, she said she had talked to Ralph and he convinced her that she should leave everything to him and he would take care of Elsa after she died. Despite this assurance from Ralph, Cleo told me she wanted to leave 60 percent of her life insurance to Elsa and 40 percent to Ralph. She was planning to fill out the form but she fell asleep.

"A week and a half later, I returned and found Cleo had tried to fill out the form but had written her social security number wrong and then had written over several of the numbers. Cleo, being a stickler for details, realized she should start fresh on a new form, so she asked Ralph to get one for her from the insurance agency. When Don arrived, he said Ralph had been carrying the completed form around in his truck and hadn't picked up a new one. I then asked Ralph if he could pick up a new form when he went to work. He yelled at me and said he was losing control. Elsa apparently didn't hear me ask him, because she also asked Ralph to pick up a new form, and Ralph blew up at her. Nevertheless, Ralph brought back the new form a short time later.

"Cleo's condition was rapidly declining and I knew it was critical to get the form filled out as Cleo wished. I called an employee in human resources asking for help in completing the form. She complied and I took the form in to Cleo asking her what she wanted for percentages. This time she chose 35 percent to Elsa and 65 percent to Ralph, saying the house would go to Ralph and she wanted to make sure Ralph could make the payments. It was clear to me that Ralph had been working on her.

"I asked Cleo about a will and whether she had specified that the things she received from her parents were to go to Elsa. Cleo said she had spoken with Ralph, who stated he was going to leave everything to Elsa in his will. I suggested she might give some things to Elsa now, and she said she wanted to keep the house intact. I filled in Cleo's designated percentages. Cleo signed, and Don and I were witnesses. As I turned to deliver the form to HR, Cleo said she wanted me to personally deliver it to a specific person in HR, and I shouldn't give it to anyone else. I left immediately and delivered the form.

It was clear that Cleo was pondering issues related to trust. It was also clear that Ralph had convinced her that he would do right by Elsa. When I returned from delivering the form, Ralph came in and asked where the form was. When I said I had delivered it to HR, he again yelled, insisting he should have delivered it. I suggested that we talk, and he said that he had nothing to say to me.

"In February, Cleo said she wanted me to write her obituary along with her trusted uncle, Jim. Jim had not seen Cleo for a long time and was shocked at Cleo's appearance. I went in to talk with Cleo alone and asked her if Ralph was drinking. Cleo wavered and said she thought so but wasn't sure. Elsa came in with Don, and they said Ralph had been drinking heavily. Don said Ralph had asked him to buy him a bottle of vodka but he refused. Cleo said Ralph had never before drunk vodka.

"We were problem solving when Jim came in and defended Ralph, saying he was sure Ralph wasn't drinking more than a few beers a night. Elsa said Ralph couldn't stop with two beers. Jim thought Cleo should confront Ralph. I knew Cleo was much too weak at this point to confront anyone, and couldn't understand why her uncle was protecting Ralph.

"Cleo's uncle and I looked at pictures with her and we took notes as she talked. She gave us the names she wanted to include as next of kin, and she didn't include Ralph's son. Cleo had mentioned that Ralph's son had recently been arrested and she didn't want him included. The next day I typed up a draft of the obituary, indicating it was just a draft. When Ralph saw that his son was not listed, he exploded. When Elsa and Jim said they could easily add his son's name, Ralph forbade them from doing it.

"I visited Cleo at her home one last time. Elsa arranged for me to come when Ralph wouldn't be there. Ralph unexpectedly arrived after I had been there awhile and started yelling that he had not given permission for me to be there. I was concerned that people Cleo knew and loved were not being permitted by Ralph to visit her, and I gave some names to Elsa.

"Cleo was admitted to hospice. The hospice case manager told Elsa the nurses felt that Cleo had some unresolved issue preventing her from dying. Elsa said she knew what was bothering Cleo, that Cleo was wondering if she had made the right choice in letting Ralph back in her life. Elsa told the case manager some of the things that Ralph had done in the prior few months but the case manager didn't believe them, saying Ralph had been through a lot and people cope differently.

"A close friend of Cleo's was there as well and said Ralph wasn't crazy but was a 'Snake Oil Sam.' She said she had urged Cleo not to marry Ralph because he'd been married numerous times before. Apparently, Ralph had rationalized his prior marriages by saying he was only trying to help lonely women. Cleo's friend told Elsa she had over-heard Ralph saying that he could get $300,000 for the house and then he was out of there.

"The following Sunday, Elsa left a message on my answering machine saying that Ralph had been in to see Cleo for 20 minutes. Ralph told Elsa that as far as he was concerned, Cleo died the day she was admitted to hospice. When Ralph left, saying he was going to a bar for a ham-burger and a few beers, Elsa had been keeping a constant vigil since her mother entered hospice. I offered to relieve her so she could sleep.

"I found Cleo emaciated and barely alive. She seemed to recognize me when I spoke to her, saying we would handle any fallout from Ralph. I reminded her that she had done her life's work and she could rest. I acknowledged to Cleo that she had been a success, that she had often held the world on her shoulders and that she was good at it. I told her everything was out of her hands. I acknowledged that she had taken Ralph back and it was the best decision she could've made under the circumstances. I acknowledged that Ralph had 'taken care' of her for the two months since her final diagnosis. I said I would be there to help Elsa and also would try to see that Ralph got help if he wanted it. I again said that things were out of her hands. She indicated with her eyebrows that I was connecting with her and she understood.

"I slept in the chair next to Cleo's bed, and Elsa slept on the couch— the first sleep she had had in 60 hours. By morning Cleo was still alive and had started a tremor that wracked her body. Her respirations were labored and she had an intermittent fever. That morning Elsa, Don, and Don's friend came. The four of us were in Cleo's room talking to her. I was leaning over the bed when I caught a glimpse of Ralph in the corner of my eye. He immediately started yelling, 'Who told her she could come? No one asked me!' Don and his friend went out to the hall to calm Ralph down. I immediately decided I had to leave so Ralph wouldn't disrupt the whole facility and wouldn't hurt Cleo any more, in case she had heard him.

"It was too late. As I looked into her eyes to say my final goodbye, I saw a look that could best be described as combined horror, shame and sadness. All of a sudden Cleo raised her long bony arms with her black fingers, and her upper torso arose from the pillow. She wanted to give me a hug. We both sobbed. I said it would be the last time I saw her. After I left, Ralph reportedly walked into the room and put his hand on Elsa's shoulder, saying, 'I was at the doctor this morning, and he's really worried about me.' Ralph reportedly stayed for 10 minutes and left.

"The next day Elsa called to tell me that after I left, she told her mom she would avail herself of hospice's counseling services and would try to help Ralph. Cleo indicated she understood by squeezing her hand. Elsa said she held Cleo's hand most of Monday night and that Cleo was alert and didn't sleep. Elsa reported that Ralph returned the next day and stood at the foot of the bed while she sat in the chair. Ralph began stroking Cleo's foot. Cleo was trying to talk to Ralph but he wouldn't look at her. She gasped her last breath and died.

"Elsa and I felt that Cleo's unresolved issue was that she wanted to believe Ralph would get help and keep his promises. When it became obvious to her that he likely wouldn't, and when she realized there was nothing else she could do, Cleo finally gave up. She had been clinging to life, trying to figure out if she had misjudged Ralph's character. It would be consistent with how Cleo lived her life to believe she was struggling to understand why Ralph had left her and what his real feelings were.

"The memorial service was crowded, with hundreds of people Cleo had touched with her humor and kindness. Less than a handful of these people had been allowed to see Cleo in her last months of life, for Ralph had been successful at keeping them away. As I approached the stage to say a few words about how Cleo had affected my life, I noticed a transient look of terror in Ralph's eyes and then his relief as I left the stage. Ralph was sitting next to Cleo's uncle at the service. Although Ralph intensely disliked him while Cleo was alive, he had befriended him for the time being. Perhaps he felt he needed an ally for the funeral.

"Ralph changed the lock access code on the door as soon as Cleo entered hospice. Next, he went public with his new girlfriend and sold the house within a week of Cleo's death. Elsa lost whatever Cleo had inherited from her parents but did inherit 35 percent of Cleo's life insurance policy."

ABOUT THIS CASE STUDY

This story demonstrates how difficult it is to break down a wall of denial when denial is serving as a way to cope with a bad situation. Cleo had been married before and seemed desperate to avoid another failed marriage. She struggled to understand Ralph and blamed herself for not being able to keep the relationship going. She was in a terrible trap of trying to rationalize Ralph's "B" behaviors.

The targets of "B"s inevitably blame themselves and obsessively reflect inward when much of the answer lies with the behavior of the "B." In a healthy state, Cleo was smart and cautious. However, in her weakened state she was no match for Ralph's sugar-coated deceit. Ralph was a proficient liar. With his strategic charm, he was able to fool Cleo, Cleo's uncle, Cleo's case manager, and perhaps even his counselor at work. They chose denial to cope with their uncertainty. Cleo had a height-

ened sense of awareness as her illness progressed, but she still vacillated between trusting and not trusting Ralph. She was keenly aware Ralph was drinking even though he denied it. Ralph successfully kept Cleo's friends at bay.

The alcohol likely enhanced Ralph's negative actions toward Cleo, and no one will ever know how he really treated her in those final weeks that she was at home. Cleo must have wondered why her friends didn't try to contact her. Cleo appeared to continually process all of this information while her health was failing.

At the same time, Cleo was continuing to hope Ralph could be helped, as is indicated by her attempts to have him see the counselor at work and her decision to leave all of her possessions to him. Unfortunately, Ralph's behavior finally proved to her he was not going to change. Perhaps that revelation was the culmination of her long and arduous thought process of breaking through her denial. Perhaps just coming to the conclusion that Ralph was a liar was the relief that allowed her to finally let go. She had figured out the puzzle even if the solution wasn't what she wanted.

Unfortunately, the healthcare providers in this case succumbed to Ralph's charms and denied, or failed to appreciate, that Ralph was using Cleo's situation for his purposes. The behaviors of "B"s are complex, with multiple permutations. Many healthcare providers are not trained to recognize these behaviors and consequently are often unable to help the victims of "B" behaviors who might be under their care.

SUMMARY

AS CHILDREN, WE ARE BORN HELPLESS INTO A WORLD in which we must bond to our caregivers. In order to survive, we sometimes learn to trust those who pretend to reciprocate our affections. Although we might be exposed to the behaviors of "B"s, we are seldom taught how to address those behaviors in constructive ways. Many of us are also brought up with religious training that teaches us to turn the other cheek, to ignore the behavior, and to forgive our abusers. Perhaps our denial is a way to discount our own misery. It's no wonder it's so easy for us to deny a "B's" destructive behaviors.

Everyone suffers slights and manipulative behaviors, and it's difficult to sort out which ones to address. Unfortunately, we often, almost by instinct, make a hasty decision to ignore "B" behaviors, thinking they're not so bad, or they won't happen again, or the perpetrator didn't mean it. We don't realize that, by cutting through the wall of denial, we have the power to prevent the domino effect. Too often, it's only when we are exhausted from being manipulated

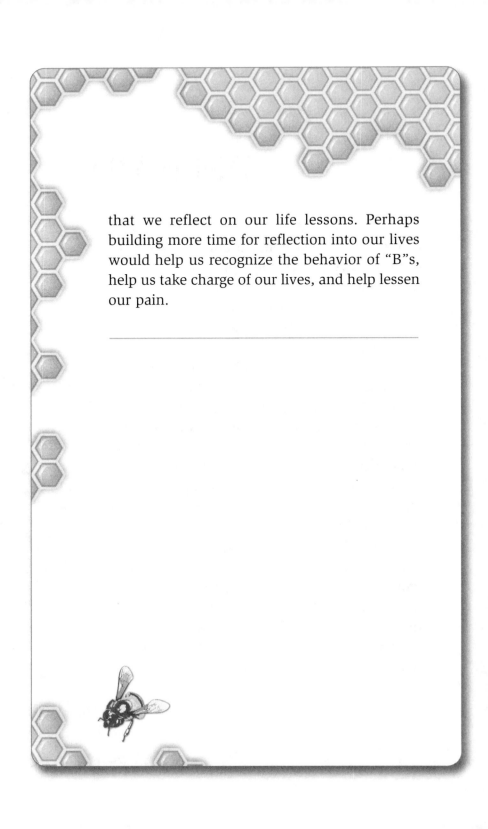

that we reflect on our life lessons. Perhaps building more time for reflection into our lives would help us recognize the behavior of "B"s, help us take charge of our lives, and help lessen our pain.

CHAPTER TEN

Tolerating "B"s

"We should not permit tolerance to degenerate into indifference."
MARGARET CHASE SMITH

Choosing Tolerance

Most of the people we interviewed remembered interactions with those who exhibited "B" behaviors. Some people had ignored or denied the "B" behaviors. Others recognized them, and made a conscious decision to tolerate them. This chapter focuses on those who recognized "B" behaviors and chose to tolerate them.

As adults, our relationships entail some element of choice. These relationships involve an initial commitment or decision such as accepting a job, having a child, volunteering to help others, or making a new friend. Any decisions we make might cause our lives to take a turn we never anticipated. When you realize you have a relationship with someone exhibiting "B" behaviors, you can usually make a conscious (often difficult) decision to either stay, and make the best of the situation, or leave.

People who choose to tolerate repeated invalidation by others frequently question themselves and their behavior, perhaps thinking they are the cause of the sting. Such people may be the "introverts" that Jay Carter discusses in his book *Nasty People*.

The introverts Carter describes look inward rather than outward for the sources of their problems. "B"s quickly focus on this quality of self-scrutiny and look at you as a potential target.

Many people, because of perceived necessity or choice, decide to tolerate "B" behaviors. Reasons for tolerating "B" behaviors include a fear of unknown consequences, such as losing a relationship; a desire for things you want, including money, excitement, sex, security, retaining a job or having a place to live; a chance to learn new things; a chance to have some power and authority; or a desire to feel special. Another reason for tolerating "B" behaviors is an appreciation of the talents many "B"s possess.

One of the biggest reasons for our tolerance of "B" behaviors is that so many "B"s are talented individuals who are difficult to discount. The question becomes whether the advantage of keeping these talented people around balances the havoc they wreak on your personal life, friendships, team performance, or a group's collective trust. You must continually weigh potential risk against potential benefits.

The Edges of Tolerance

In his book *Wingnuts*, John Avlon discusses the behaviors of media and political representatives who rant and rave, appealing to a narrow but intense share of the population. The author proposes taking America back from extremes, such as professional partisans and unhinged activists.

Many of the behaviors that compose the lunatic fringe are "B" behaviors described by Dr. Martin Kantor. Kantor writes that we may tolerate and encourage "B" behaviors by being either too liberal or too conservative. Our liberal behavior is born in the belief that individual rights are paramount over the rights of the community. For example, we fail to see the unintended consequences of encouraging our children to be free and do whatever they want to do. According to Dr. Kantor, our conservative behavior is seeded by immutable rules we set or that are set by the organizations to which we ascribe. For example, our religion forbids certain behaviors, so we want to assure that everyone conforms to those behaviors, whether or not they ascribe to our religious beliefs. We ascribe to certain political beliefs and think those who don't share our views are bad .[48] Rigidly following *and* rigidly not following rules allow us to be perfect narcissistic "B"s.

The Learning Curve

JESSE

"When I was fairly young I remember working for a guy who was a holy terror. He was obnoxious and would yell at his employees. He was not only loud and obnoxious but he was also a con artist. I remember one time he had an entire store emptied of its merchandise. He then filed an insurance claim, moved the stuff back into his store and used the insurance money to buy more merchandise. I worked for him for nine years. I was a young contractor and had the opportunity to build a three-story building. I had 30 guys working for me, and it was fun. I had to put up with his yelling and screaming for an hour every morning and then I could just do my job."

[48] Kantor, *The Psychopathy of Everyday Life*, 128–129.

ABOUT THIS CASE STUDY _____

Jesse was young, and the opportunity of working for a "B" provided him with needed excitement and experience. Since Jesse was learning new things and felt the abuse he suffered was tolerable, it became a win-win situation.

CORRINE

"I have always been pretty tolerant and trusting of people. Sandra was my best friend in high school, and there was this boy she really liked. The problem was he didn't want to date Sandra, and kept asking me out instead. Finally, I went out with him after talking to Sandra about it. I was never in love with him—we were only good friends and had fun together.

Toward the end of high school Sandra made friends with a guy who worked at a gas station, and he started functioning as Sandra's pimp. One day Sandra came into my room and threw a fifty-dollar bill on the bed, saying, 'Where do you think I got this?' I tried to talk some sense into her but she said she knew exactly what she was doing. Sandra and I stayed off-and-on friends. Fifteen years later, when I was ready to be married and had already chosen my maid of honor, Sandra laid a guilt trip on me. I ended up asking Sandra to be my maid of honor. On my wedding day, Sandra told me that my new husband had made a pass at her. She must have been holding a grudge all that time and thought she could get to me. After I was married, my husband and I compared notes on Sandra and we both realized how crazy she was. She would call me from time to time after that. I was always nice to her but refused to let her back into my life."

ABOUT THIS CASE STUDY ———————————

Leave it to a "B" to target your vulnerabilities by laying down a smokescreen of guilt. "B"s love trusting and tolerant people like Corrine. Fortunately, Corrine had a limit to her tolerance of Sandra's "B" behaviors, and in the final analysis didn't let Sandra's lies affect her relationship with her husband. Corrine finally established her boundaries with Sandra by not letting her back into her life.

MALLORIE

"Shortly after graduating, I received a call from the chairman of my department, offering me a job on a grant. Desperate for a job, I simply asked, 'When do I start?' The chairman told me to show up the next day at one o'clock in a building on campus. He said the grant agency was making a site visit. I didn't know what a site visit was and didn't ask the chairman for fear I would sound stupid and he would rescind his offer. I said I would be there. I felt somewhat honored that I was called for a job without actively seeking one out.

"I arrived the next day at the designated time and place. The room was full of people sitting at a large table. I joined them and introduced myself. They proceeded to ask me questions that I answered as well as I could. It turned out the site visitors were from the granting agency, and they were there because the grant was in jeopardy, as it had not fulfilled its mission. I quickly learned the meaning of a site visit and realized the only reason I was hired was because the grant administrators needed a warm body to fill a vacancy for the visit. The granting agency narrowly approved the grant for another nine months. I realized I was a pawn but tolerated it because I wanted a job."

ABOUT THIS CASE STUDY ──────────────────────

Mallorie tolerated a minor sting from the director of her department, who was less than truthful with her. This is a good example of how intersecting needs will cause us to drop our guard, opening us to the behaviors of "B"s.

TIM

"I have found myself in relationships with women who seemed to have manipulative personalities. In recent years, I had fairly serious relationships with a number of different women. They all seemed to have similar qualities. They were well-educated, bright, sophisticated, world travelers, sexy and exciting. There was also an element of danger in each of them. In general I got a lot out of the relationships, and they all seemed to like me. However, I broke up with all of them because at some level they all seemed to be rather needy.

"My last relationship was with a woman named Hazel. Hazel was a history professor like me and she had a level of knowledge that far surpassed anyone's that I knew of at the time. Also, cognitively and intellectually, I had more in common with her than anyone else. As a bonus, she had a great body. The problem with Hazel was her lies. I couldn't tell which lies were conscious and which were unconscious.

"Hazel lived in an apartment and would leave the back door open so her dog could get out. The upstairs tenant thought it was wasting heat, so she asked Hazel to keep the door closed. Hazel promised the woman she wouldn't leave the door open anymore. Somehow I knew she was lying and that she had every intention of continuing that practice. The next time Hazel left the door open, the tenant upstairs (who had control of the heat for the building) turned off the heat, and Hazel froze.

"I felt sorry for Hazel because she had been abused as a child. She said she had lost substantial income because her first husband was an alcoholic and was in Alcoholics Anonymous. Before they were married he promised to stop drinking, but after they married he continued drinking and abusing drugs. She said her husband had found a way to tap her kids' trust fund to fuel his cocaine addition. Yet she later told me she hadn't known her husband was using cocaine. That lie was significant because I started wondering how many other things she had told me might not be true.

"One day I was driving somewhere with Hazel, and she got really mad, saying I was dismissing her observations when in fact I was agreeing with them. She would distort details of events, and her revised details would put blame on me when in fact that wasn't the way it was.

"Hazel and I split up when she assumed a new faculty position. Later, two faculty members in her department stopped speaking to her because since she had taken the position she had broken up one marriage and almost broke up another. One day Hazel called me out of the blue to tell me she had remarried. Then she immediately changed the subject and started talking about her cat. The worst thing is, I'm still attracted to her but now I realize I could never have any real relationship with her. The reason I stayed friends with her as long as I did was because I thought I could save her. I guess I get sucked into relationships when people are needy.

"Hazel called me again to say her new husband left her after nine months. She actually seemed to revel in revealing that her husband told her that living with her was like living in an emotional minefield. Six months later, Hazel called me again to say she and her husband had reunited."

ABOUT THIS CASE STUDY

Hazel exhibited many of the chaotic behaviors of a borderline "B." Although Tim recognized Hazel's "B" behaviors, he admitted how difficult it was for him to let go of his relationship. It's important to highlight again that we tolerate relationships with "B"s because those "Bs" portray themselves in ways that tap into our needs. In this case, Tim wanted to feel special by dating someone who was his intellectual equal. He also had a very strong need to rescue people. His relationship with Hazel met both of those needs. In addition, Tim's love of excitement drew him right into chaotic borderline behaviors. Like Tim, you can enter in the role of rescuer and end up in the role of victim when the victim you try to rescue becomes your persecutor. Ultimately, Tim realized that he didn't want the chaos in his life.

◉◉◉◉◉◉◉◉◉◉ ORVILLE ◗◉◉◉◉◉◉◉◉◉

"When I attended a college dance with a fraternity brother, Peter, he asked me who the richest girl in the room was. I pointed to a girl named Hallie who had inherited a lot of money and was independently wealthy. Peter told me he was going to marry Hallie. I remember this story because I ran into Hallie and Peter many years after they married and had three sons. I discovered Peter handled all of the finances, including Hallie's inheritance. Since they were married, Peter had only worked for a brief time. I discovered that Peter verbally abused Hallie, often waking her up in the middle of the night to yell at her. Peter seemed to control Hallie. He threw Hallie out of the house numerous times and later accepted her back into his life.

"I was quite blunt with Hallie, telling her that Peter was abusing her. I told her to leave the relationship or at least get some counseling.

Some years later I discovered that Peter had thrown Hallie out of the house for some insignificant thing. Hallie then decided to move to another state to be near one of her children, and Peter followed her. One day I received a bizarre email from Hallie, saying she could no longer be my friend because my wife and I didn't have a good marriage. But a few months later, I received a Christmas card from Hallie like nothing had happened.

"I believe Peter had told Hallie to end her friendship with me. Several of Hallie's friends have encouraged Hallie to make a break with Peter but she seems unable to permanently let go."

ABOUT THIS CASE STUDY

One of the most difficult things to accept is the inability to convince an adult who is being manipulated by a "B" to leave their abusive situation and get help. Sometimes the two people in such a relationship have co-dependent personalities. In this case, one of them exhibits the narcissistic behavior of needing total control, while the other needs to be controlled. When you encounter such a dyad, you can suggest help and offer your support, as long as you know your boundaries. In this case, it's important for Hallie's friends to draw their boundaries firmly before being enticed into the "B's" nest as the rescuer. Otherwise, they'll end up as victims and the persecutor might turn out to be Hallie.

Overcoming the Past Is Not Easy

ANGELA

In some ways, it was a relief to have my nine-year relationship end because I always felt I was walking on eggshells. My boyfriend, Shaun, was extremely critical of me no matter what I did. He had promised me things for years that would have moved our relationship forward but never followed through on those promises. Shaun made me feel inadequate, like I was never quite good enough. Although I was in a lose-lose situation, I also felt addicted to this relationship and had difficulty getting out. I had difficulty verbalizing negative thoughts about Shaun. I would think he didn't really mean it that way; he is a good person, he is just anxious, depressed, or dealing with physical problems.

"My best times with Shaun were in the beginning of our relationship. He was very attentive and made me feel special. He would buy me nice things and take me out to eat. He brought me into his world by introducing me to his friends and family. I felt I had become a part of Shaun's family. I had dinner with his family weekly and I got the sense his parents were very pleased with our relationship. However, they too seemed to walk on eggshells around Shaun.

"They appeared to have high aspirations for him but had learned over time to lessen their spoken expectations for fear they might drive him away. They seemed to set very few limits with him, and just seemed grateful he came to see them and had a stable relationship with a girlfriend. They treated me in a very welcoming manner, and Shaun's mother treated me as a confidant. I often had success getting personal information from Shaun, and at times his family turned to me for answers. I felt proud of him and was happy to share what I knew with his mother. I reflect on my times with his family as some of the happiest times in our relationship.

"On the other hand, I found it difficult to integrate Shaun into my family even in a minimal way. I worried that he would view my parents as less progressive than his parents. I was fearful this might reflect badly on me and jeopardize my relationship with him. I would always invite Shaun to family events but I'd be on pins and needles wondering how he'd judge me afterward.

"I didn't realize until after my relationship with Shaun ended that most people who came in contact with Shaun were very quickly turned off by the way he made them feel about themselves. Shaun had slow mechanical responses to questions. He seemed to be rolling his eyes at people through his words or lack of response. After I stopped talking to him, I started asking friends and family for honest feedback about him. I was surprised by the overwhelming responses that Shaun was difficult to get along with because he always seemed to be judging everyone. When I was with him I was always second-guessing myself and wondering if I deserved his cruel behavior toward me."

"I now question why I was drawn to Shaun. When I analyze my relationship with him, I realize the way I describe this relationship is remarkably similar to my relationship with my father. For my entire life, I felt as though my father had judged me. My father had expectations about what I should be like and didn't respect or acknowledge my wishes. I felt as though I didn't choose this type of relationship with my father but I was born into this situation. I learned to cope with it by trying to please my father. I didn't push back but tried to keep the peace. I'm left to wonder why I willingly engaged with Shaun when I had worked so hard at distancing myself from my father, who exhibits the same distasteful behaviors toward me."

ABOUT THIS CASE STUDY ——————————————

Angela was a magnet for Shaun, who could read her like a book. He manipulated her with her need to please. Angela had difficulty establishing her personal boundaries with Shaun, and this caused her to tolerate his manipulative behaviors. Like a good narcissistic "B," Shaun also used Angela's prior conflict with her father to separate her from her family. Perhaps Angela was so used to the judgment that came from her father she didn't recognize it when it came from someone else.

Angela's struggle will likely intensify as she tries to heal herself from years of manipulation by Shaun and her father, while attempting to remain in a familial relationship with her father, a reminder of the behaviors she is trying to eliminate from her life. Hopefully, Angela will seek therapy to learn from her experiences and help ease her pain.

The Long-Sufferers

RITA

"My father was a very gruff and aggressive person, and that's how he dealt with life. I have often thought my mother, in order to cope with his aggressiveness, was the most passive-aggressive person I ever knew. Once I asked my mother why she didn't drive a car. She told me that when she and my father were first married, she did drive. One night, as she was putting the car in the garage, she scraped the side of the garage and scratched the car door. My father scolded her, telling her she was a terrible driver, and she never drove again. So for the next forty years, every time she had to go somewhere, my father had to drive her. I don't know if he ever recognized his burden as a consequence of his behavior but that is what it was, and he complained plenty about it for the rest of my mother's life. I doubt my mother's passiveness solved any of her problems, because she often had to wait for my father to pick her up."

CELINE

"I feel like I have a very high tolerance for and possible attraction to people who are manipulators. I wonder if it's caused by the childhood message my sister, brother and I received, which was that everybody was better than we were. Hence, who were we to reject anybody, except people receiving welfare. Those folks were the only group my father belittled. I guess we were at least better than those people who 'depended on the government to survive,' as dad would say.

"The other childhood message we received loud and clear was, 'You are not good enough, smart enough, blah, blah, blah.' I am realizing my new motto probably shouldn't be 'make it happen,' but should be instead 'enough already.' "

ABOUT THESE CASE STUDIES

While Rita and Celine's stories involve willing tolerance of "B" behaviors, they have different endings. Rita's mother tolerated her husband's aggressive behavior in a passive way and, as a result, reduced her independence. Celine had the insight to question belittling messages that still haunted her from childhood. This could go a long way toward preventing her from assuming a victim role when exposed to manipulative behaviors. Hopefully, Celine was also able to discuss her insights with her siblings, for exposing "B" behaviors is helpful in alerting us to our tolerance.

Tacit Approval Through Inaction

LILA

"I recently married and moved to the town where my husband worked. One day, shortly after I moved, I attended a social function at the country club. I was talking with a group of women when one of the women looked at me and said, 'Ever since you've come to this town, you've created a real negative undercurrent.' I noticed the mouths of the other women collectively fall open and I asked the woman if she was serious. When she said yes, I walked away and she yelled, 'Nothing personal!' I left immediately and went home. A short time later, some of the women who had been in the group and had said nothing showed up at my house to give me moral support. I still don't understand why they just stood there tolerating her behavior, not saying anything.

"The next day I sent an email to the woman who had verbally attacked me and told her if she feels the way she said she did, we should discuss it because I didn't know what she was talking about. She sent me an email in return and told me I was making a big deal out of nothing, and not to get my dress over my head. She never made any effort to talk with me about it."

ABOUT THIS CASE STUDY ——————————————

In Lila's story, the other women in the group had the chance to actively defend her but they chose not to. Perhaps they were guarding their social status or were afraid of being stung by the "B." Lila would be wise to observe their behaviors in the future for signs they might be guard "B"s who guard themselves from being stung. *Lila chose to tolerate her friends' inconsistent behaviors. However, by sending the email, she put the perpetrator on notice that she wouldn't tolerate such attacking behavior in the future.*

Knowing the Inevitable

JOHANNA

"I managed a hair salon in a lovely southern town, and one day I arrived at work to find a note from Shelby, one of my hairdressers, stuck to the mirror. The note simply said, 'I won't return.' I first met Shelby at a soccer tournament. She was at the end of her marriage and going through some tough times. She was gifted at finding key words to say to someone in order to befriend that person. I was overweight, and Shelby said something about my beautiful womanly figure. In our subsequent conversations, Shelby seemed to zero in on the value I placed on loyalty, mentioning how loyal she was by saying she would take care of her ex-husband until he died.

"I urged Shelby to go to beauty school. After she enrolled, she came to me, saying she wasn't making any money. I said I would apprentice her and, against my policy, I paid her while she was an apprentice. I taught her how to cut hair and worked with her to teach her the business. Although Shelby didn't have much money, she somehow maintained five show dogs, keeping them at some guy's house. The guy ended up paying her tuition to beauty school.

"Shelby was somewhat guarded around me but over time she told me that during childhood her siblings had abused her. She also said in one of her previous jobs, the women were really mean to her. I had

301

compassion for Shelby, even paying her medical bill when she was faced with an unexpected expense. I knew she was raising her sons alone and I was somewhat tolerant of her coming in late, often smoothing things over with clients.

"When Shelby remarried, I discovered she had invited a very wealthy client to her wedding even though the client didn't know her. Shortly after her wedding, Shelby's new husband accused her of physical abuse. Shelby somehow convinced us to feel sorry for her, and even though the staff was really starting to dislike her, they were nice to her, giving her the benefit of the doubt. Shelby even talked her husband out of the abuse charge.

"Shelby saw herself as shy, saying people experienced her as being aloof. I saw her as anything but shy, especially when she had something to drink. One glass of wine would obliterate any filters she had on her behavior. On one occasion, after a glass of wine, she called her son and screamed at him. She was berating her son and telling him he was useless. Others said she did this all the time.

"She had an uncanny insight into human behavior, almost like a sixth sense but in a convoluted way. She had an odd clarity about difficult clients and you would think, maybe she is right. Shelby was exciting, flamboyant, and very pretty in an exotic way. After a while, however, all I could see was dysfunction. She was really good at befriending and gifting the front desk staff. She did it so they would give her preference with clients. She also ran another business on the side and would have supplies delivered to the salon. One day she didn't have the money to pay the vendor, so she dipped her hand in the till. Fortunately, the cashier on duty had the sense to stop her from stealing the money.

"One of the stylists commented that every woman wants to be a little bit like Shelby. Clients think, 'Maybe I can be a little like that if she cuts my hair.' She had clients who loved her. One client actually bought

Shelby a $200 handbag for Christmas because Shelby was so good at drawing clients in and playing the role of victim. She was a great sales-person, selling things to clients that I certainly wouldn't have sold them. She had a way of convincing people that she liked them even when she didn't.

"Shelby convinced this woman with beautiful black hair that she'd look great as a light blond. All hairdressers know that when someone has really dark hair you don't dye it blond, because it will look absolutely terrible when it starts to grow out. Shelby, however, con-vinced this woman her hair really looked nice dyed that way. The hairdressers who stood on either side of Shelby noticed she would tell customers the same story with a different twist based on what she thought the client wanted to hear. It was like a game to her. She would lie and make up stories at the drop of a hat.

"I did recognize Shelby's faults early on but I chose to tolerate them because by that time I had put a lot of effort into her development. Shelby also had a cadre of clients, so it would've been very disruptive to get rid of her. At one point, her ex-husband called to tell me she was-n't who I thought she was. I should've known something was up when Shelby convinced me she needed an advance on her pay to fix some-thing in her house. That was three weeks before she left."

ABOUT THIS CASE STUDY

The major lesson in this story is that making exceptions to the rules you've carefully established is a sign that you're dealing with a "B." As soon as you start to see an employee as so special that you're willing to break the rules for that person, it should be a red flag to stop and re-assess the situation.

Shelby was transparent to her coworkers and to Johanna. However, Shelby knew how to target Johanna's nurturing spirit to get her to make exceptions to the rules. Shelby portrayed anti-

social, histrionic, borderline and narcissistic behaviors. She was showy, melodramatic, seductive, overly emotional, often child-like, impulsive, and very good at portraying herself as needy. She was also uncaring and deceitful. Being beautiful and talented drew people to her. Shelby's "B" behaviors were overt to those who took the time to look. Johanna was well aware of Shelby's maladaptive behaviors and was willing to tolerate them, but this knowledge didn't prevent her from being stung.

Narcissistic Rage

CORA

"I was involved in planning a large national conference for neuro-science research centers. Although all the centers were involved in the planning, not all of them participated fully. During the conference, I was leading one of the large breakout sessions and things were going well, until a nationally renowned researcher, who controls a lot of research funding, came in late and sat in the back of the room.

"He raised his hand and berated me for twenty minutes about how the conference was being run. The rows in front of him were full of male researchers and educators, and no one spoke to counter his rage. Finally, I turned to a research colleague next to me and asked him if he would like to clarify. He declined to say anything and kept his head down. After the breakout session, I had to organize a poster session, and this raging researcher came in, stood about six inches from my face, and pointed his finger at me, saying, 'Do you know you are dangerous?' I remained silent, thinking my job was to be in control and respectful.

"One of the other researchers finally cornered this man and asked if she could talk to him. She told him his behavior was out of line, and he responded with a cold stare. For the remainder of the conference, attendees streamed to my room to empathize with me and to tell horror stories about their encounters with the rage reactions of this same researcher. As I reflected, I think he was upset that he hadn't been asked to give a presentation at the conference. When I returned to work, I found out this researcher had called my boss to tell him I was dangerous. Someone made me a bracelet with the word 'DANGEROUS' on it, and now I wear it as a joke. It adds a little humor to what I consider to be the worst experience of my professional career."

ABOUT THIS CASE STUDY

When you encounter a raging "B" who has assumed the role of persecutor and is trying to draw you in as a victim, it's always a difficult situation. In this case it was in a public forum and everyone in the room, by their silence, became the guard "B"s for the persecutor. Oddly, when you have witnesses and a "B" attacks you in an angry way, silence might be the best response. Unless she could have come up with a humorous quip, there is little Cora could have said in this forum to calm down this researcher. When someone is raging in front of others, he is showcasing his "B" behaviors for everyone else to witness.

When the researcher verbally attacked Cora in the poster session, she could have established her boundaries by stating she would not tolerate being berated and requesting that he back off and speak to her in a normal voice. However, to do this she would've needed at least one witness. Otherwise, the researcher would've interpreted whatever Cora said to him differently than she intended. In this blatant case of abuse, someone should have filed a complaint. Perhaps Cora had other things to tend to or didn't want to make waves. Perhaps those who witnessed this abuse could have collectively signed a statement chastising the researcher's behavior. It's much more difficult to retaliate against a group than it is to retaliate against one or two people.

When money and jobs are on the line, a "typical" response is to tolerate the behavior and avoid conflict at all costs. This is unfortunate because it only encourages more malicious behavior by "B"s. We need to keep in mind that enraged "B"s, when pushed far enough, can become violent. The news is full of stories of "B"s bringing guns to work, schools, and shopping malls and killing people. It's difficult to tell when an angry "B" might enter a psychopathic rage. It's most unfortunate when this type of "B" is given credence by gaining a position of power. Collective tolerance of a killer "B" doesn't provide protection against violent acts.

A Politician and His Guard "B"

ANDIE

"We live in a rather small city, and my husband was running for elected office. A week before the election, the wife of the other candidate started a whisper campaign in town insinuating that my husband couldn't manage this elective office because he couldn't manage his marriage. Many of my friends mentioned that this woman had whispered her gossip to them. However, they seemed to tolerate her bad behavior. I decided I would write her a letter after the election but I never mailed it. I felt better just having written it."

Hi Rosalind,

   While I congratulate Aaron on his victory, I need to tell you I am disappointed to learn of the rude things you said about Jonathan prior to the election. At least several people with whom you spoke have told us you commented, 'How can Jonathan manage being a supervisor when he can't even manage a marriage?' And to one person, you indicated, 'I hope this doesn't get ugly.'

   I must say those comments are tacky and unkind. And given that you know nothing about Jonathan's history, our marriage and how expertly Jonathan has managed his professional career, your comments are especially ugly, vicious and out of bounds. I would also like to add that belittling the competition is neither an effective nor a mature campaign strategy.

   I am Christian, as you are, and I was not taught to leave my Christian kindness at the door when leaving church. I had thought you were a more professional and enlightened person than this. I am disappointed to learn this is not so.

Sincerely,

Andie

ABOUT THIS CASE STUDY

Rosalind used the antisocial behaviors of deceit and gossip as a campaign tool. It is interesting how people accept the destructive lies that accompany political campaigns and just assume they represent politics as usual. The lies keep coming because they influence the voters' choice of candidates. Even though people profess to disliking negative campaigns, they often raise enough doubt in the public's minds to have their intended effect. Next time you encounter a negative campaign or lies and smears that often accompany negative political advertising, think about your role in tolerating these "B" behaviors. Perhaps if people checked the facts and didn't vote for untruthful candidates, local and national governments would be better managed.

Limited Tolerance and Trigger Points

SUZANNE

"I had just started taking full-time coursework for a degree. In addition to working full-time, I wasn't feeling well, because I had broken my leg three days before classes began. I had enrolled in a decision-making class that involved complex math skills. I was clearly the only older student and one of only a few females in the class. Because of my broken leg, I sat in the front row, right in front of the professor.

"He began with an introduction to the course, and after his initial comments he said, while looking directly at me, 'The only people who do poorly in this class are middle-aged women.' Under ordinary circumstances, I would've taken his words as a challenge and remained in the class. But in that instant I decided I had no energy to deal with his prejudices against women, and I took my crutches and noisily stomped out of the room. I still regret not reporting his behavior and often wonder how many other older women he went on to harass."

LIZBETH

"I am a foster parent for a child whose father has spent time in jail. His long rap sheet portrays him as one who likes to play games with people's minds and who enjoys harassing and abusing women. At one of the court proceedings to restrict visitation rights to his biological child, to whom he had never been a father, I was left in a room with him by accident, and he began to harass me. I really tried to tolerate his insults and keep my cool but finally his taunts made me so angry that I responded by telling him he was nothing but a sperm donor. Despite his arrest record, he seems to have the capacity to draw in counselors and make them believe his bullshit."

ABOUT THESE CASE STUDIES

Both Suzanne and Lizbeth were at low points in their lives when a "B" stung them. Feeling weak or down limits your ability to either tolerate or appropriately confront the behavior of "B"s. Each of them lost their cool, and this gave an exciting charge to the "B" who was harassing them. Many "B"s rely on the element of surprise, so it's difficult for you to plan your response. However, losing your cool can interfere with you reaching your broader goals and might not be worth the satisfaction of confronting the "B." If you suspect that someone might be a "B," you can anticipate some of the types of behaviors they might use against you. The phrase, "Don't get mad, get even," is appropriate in these situations.

Fighting back against "B" behaviors is difficult, and a lack of energy is a reason to tolerate them, at least for a while. In tolerating such behaviors, you need to assess the importance of the situation to you and to others. Combine that information with your energy level, your stamina, and the potential of ever being stung again by this "B," and that'll help you make a decision. If you have the energy and there is high potential of being stung again, you might choose to fight back at a time of your own choosing.

Those Charming "B"s

Why do we fall in love with "B"s, put them on pedestals and tolerate their bad behaviors? Consider the stories of illegal drugs, physical abuse and philandering that are reported about movie stars and sports figures. We complain and buzz about their behaviors but ultimately we tend to forgive them because of their talents. When we look in the mirror and actually see ourselves, we realize our responses to "B" behaviors are usually consistent with the person we have chosen to be.

"Consider the people who write love letters to convicted murderers. If you are drawn in by charm, excitement and games, then you may have high tolerance for "B"s with antisocial behaviors. If you admire people who strive for great accomplishments no matter what the cost, then you admire "B"s with narcissistic behaviors and will likely have a high tolerance for manipulative tactics, even when you've been stung multiple times. Or maybe you haven't been stung because you pose no threat to their self-image and you continuously shower them with compliments and favors.

"B" Apologies

Everyone makes mistakes, and it's charitable to forgive. However, when behaviors are repeated over and over, it's time to question our tolerance. It's easy to recognize "B"s by how they word their apologies. They will typically avoid admitting any personal responsibility for their bad behavior. They will cleverly twist words to make it seem like the ill deed accidentally happened.

A business was under criminal investigation for creating an outbreak of salmonella caused by tainted food produced at their facilities. The owner declined to discuss events leading to the outbreak, saying in a statement: "We are sorry our process fell short of not only our goals but more importantly, your expectations." When appearing before Congress, the CEO took the Fifth Amendment and didn't testify. Later that week the company declared bankruptcy, further lessening his company's responsibility.

It's important to listen to the words that people choose when they "apologize for misbehavior." In this case, the CEO's placement of the blame on a "process" was totally impersonal, as if the process had planned itself. Someone, or a group of people, plans a process, and ultimately the owner is responsible for the process and how it's carried out. Be very wary of someone in charge who assigns blame using impersonal language, without a follow-up statement of personal responsibility.

Blinded by Good Faith and Charm

DOUG

"I was in a position where I shared a supervisory role with Francesca. Francesca worked onsite with the people we supervised, and I worked across town in another building. Because of this, I relied heavily on Francesca's reports. Francesca was guarded with her information and would tell me things were going well. But as a result of downsizing, Francesca left the company. That's when I learned she had been saying things to the employees we supervised that indicated she was the only one who could help them. She had failed to share information regarding complex employee situations in which I could've provided much needed support to the employees. Consequently, many of the employees had lost all faith in me and were convinced I was unwilling to help them.

"There was a lot of damage to repair when Francesca left the company. Some employees, upset by her departure, also left the agency because they viewed her as their savior. It was a delicate situation because I wanted to defend myself and explain how Francesca hadn't shared important information that would have allowed me to help. Instead, I just tolerated the fallout because I was afraid it would be unprofessional to tell the staff the truth. I also had a sense the staff members who took Francesca's leaving the hardest were also dysfunctional. They could've come to me directly with their problems but instead chose to believe Francesca's report that I didn't want to help them. It was almost like some staff enjoyed the drama of the whole thing."

ABOUT THIS CASE STUDY

This is an example of how the seductive actions of a "B" without boundaries can lure employees into the guard role. This is similar to the hairstylist example from chapter seven. A swarm of guard "B"s is a very serious situation because it can cause high turnover in a company. In a smaller company it can be devastating. While Doug was unhappy with Francesca's performance, he tolerated the fallout rather than using it as an example to teach the staff.

GRANT

"My law firm partners and I hired Stewart, an office assistant, to help with incoming calls and billing. Stewart was single, with an invalid mother to support. He was very engaging and a very hardworking employee. He was the first one at work every day, making coffee and greeting us as we arrived. He was cheerful and respectful to clients and quickly learned his job, doing everything we asked him to do.

"One day I received a call from a parole officer asking to speak with Stewart. I inadvertently discovered from the caller that Stewart was on probation for embezzling money from his prior workplace. He had been ordered to avoid any job in which he would be responsible for handling money. My partners and I knew we would have to fire him. We came in early the next morning and called Stewart into an office. My partner opened the conversation by saying, 'We know everything.'

"Stewart immediately replied, 'I'm sorry for stealing the $15,000 from your agency. I needed it for my mother's medical care.' We were flabbergasted, because we hadn't known he had been stealing from our firm. We immediately escorted him out and didn't report the theft to the parole officer because we felt terribly sorry for Stewart's mother. We let him go with no other repercussions."

ABOUT THIS CASE STUDY

Unfortunately, Grant and his partners didn't hold Stewart accountable for his behavior. While Stewart's story about needing money for his mother's medical care might be true, it's possible it was a lie he used to evoke sympathy. By having the tolerance to keep quiet about Stewart's behavior, Grant and his partners might have unknowingly set up Stewart's next target.

LEZLIE

I worked for a department store chain where I met Cynthia, a longstanding employee. Cynthia knew every employee on a first-name basis and was friendly to everyone. She planned many of the company celebrations and was always making treats for staff. I liked her and felt we had a good relationship. We shared stories about our families and often sent pictures to keep each other up to date on how our children were growing. I never really demanded much of Cynthia because I wasn't her superior and I had little reason to talk to her about anything work related. But this all changed suddenly when I needed to depend on her for a high-level project.

"I would call Cynthia and email her but would receive very little response. This seemed strange because when I had emailed personal information to her, the responses were instantaneous. I finally met with her, and she offered information that was confusing and incomplete. Once I started discussing Cynthia's lack of helpfulness with other coworkers who had worked directly with her, I learned they had had similar experiences. They had learned the hard way that if confronted, Cynthia would make your life miserable for the remainder of your tenure at the company. Also, staff warned me that no one else would believe it because of her reputation as such a friendly, helpful employee.

"I never confronted Cynthia and found other ways to get my needs met without having to rely on her. I remained on friendly terms with her but decided to no longer share personal information with her. Months passed and an announcement was made: 'After 25 years, Cynthia was no longer at the company, effective immediately.' Staff members were hurt and angry about this sudden change. They took Cynthia's leaving extremely personally. They viewed her as someone in a managerial position who was 'one of them.' Very little information was disclosed about her departure. Staff speculated and believed that upper management had wronged her. Staff rallied to figure out how to contact her and support her.

"Eventually, staff learned that Cynthia was under investigation for embezzlement. She had stolen personal information from staff and created an intricate scheme that allowed her to steal funds from the company. Nobody saw this coming unless they had somehow raised Cynthia's ire in the past. Those people seemed less than surprised. Once the story broke about what actually happened, it was revealed that this wasn't Cynthia's first offense. It left me wondering how someone with Cynthia's history got into a position with access to all the information that would allow her to continue to embezzle."

ABOUT THIS CASE STUDY

Like Stewart, Cynthia tricked her boss and fellow employees into thinking that she was a great employee. Irritability and anger at being questioned about work processes were a signal to some that there was something wrong with her. Antisocial "B"s are great pretenders and regard tricking people as just another game. They display superficial charm, produce tears at the drop of a hat, and know where your soft underbelly lies. Their charades prompt you to tolerate behaviors that you might otherwise question.

Even when punishment is administered to "B"s, they often manage to trick those in charge to lessen their punishment. This skill is even more advanced in the most hardcore criminals. Canadian researchers discovered that psychopaths, even though they were much more likely to re-offend and their average return to prison time was one year versus two for non-psychopaths, were more than twice as likely to fool parole boards for early release than were ordinary criminals.[49] The researchers also speculated that psychopaths may have been better than other inmates at pretending they were responding to therapy and therefore were better at deceiving decision-makers like prison therapists and parole officers.

Dealing With the Defenders

The longer a "B" is in a particular work or social situation, the larger their nest will be. It becomes an extremely difficult task to break through the protective guard "B"s that shelter the queen. This message becomes even more poignant when you observe that even criminal acts committed by "B"s don't get reported. Why do agencies delay or neglect reporting criminal behavior by their employees? Why do workers in agencies decide to tolerate "B" behaviors in coworkers? Why are we so willing to tolerate the consequences of bad behavior? Realistically, if we see our association with a "B" as something that benefits us, we are more likely to tolerate the "B" behaviors. Perhaps the only thing worse than having a relationship with "B"s is trying to understand and deal with the tolerance of their defenders.

It appears that companies just keep passing "B"s on to other companies. Do these employers choose to ignore the facts and quietly pass the "B" on to some unsuspecting company because they assume they will avoid retaliation from the "B"? Were Grant and his law partners, as well as Cynthia's previous employers, unaware that there is greater than a 75 percent chance Stewart and Cynthia will steal again?[50] Our litigious society has made it very difficult for new employers to obtain the facts about an

---

[49] Porter et al., "Crime Profiles and Conditional Release," 113.
[50] Langan & Levin, "Recidivism of Prisoners Released in 1994," 51.

employee. So "B"s fly to new companies where they can access fresh pollen.

Our Achilles' Heels

We need to become aware of the enemy within, whether it's our own narcissism, our insecurities, or our vulnerabilities that allow us to be charmed and subsequently tolerate someone's lies. The enemy within differs in each of us. Whatever our particular weakness, it can cause us to be blindsided, trust someone who is untrustworthy, and see someone as our friend when he is not. One of the most destructive consequences of tolerating "B"s is that tolerance gives credence to their behaviors. By lending credence to their behaviors, we sometimes end up as perpetrators, just like the children who turned aggressive in the book *Lord of the Flies*.

Those with "B" behaviors have a way of zeroing in on people they perceive as either potential supporters or potential threats. They target a person's most powerful desires, susceptibilities and accomplishments and turn those qualities into power sources for their own gain. We might wish to be or see ourselves as intelligent, pretty, physically strong, energetic, tactically skilled, an expert in something, a caring person, a born leader, observant or ethical. Whatever is your Achilles heel, the "B" will capitalize on it by charming you with praise for your skill or desire. Or if a skillful "B" perceives you as a threat, he'll turn your susceptibility or even your accomplishments against you. In some circles it's a detriment to be intelligent or learned. In the 2006 presidential campaign, John Kerry's war hero status was a source of power that writers of political ads used against him.

A higher functioning "B" lures his targets by using charm to draw them in. If someone is vulnerable to cries for help from others, the "B" will find a way for him to help a noble cause. Only after the target has done all the work will he realize the "B" has taken all the credit. If someone isn't in a "B's" favor or if the "B" is in a power position, the "B" might manipulate him with coercive tactics. In this case, if he is vulnerable to cries of help from others, the "B" will say how disappointing his efforts have been to those in need. When he does the work, the "B" will take credit but berate him because he didn't do enough. Those who are unlucky enough to be drawn into a "B's" radar will need to examine their own vulnerabilities, because they can bet the "B" has already figured out how to manipulate them.

The Influence of the Internet and Blogs

Since the introduction of the Internet and the rise of mainstream blogging in the late 1990s, there has been an interesting twist to the "B" experience. Theoretically, anyone who wants to put forth a viewpoint can start a blog and can literally overnight gain a lot of attention and sometimes even gain instant fame. On the social networking sites, people can friend and de-friend anyone they choose. People can join dating websites and be anyone they wish to be. If you are a "B" and aren't happy with the treatment you're getting from coworkers or friends, you can find new friends on the web and wow them with your wonderful qualities. You can start your own business and swindle anyone who wants to send you money. People can publish videos on YouTube or other sites and become overnight sensations. It can be a virtual candy store for "B"s who crave attention and want to be noticed.

There is another side to the Internet and all the different venues for reaching many people in a short time. People who have been victims of "B" behaviors have started to use the Internet to fight back. Perhaps the Internet has inserted some cracks in the wall of tolerance by allowing people to share information about "B"s.

A Blog as Watchdog

An anonymous blogger had been blogging about a large multi-site company. Many people posted stories to the blog about purported inefficient and unethical activities in the various divisions over the years. Bloggers indicated that numerous employees were forced out or resigned because they refused to follow the whims of those who ran the company. The following topics were addressed by the blogger:

- A new CEO without proper credentials was appointed by the corporate president to run a large division in the company.

- A member of top management who was rumored to be having an affair with the CEO retired and moved to another state. Despite this, the CEO kept him on the payroll for months as a consultant. When the former member of top management returned to the state, the CEO attempted to rehire him. Later the offer was rescinded.

- An employee in the division reporting to the CEO found that another employee handling financial accounts was not following proper procedures. The CEO eliminated the position of the employee who had reported the behavior of the employee mishandling financial accounts.

- The employee suspected of mishandling financial accounts was indicted for embezzling tens of thousands of dollars from the agency but was allowed to remain on the payroll until the end of the year, ensuring a larger pension.

- Both the division CEO and the corporate president lobbied for, and were each voted into, officer positions in national organizations.

After several years of blog postings, some posts were picked up by the national press. During this time, high-level employees left the company because of conditions they refused to tolerate. Most employees stayed and remained silent for fear they would lose their jobs. Whenever a new event hit the blog or the press, administrators warned employees to keep silent. Despite these warnings, more blog postings followed regarding the CEO's and corporate president's alleged incompetence. Finally, after four years of revelations by the blog, both the CEO and the corporate president were fired. While there is no proof that the firings were the direct result of the blogs and the press, they likely had an effect on the outcome.

If there are many interlocking "B"s administering an organization, it often takes years to break through the tolerance by employees who fear for their livelihoods and their reputations. Even the anonymous nature of a blog can be intimidating for those who need their jobs and fear being identified as a source of information. Employees who come forward to provide information deserve credit for their willingness to take personal risks by standing up to the behavior of "B"s.

Tolerance Crumbles Slowly

When a university wants to increase its research status, it attempts to hire researchers who have the potential to bring in grant money. Sometimes that involves a lot of denial and a blatant tolerance of

"B" behaviors. Over a 30-year period, Robert Felner, a researcher with a reputation for obtaining grant money, accepted professorships, directorships, deanships and a chancellor position at numerous universities, including Yale, Auburn, University of Illinois, University of Rhode Island, University of Louisville, and the University of Wisconsin–Parkside. Everywhere Felner went there were accusations that he abused faculty members, staff and students. For an expose of Felner, reporter Katie Mulvaney interviewed the only person who came close to successfully suing Felner for his "abusive behavior, intimidation and sexual harassment."[51] A very courageous Theresa Watson had to file a civil suit after university affirmative action officials dismissed her complaints and those of two other female students. The suit was reportedly "settled in 2008 under undisclosed terms," and Ms. Watson indicated that those surrounding Felner "took him for a hero."[52]

According to reports, Felner was usually able to assemble a cadre of guard "B"s, i.e, other professors, administrators, or support staff who would not only tolerate his abusive behaviors but, by praising his achievements, would protect him from those who accused him of such behaviors. The higher the positions of his guard "B"s, the better Felner could control those who were under his power. Instead of being supported, Felner's accusers were allegedly made to feel inferior, were denied promotions, or were excluded from the inner circle of faculty members.[53] The one exception might have been the University of Illinois, where the head of the psychology department had removed Felner as director of clinical training because Felner had a disagreeable personality and also because he was sloppy in his management of grants.[54]

[51] Mulvaney, "Robert Felner's Trail of Deceit," *The Providence Journal.*
[52] Ibid.
[53] *Page One Kentucky* blog posts, July 14, 2008 and August 13, 2008.
[54] Ibid., August 13, 2008.

At the University of Rhode Island and the University of Louisville, Felner was allegedly able to draw enough support from some professors and administrators that he had treated well, to stave off complaints from those whom he had terrorized because he didn't think they were powerful enough to be of any consequence to him. At the University of Louisville, officials dismissed 33 grievances that were filed by faculty, students and parents against Felner. He claimed he was mistreated and misunderstood.[55]

Despite all of the tolerance for Felner's behavior, someone or something tipped off federal investigators that Felner had been mishandling grant funds. As federal investigators moved in and Felner saw the noose tightening, he didn't go into hiding. Rather, he boldly sought positions at numerous other universities. He finally landed a chancellor position at the University of Wisconsin–Parkside and was within a week of being sworn in when he was indicted.

In the midst of this chaos, something amazing happened. Jacob Payne, a reporter for *Page One Kentucky* picked up the investigator's trail and doggedly stuck with the Felner story.[56] The blogs that ensued became a flood of reports on the scope of Felner's "B" behaviors. Abused faculty, students and staff from the universities in which Felner had served over the years poured out their stories on the Internet. Within weeks, hundreds of stories had been entered into the blog. Some questioned the veracity of Felner's degrees. Others were angry with administrators who had allowed and encouraged Felner's abuse of faculty members, staff and students.

Bloggers on Payne's blog strongly suggested Felner had many affairs with students and faculty over the years. Others reported leaving their positions because of his abuse. Still others ques-

[55] Ibid., July 14, 2008.
[56] Ibid., May 17, 2010.

tioned the selection process at various universities, saying an unyielding desire for grant money and fame had prevented an adequate vetting process. A contributing blogger who had left the University of Louisville because of Felner posted his comments. This blogger was one of many who chastised both administrators and faculty for tolerating Felner's behavior and for allowing Felner to sting so many with his venom.

> "Indeed, it is the cultural corruption of the U of Hell, which allowed the 'Robert Affair' to happen. It's not just little Robert's fault! Many of the faculty who are whining now about how badly they were treated by Little Robert, were the ones who ignored the facts and ignored the warnings they were given before he was hired. Many were also willing to look the other way when Robert's abuse was directed at others but they thought they were immune. So you faculty stop trying to blame this train wreck on Little Robert or on anyone else alone. You all have to take responsibility for the systemic sickness that is this university. You had your chance before Robert arrived to treat the cancer that plagues the place, but were too weak to step up to the plate."[57]

Felner left a lot of clues in his wake. As we read hundreds of complaints from faculty who had experienced Felner's behavior at other universities, it's curious that many professors and students across the country had also tolerated Felner's "B" behaviors. It's likely that some of those who didn't speak up were benefiting from Felner's successes and didn't want to upset the status quo. Perhaps Felner only showed those individuals his good side.

Many years before Felner was indicted for financial crimes, we had heard stories from various faculty members throughout the

---

[57] *Page One Kentucky*, July 29, 2008.

country about the abuse that they had suffered under Felner. Although we asked some of these people to share their stories for this book, none did. Several said they were too traumatized and still afraid of those who had supported Felner.

It was clear from the blogs and from the anonymous concerns in the open records that many people were simply intimidated and afraid of retribution for speaking out. In cases like this, a feeling of isolation and uncertainty often prevents people from coming forward when the abuse first begins. By reading the comments on the blog, it was obvious that hundreds of faculty, students and staff members felt intimidated and trapped.

Many bloggers expressed helplessness. They indicated that there was no one to go to with their complaints since Felner had the power brokers in his pocket. Did Felner hide his "B" behaviors from the top power brokers? The University of Rhode Island, swindled years earlier out of over a million dollars by Felner, finally called to warn the University of Wisconsin–Parkside about Felner. By then the federal investigators were ready to hand down their indictments and UW–Parkside had already realized their mistake. In 2008 Felner was indicted on charges of misusing federal grants, 10 counts of mail fraud, money laundering, conspiracy, and income-tax evasion, all counts that involved money and not human suffering. Felner was sentenced for his money crimes in 2010.[58]

It's common for people to tolerate or defend "B" behaviors without actually investigating whether or not allegations are true. Perhaps it's because people who hear the stories don't want them to be true. Somehow, the truth will change the world as they know it, making the comfortable, somehow less comfortable. People don't like to talk because they might look stupid or they fear for the reputation of their institution. After the story broke, numer-

[58] Huffingtonpost.com, "Robert Felner Sentenced," May 18, 2010.

324

ous administrators from institutions that had employed Felner in the past asked their faculty members not to talk about his tenure there. Despite their reasons for silencing their faculty, this closed-mouth attitude only perpetuates more cover-ups. Unfortunately, once you discover an abuser, you can usually bet they are abusing others. If you suspect someone of wrongdoing, they bear watching to see if they repeat the behaviors with others.

Another theme that was common in the blogs and the newspaper articles was that professors and administrators at the various universities affected by Felner said that no one had ever asked them about Felner. This speaks to a passively inadequate vetting process. On the other hand, until the University of Rhode Island came forward to warn the University of Wisconsin–Parkside, we could find no evidence that anyone in power had actively tried to stop this "B" from perpetrating his stings on another institution.

While "B"s can use the Internet to ruin someone's reputation, the Internet can also be a tool for shedding light on the truth and easing the pain that a sense of solitary suffering creates. In the first blog example, one has to think the unrelenting stories had put pressure on the oversight agencies to investigate the charges. The fact that several administrators who had been causing the problems for the multi-site agency were fired, suggests that blogs are useful to counter "B" behaviors. In the case of Felner, the sheer volume, variety, and poignancy of the stories spoke to their veracity.

Actions Speak Loudly

PAGE

"I had a friendship from childhood with Gladys, who could be fun but at the same time disrespectful of me. I tolerated Gladys's behavior because I value close friendships and am determined to keep them going, at times at my own expense. Over time, Gladys offended me or insulted me too many times and I decided to let the friendship fade. We have not been in touch for years and that has suited me just fine.

I was recently watching an old video of an event we both attended while still friends. It included many of our mutual friends and one in particular, Jana, whom Gladys always seemed to hold in high esteem. In the video we were greeting Jana, and in my excitement I put my arms around Gladys. Gladys sneered and rolled her eyes at me as I walked away from her and then, looking angelic, Gladys turned to Jana with a huge smile on her face. It was extremely validating to know my instincts were right to end our friendship. Gladys was never a true friend, and now I have the videotape to prove it."

ABOUT THIS CASE STUDY

When you discover someone in your life showing a bad side to a chosen few; when you find yourself walking on eggshells to avoid mood shifts; when you incessantly blame yourself for another person's bad behavior; when, despite their malevolence, you continue to assume that friends are well-intentioned, it's time to question your level of tolerance for "B" behavior. Sometimes, just observing a "B's" behavior will give us more clues than listening to her words.

Tolerance Has Its Limits

NOREEN

(FROM CHAPTER SIX)

"I was working in a mental health facility and Mel, the administrative director for mental health, was verbally harassing me and several other women in my area. One day Mel told me he was responsible for me getting my job with the facility and I should give him two big kisses for that. I told him I thought I got the job on my own merits and not his. Afterward I wished I would've purchased two of those giant Hershey's kisses, placed them on Mel's chair, and told him there was one for each cheek. Anyway, his comment set the stage and he continued his harassment.

"In a meeting with new employees, Mel asked a question and then quickly told them they should ask me for the answer. He just as quickly followed with the statement that they wouldn't have anything to gain by listening to me. I was speechless. I returned to my office and was furious. Mel would come in and tell me he was going to change my position to a limited term appointment because he had to reduce the number of people who worked at the facility. By this time I realized I had learned a lot working for this agency and I was also smarter than Mel. So in response to his statement, I said, 'Go ahead and try it.'

"If women were in the room, Mel would totally ignore them. Because of his continued harassment of staff, particularly women, I told everyone who came to my division they had to read Machiavelli's The Prince so they would know how his head worked. After three years of tolerating Mel's verbal harassment, I finally went to the director of our division and told him about Mel's behavior. None of the other women would go, and I could understand because Mel was their boss. They said they were afraid of losing their jobs. Although Mel thought of himself as my boss, he wasn't.

"He has since been demoted and relieved of his administrative duties. Management told him he could retire or take another position, or they would terminate him. He was going to retire until the economy tanked and then he decided to stay. This whole process took three years, and a number of valuable employees quit because of Mel's behavior. Although he is no longer in our division, his presence in the facility gives those he harassed the creeps, and they are all hoping for the economy to pick up so he'll leave. I think my past experiences have given me an intuition about people. I quickly get an accurate read on their characters."

ABOUT THIS CASE STUDY

In this story, Noreen demonstrates how experiences over time can alter how we might address the behavior of "B"s throughout our careers. In chapter six, a relatively younger Noreen was more aggressive in her dealing with a "B," while the older Noreen in this chapter was more studied and somewhat more tolerant until she was sure her aim was accurate enough to swat the "B."

Reasons for Tolerating "B"s

Some "B" behaviors seem positive at their face, as when their empathic gestures help you obtain what you need while ultimately luring you into becoming their guard or rescuer. Part of the seductiveness of "B"s is convincing you they are special. In turn, you also feel special just to be with them, protecting them from negative feedback.

The more successful "B"s can direct cruel behaviors toward some people while simultaneously directing nice behaviors to others. Often they are nasty down but not up. This means that people they think are beneath them will likely be the recipients of their worst behaviors. The up-people will think they are wonderful.

There are countless reasons people give for tolerating the "B"s in their lives. People who assume everyone is good or can be saved believe a "B" will change. Others stick with a "B" in hopes of resolving unresolved issues with another "B," often a parent or sibling. Of those we interviewed, even in old age, some never considered excluding individuals from their lives who repeatedly exhibited "B" behaviors. Even when the "B" harmed them emotionally, if not physically, some people continued to tolerate the abuse.

People who decide to tolerate "B" behaviors, for fear of losing their jobs, because they are afraid of greater abuse, or because they feel helpless, are often the people who secretly wish evil on those who subjected them to "B" stings. We spoke with numerous people who, after being subjected to "B" behaviors, expressed a variety of emotions, like being happy the "B's wife was filing for divorce, or wishing a former boss would drop dead. A nurse who had worked for an abusive physician wanted him to have a stroke so she could give him an enema. A man who had remarried and bought his new wife a house, subsequently had his money stolen by her, so he wanted to hire a military helicopter to pick up the house with her in it and drop it into a lake.

SUMMARY

WHEN YOU GIVE CONSTRUCTIVE FEEDBACK TO SOME-
one and they interpret it as an attack on them
rather than an effort to solve a problem, this
person bears watching to look for signs of retaliation or repeat patterns of such behavior. If this
person is a "B," the result of your feedback will
likely be a sting out of the blue. The sting can
take passive or aggressive forms. Repeated stings
can go a long way to prevent you from ever again
giving feedback to a "B." If your willing tolerance
pulls you into the "B's" nest by making you a
permanent victim or a guard for the "B's" behavior, you might want to reassess your situation.

If you decide to tolerate a relationship with a
"B" and can preserve your self-esteem, it might
be worth the effort. If you're getting what you
want from the relationship, you likely won't
suffer unless your relationship with the "B" is
also negatively affecting your friends, family or
coworkers. However, as these stories demonstrate, maintaining your self-esteem when you
are involved with a "B" isn't easy. "B"s have a
tendency to create smokescreens that can con-
fuse your goals. Maintaining your personal

boundaries in a relationship with a "B" takes constant vigilance; can become tiring; and depending on the relationship, might not seem worth the effort.

It's important to realize you have a choice whether or not to tolerate a "B's" behavior. While some of the people we wrote about in this chapter chose to tolerate "B"s, others realized that, in the end, it wasn't worth the damage to their self-esteem or even to their health. In chapter eleven we focus on those who decided to fight back.

CHAPTER ELEVEN

The Courage to Fight Back

"Growth demands a temporary surrender of security."

GAIL SHEEHY

Whistleblowers Are Not Always Welcome

Some people have the courage to fight back when "B" behaviors are negatively affecting their lives. However, many "B"s are powerful, and the voices of the heroes who choose to fight back aren't always heard. It's difficult to know if some people are born with the inclination to fight back when they are negatively affected by "B" behaviors, or if that inclination develops out of personal experience. Fortunately, when "B" behavior is negatively affecting a lot of people, some heroes feel compelled to act. Unfortunately, we don't always choose to listen soon enough to prevent the fallout.

Sharon Watkins, a former employee of Enron, lamented that she didn't act sooner and that she didn't take her concerns to the audit board outside of Enron.[59] Initially, no one listened because either they were collaborators or they didn't want to face the horrible truth that Enron was ready to collapse and take the savings

---

[59] CNBC, Sharon Watkins interview, March 1, 2010.

of thousands of unsuspecting people. Ms. Watkins complained that CEOs were never penalized for taking exorbitant risks.

Harry Markopolos worked for a securities firm in Boston and noticed that Bernie Madoff's New York firm was attracting all of his firm's clients because their continued payoff was greater. He investigated and knew Madoff's percentages weren't possible. Markopolos went to the Securities and Exchange Commission four times and was ignored each time. It took eight more years for the federal government to charge Madoff for conducting his immense Ponzi scheme. Reportedly the hush-up was directed by an organization of crime and greed, because 90 percent of the investors' money was going to those who were feeding victims into the scheme. Markopolos said, "The SEC didn't want to ask questions they didn't want to know the answers to."[60]

The Immune Response

Brent (from chapter two) first recalled being stung by his friend at age 12. As an adult he regarded "B" behaviors as normal, because "this kind of thing happens all of the time." Could it be that "B" behaviors don't alarm some adults, just because they see "B" behaviors as normal? If this is the case, it might explain why so many people, even those you consider friends, don't intervene. Sometimes someone who observes "B" behavior will warn you first and then stand back and watch, thinking they have performed an act of courage by warning you of the impending sting.

"B"s are people who know the rules and decide the rules don't apply to them. Someone who figures out who the "B"s are might get laid off while the "B" gets promoted. In 1989 Jerry Harvey published an article titled, "How Come Every Time I Get Stabbed

---

[60] *The Today Show*, Harry Markopolos interview, March 1, 2010.

in the Back My Fingerprints Are on the Knife?" In the article, Harvey told the story of getting stabbed in the back as a young schoolboy. Another classmate had spread the rumor that Harvey had not contributed his fair share while working on a class project, when in fact he had contributed fairly. Harvey's friends had told him (in strictest confidence) that another boy was going to spread these false rumors about him and then they asked Harvey not to betray their confidence. Essentially, they were allowing the boy to get away with his behavior. Because Harvey respected his friends' requests for confidence and because he didn't confront the perpetrator, he allowed himself to be stabbed in the back, placing his own fingerprints squarely on the knife.

This story fits perfectly into the drama triangle of persecutor, rescuer/guard, and victim. The boy who told the lie was the persecutor, Harvey's friends were the rescuers, and Harvey stepped into the "B's" nest by becoming the victim. The most important lesson in these stories is the message to stay out of the "B's" nest. If you find yourself being repeatedly drawn back in or see others being drawn in, you have a pretty good idea that more than one "B" is involved. This is the same kind of "B's" nest that is consistently built by aggressive "B"s, the helper/guard "B"s, and those of us who become complicit victims.

Staying out of the "B's nest is easier said than done, especially when someone stings you when you least expect it. It's important to remember that staying out of the "B's" nest is a constant struggle. Whenever you feel dread in the pit of your stomach, it's time to examine the situation and figure out if you have been inadvertently lured into the drama. Too often, "B"s are referred to as bullies, and the process of getting stung is made to seem obvious. However, getting stung can be far from obvious.

Our psyches are filled with messages from childhood. Some of these were adages from our parents, such as be nice to others and others will be nice to you. Our religious beliefs left their imprint: turn the other cheek. Then the culture of our organizations threw in its two cents, by urging us to always present a positive attitude. Remember, high-functioning "B"s will avoid entering the "B"s nest as persecutors when it's easier and more effective to enter as a victim. In this way they can skillfully play the game "Ain't It Awful?" as noted by Berne.[61] They adapt it well: "I worked so hard to turn this organization around, and look what they're doing to us"; "They gave me this loan even though I couldn't afford to pay my mortgage, and now they are taking my house away." We who have a need to rescue others or to guard the moral character of our family, our organization, our church, or our country, will happily jump in to offer our moral support or tacit agreement in supporting whoever appears to be a victim. Unfortunately, we often jump in without thoroughly investigating the situation. We might not notice that the victim we are rescuing has suddenly transformed into our persecutor.

It's important to remember that it isn't the single occurrence that defines the "B's" nest but rather a swarm of occurrences. The difficulties inherent in avoiding the "B's" nest are what make the following stories so extraordinary. Sometimes you can make a difference by fighting back. The effectiveness of your fight takes courage, timing, skill and luck. Many of the following stories involve the same people who told us stories in previous chapters.

---

[61] Berne, *Games People Play*, 29.

Overcoming and Integrating Voices from Our Past

JULIANA

(FROM CHAPTER FIVE)

"As a freshman in college, I dated a guy and we became friends. When I was a senior we were in a bar drinking and talking to a group of friends. I was talking to this woman when suddenly he called me a 'fucking bitch,' just out of the blue. I said, 'What?' and he again said, 'You bitch.' I remember I was wearing a new navy blue body suit my mom had given me. He pulled the sleeve and ripped it out. I left the bar and he followed me out. I returned to my dorm totally mortified. Since the bar was across the street from my dorm, when I looked out the window, my boyfriend and his friends drove by and they were all waving to me. I was confused, hurt and very angry.

"We were taking astronomy class together and sharing a textbook. We met in class and I told him he was never getting the book again. But he made light of it, and I continued to see him. My self-esteem was so low back then. He was my first love, the first man I had ever slept with. Because of my upbringing, I was used to being treated with disrespect, and his behavior seemed normal to me because my dad was cruel to me and I was able to overlook it.

"I ended up marrying someone else who also didn't have a capacity for caring. My husband was handsome, rich and well educated, but I didn't like who he was. We were living in a beautiful house, and I remember the ugly scene in the kitchen when he said something to me and I shouted, 'You are not a person, you are just a shell of a person. There is nothing in there.' He had no affect or emotion.

"On a Sunday afternoon in August when our son was one, I was sitting on the deck and my husband had been grilling. Out of the blue, as he brought the platter of chicken up, he said, 'I don't care if we have affairs, as long as we stay together.' I was shocked. A month or so later, I watched him plant tulip bulbs and I remember dreading that I was going to be there when the tulips came up in the spring. That was when I decided to leave. I realized my parents had this same type of relationship and I had thought this was how it was supposed to be. I finally realized that I could no longer bear a loveless union.

"Before I left my husband, I had a conversation with my mom in which I told her things were not going well in my marriage. My mother replied that she and my dad had had a good marriage in spite of the fact that they never could communicate. After I told my mother I wasn't happy, she said, 'Well, you should just have another baby.' Many years later, when I met my current husband, I wanted to tell my mom about him, but she said I had had enough relationships. I wanted to tell her I didn't have any role models and that I seemed to flounder until I accidentally found genuine love. I think I finally attained my self-esteem when I taught at the university and was proud of myself for what I was doing professionally. I was proud of myself for deciding to leave my first husband."

ABOUT THIS CASE STUDY

Clearly, Juliana's father, from the story in chapter five, had a major influence in suppressing her self-esteem. By saying her teeth weren't white enough, he implied that nothing she could do would be right. Our parents are such powerful forces in our lives, whether our relationship with them was constructive or not. It's often not what they said but what they didn't say that has the most impact on us, and it behooves us to think about how the things we do and say reflect our past experiences with them. Often, what we view as normal, because it came from our parents, doesn't serve us well in our current situation. From time to time, it's wise to question whether we want to keep old roles we played with our parents, or whether we should discard them from our psyches. Eventually, Juliana refused to be stuck in the role of victim and she fought back by leaving her husband, building a new life, and gaining self-esteem.

The Difference Between Believing and Acting

If we see someone being physically attacked and do nothing, it might make headlines. However, if we see someone being attacked emotionally and ignore it, it's often viewed as just another day at the office. It occurs to us that merely *believing* in what is right is very different than *acting* to renounce or prevent behavior we believe is wrong. For example, if a "B" is attacking another person and you believe it's wrong to do so, you can actively do something to stop the attack. Or you might say to yourself, "It's wrong," and make a commitment that you'll never do such a thing to another person. If you then decide to avoid the situation by walking away, content in the knowledge that you're better than the "B" who is engaging in injurious behavior, are you passively collaborating with the "B"? Actively renouncing or preventing the malicious behavior of a "B" is an entirely different level of response. It's also one that is frightening and fraught with danger, especially if the "B" is someone who is above you on the organizational ladder.

Tony and the Chief Reprise

In chapter one, the police chief surprised Tony by stinging him when he least expected it. In this story, Tony decides to hold the chief accountable for his arrogant and demeaning behavior toward African Americans.

TONY

"Ever since making lieutenant in the department, I've tried to do my job to the best of my ability while avoiding the wrath of the chief. I led the effort to computerize policies and procedures. I wrote a grant to bring exercise equipment into the facility to improve the physical condition of the police officers, all with no recognition from the chief.

"One day an officer came to me complaining the chief had used racist language in his presence. Although I didn't want to tangle with the chief, I strongly objected to the language the chief had used and felt obligated to report the incident to the captain on duty. When the captain spoke to the chief about the incident, the chief again used a racial slur. At that point the captain was obligated to go to the city mayor, who was the chief's boss. The mayor, who was also a friend of the chief, met with him and gave the chief a three-day suspension with the requirement the chief apologize collectively to the police officers. The chief's apology was weak and without feeling. Instead of apologizing for his behavior, the chief used the opportunity to rationalize what he had said. He remarked that it wasn't that bad compared to what others in the department had said in the past. The chief also indicated he was going to punish some of the other officers.

"As more evidence of the chief's racial slurs surfaced, I knew the union needed to act, and so I met with the police officers. They unanimously voted to file a grievance against the chief. The grievance stated this:

The chief of the police department intentionally and repeatedly used racist language and expressed a racist attitude in the course of his employment, in front of his subordinates, thereby compromising his ability to effectively command and supervise the department. The chief had used the racist language numerous times while speaking with various police officers under his command. In one instance the chief even made derogatory racist remarks during an officer's annual review.'

"The police officers felt strongly that the chief's ability to run the department had been compromised and they should be able to work in an environment free of race-based hostility. The police officers agreed the chief should be held to the highest standard in promoting this type of work environment.

"Several months later, the case was presented before the Police and Fire Commission. When I walked into the room, there were approximately 50 people in the room who were wearing stickers on their shirts in support of the chief. At least three of the commissioners were in the same yacht club as the chief. The mayor and the chief were friends. One of the first witnesses was an African-American resident who voluntarily came forward and asked to testify to the discrimination his children suffered as they attended school in the city where this occurred. As I approached the witness stand, I heard hisses from the crowd.

"While the questions were straightforward, the answers were not, and as hard as I tried not to, I would often elaborate on the answer. Finally, the chief's attorney asked me if I could either answer yes or no. I realized the attorney was trying to train me, so I said, 'Well, ask me a question.' The attorney repeated his admonition, 'Can you answer either yes or no?' I said, 'Yes, sir.' The attorney then asked me if I objected to entering into the record all of the letters of support for the chief. I leaned back on my chair pondering my answer and finally said I didn't mind as long as he also included the letters from all the minorities in the chief's church that were subjected to his racial slurs. The chief's attorney went berserk, telling the commission to strike that response from the record.

"The hearing lasted five hours, and despite the friends the chief had on the commission and the supporters he had brought to the hearing, he received a 90-day suspension without pay. The police officers had wanted the chief fired. However, our officers had sent a strong message, not just to the chief but also to the entire community. They would not tolerate racial slurs and ultimately the city needed to look at its policies because there were no minorities in any public department within the city.

"After the chief had served his three-month suspension, he resumed his position as chief. He acted quite differently from his usual boisterous self by avoiding socializing with the police officers and by hiding out in his office. The chief immediately set out to retaliate against some of the police officers that had testified against him. I was one of the chief's prime targets, and he wrote me up for some rule infraction no one had ever enforced. I filed another grievance against the chief and awaited its resolution. Many of the officers just wanted the atmosphere at the station to return to normal. As the chief acted more like he had been victimized, some of the police officers on other shifts started to turn against me, silently blaming me for the disruption within the department. When I addressed this issue at a union meeting, the police officers said their comments were all in fun. However, I asked them to stop because it was all too painful for me.

"A month or so after the commission hearing, one of the off-duty police officers saw a huge card being delivered to the police station. The fire chief had initiated a huge sympathy/support card and had all of the city workers sign it. The card was eventually delivered on city time in a city vehicle to the police chief.

"When the most recent grievance came up for review, my attorney knew the judge would rule against the chief. Finally, when the judge recommended the chief drop the complaint, the chief knew he had been defeated again. After this last grievance was stopped, the police officers seemed to understand why we did this in the first place. Since then, they have been more supportive of me. The chief has given no indication that he will retire anytime soon. I am waiting for the next shoe to drop."

TONY, AS A YOUNG BOY

"I was 10 and my parents were getting ready to go to a party. They had a large tray of appetizers on the table, and as they were preparing to leave, my father turned to pick up the tray. Our dog had eaten everything on the tray. I only remember hearing my dad screaming as my siblings and I hid. We never saw our dog again.

"My dad abused me many times as I was growing up. When I finally felt secure in myself, I wanted to tell my dad what his actions did to me. However, by that time he was too demented to understand what I was saying."

ABOUT THIS CASE STUDY ───────────────

Ironically, the impetus for Tony's strong reaction to the chief's "B" behaviors was likely his unresolved issues with his father's abuse. Tony was still furious at his father for abusing him, his dog, and his siblings. As an adult, Tony must have thought through many of the issues with his father and established strong boundaries against abuse by others.

Tony is a true hero who risked his career by fighting back against the "B" behaviors of his boss. It's remarkable how many of the city employees sided with the chief when he assumed the role of victim. It's also interesting to note how some of the police officers temporarily turned against Tony when they realized the atmosphere in the department had changed. To Tony's credit, he remained true to his values and to the boundaries he had for ethical behavior. Eventually the police officers came around.

This story highlights the difficulties inherent in fighting back. It also demonstrates how bystanders can be pulled into the buzz of the "B's" nest as rescuers, and how important it is to examine the facts of a situation before you jump in.

Students Fight Back

ANNMARIE

"I was taking a university class to renew my teaching certification. I had previously taught classes at this university and knew a number of the faculty in the department where I was taking this course. During one class a guest lecturer harassed me. While the other students tolerated the lecturer's behavior, I responded by writing the following letter to the professor responsible for the class. Within several days of receiving my letter, the guest lecturer read his letter of response to the entire class. My letter is here:

June 4

Dear Dr. Brimes,

On Monday June 4, I was enrolled as your student in E862. I asked Mr. Seneth, the guest lecturer, the following question: Can someone have too much intuition 'N' on the Meyers Briggs Type Inventory?

In discussion previous to my question, he was discussing the process whereby you begin with S (sensing) to gain facts and move to N (intuition) to assess alternatives, then to T (thinking) for rational ideas and finally F (feeling) for how it'll affect individuals. He called Ns the witches. He asked who the NTs in the class were. A student volunteered she was an INTP type. He asked if there were any other INTPs in the class. I raised my hand.

The Ts he said were rational, logical, firm and fair, and were product oriented. He added they are female bitches. He stated I was both an N (a witch) and a T (a bitch). He then said my former students called me worse in words he couldn't mention here. The class laughed. I stated that I assumed these comments had been made in his office. I don't recall his response.

His words were embarrassing and demeaning. His expressed opinion failed to reach the threshold of sharing with me (through professional channels) when we were then colleagues at this university. He instead chose to publicly humiliate me when I was in the role of student. I consider his expressed opinion and insults to be an amazing breach of confidentiality between professional colleagues and an unacceptable insult to a student asking a question.

I request he apologize to me at an upcoming class meeting, and in writing. Failing this, my next recourse will be to address this issue with the affirmative action officer at this university and with his supervisor.

Sincerely,

Annmarie Frinder

"Two days later, I received a letter from Mr. Seneth, apologizing for having humiliated me and the other students by his presentation. He subsequently stopped by Dr. Brimes' class and apologized to the entire class. Initially, his apology seemed genuine. He said that there were never any comments made by his students to him. He commended me for writing the letter. However, as his apology continued, he tried to explain why he had made these comments, saying he was only trying to illustrate extreme examples of the principles he was explaining and to show the strength of certain personality types. I felt that he was just trying to justify his behavior."

ANNMARIE, AS A YOUNG GIRL

"I remember coming in from outside in the wintertime. I couldn't get out of my snowsuit in time and urinated in it. My mother surprised me with a spanking. However, she later apologized."

ABOUT THIS CASE STUDY

Annmarie responded very appropriately to the verbal abuse she sustained in class. Perhaps Annmarie's experience with her mother apologizing for spanking her, led her to understand she could expect an apology when she was wronged. If you are to make any headway against the type of "B" behavior that unfairly denigrates you, the response must be swift, specific, and consistent with the insult. Annmarie, simply and without emotion, presented the facts as she had experienced them.

While a straight apology by Mr. Seneth would have been appropriate, he felt the need to elaborate and justify his actions and motives for using Annmarie as an example. Thus, his letter raises some skepticism as to whether he was truly sorry for his "B" behavior or had simply been 'caught in the act.' On the other hand, the students had remained silent about Mr. Seneth's remarks, in effect, tolerating and tacitly condoning them. By requiring Mr. Seneth to read his apology in class, Dr. Brimes, the responsible professor, served to teach the students they did have some power to respond to "B" behaviors in the classroom.

Revisiting Isabel

(FROM CHAPTER TWO)

In chapter two, Isabel, at eight years of age, could not recall anyone having been mean to her. From time to time, her parents would ask Isabel the same question, querying about whether or not anyone had ever been mean to her. One night at the dinner table, Isabel's answer was yes. After listening to Isabel's story about a girl in her class who was bothering her, Isabel's parents encouraged her to write a note to her teacher describing her problem:

Dear Ms. Lamy,

I need your help. There are times that Irena does things to me that frustrate me. Sometimes in music class she sits in my chair and won't get out. This week, since I was the leader, I got to sit in the green chair and sometimes when you called us down to the rug, Irena would sit in the chair and ask me, "What's the password?" and I would say, "I don't know. Please?" and she would say, "No," and then I just don't know what to do about it.

One time Irena took my eraser and hid it in her desk. I saw her take it and she said she didn't take it, and then I told her, "Yes you did because I saw you take it." Then she gave it back but before she gave it back she said, "Will you let me have it?" I said maybe but I didn't really want to give it to her. I just didn't know what to say. Then Ms. Schwartz gave Irena *an eraser to keep. As these things keep happening, I want to have some ideas about the best way to respond. I like Irena and want to be her friend but I think she might be taking advantage of me being her friend. Can you help?*

> *Thank you,*
> *Isabel*

Ms. Lamy's response:

Dear Isabel,

I am so glad you wrote me to tell me how frustrated you have been with Irena. I appreciate how specific you were of the times there have been problems. I am going to sit down with Ms. Schwartz and Ms. Kaiser to talk about the issues you've had with Irena.

I'm proud of you for being assertive and upfront with Irena. Most importantly...you let me know. I will try to be more aware of Irena's behavior and will sit down with you on Monday to talk more about the situation.

I'm also proud of you for being a problem solver and being so patient!

Sincerely,

Ms. Lamy

ABOUT THIS CASE STUDY

Isabel's story illustrates that we shouldn't underestimate a child's ability to understand "B" behaviors. Isabel's story also exemplifies how it's never too early to start discussing "B" behaviors with children. The sooner we learn to recognize "B" behaviors, the more quickly we can learn ways to avoid being stung by "B"s. By learning how to constructively address attempted "B" stings, perhaps we can influence the messages children take from their childhoods. Instead of remembering messages filled with dread, they will remember the courage they showed in blocking an attempted "B" sting.

Rejecting Abuse

SALLY

"I was sitting at my desk one day when George, one of the agency counselors, walked into my office. George was concerned because he had noticed Desiree, one of the other counselors, seeing a patient on a unit she wasn't assigned to. George was curious as to what she was doing on that unit.

"Desiree had been a problem for the department for years. She often didn't show up for work, and it was common knowledge that her sick leave and vacation time were always at zero days. Desiree was a middle-aged woman who was boisterous and who had an imposing physique. Everyone on the staff seemed to be afraid of her, and the department director was no exception. She should've been held accountable for her poor performance but that had never occurred.

"I wasn't sure why George decided to tell me the story since I had no oversight over Desiree. However, I asked George to obtain the chart of the person Desiree had seen on the unit. In reviewing the chart, I could see nothing out of line and simply made a mental note of the patient's name and returned the chart.

"I had a neighbor, Lorraine, who happened to be a counselor at a local social services agency, and most evenings after work Lorraine and I would visit over the back fence. One day we were shooting the bull and she asked me if I had seen the story in the paper about the woman who had tried to bite off her boyfriend's tongue. I said I had not seen the story but it sounded painful. Lorraine said she would find the story for me. The next day we again were talking over the back fence and she brought the story. Lorraine asked me if I knew a Desiree Lofran, the woman named in the story. I said the only Desiree I knew was the counselor who worked at our facility, and her name was Desiree Pelipson. Lorraine said she knew Desiree Pelipson because she was a foster parent with her agency.

"That night I awoke, realizing the last name of the patient's chart I had reviewed was Lofran. The next day I spoke again with Lorraine, and told her my concern that Desiree Pelipson might have married a patient. I had remembered in reading the chart the patient was receiving a lot of monetary assistance for a disability, and I was now very curious about Desiree's motive in seeing him on the unit. Lorraine had friends in the county clerk's office and she said she would search the public database for any marriage with the names of Lofran and Pelipson.

"The next day Lorraine struck gold. She discovered Desiree Pelipson had married Mr. Lofran, and that was why her name appeared in the newspaper as Desiree Lofran. Desiree was milking the social service system, the agency she worked in, and her new husband. All the while, she had a boyfriend who she had attacked. It was obvious that Desiree didn't want the people at work to link her with this story. Lorraine was concerned about Desiree's capacity to raise foster children, especially because she demonstrated a serious violent side. Concerned about Desiree's fraud and her unethical behavior, I felt I had to report my evidence to the director of the agency.

"The director called in an outside investigator, and Desiree was fired. Unfortunately, at that time Desiree's profession was unlicensed, and Desiree walked free. Lorraine made sure that the foster children were

THE COURAGE TO FIGHT BACK

removed from Desiree's home. Lorraine was furious that Desiree did not get any other punishment for her behavior. Fortunately, Lorraine was a member of many social service boards in town, and was able to prevent Desiree from obtaining several jobs for which she later applied. I spent the next few years looking over my shoulder worried that Desiree would take revenge if she found out who uncovered her unethical behaviors. Eventually Desiree disappeared from town and neither Lorraine nor I ever saw her again."

SALLY, AS A YOUNG GIRL

"In third grade, one of the kids in my class acted out in school and the teacher made the entire class take out a textbook and copy it. I felt like I was being tortured as we copied the text from that book all day, every day, for a week. I only remember the helplessness I felt and the stupidity of the task. I was left feeling, even 50 years later, that the teacher was the worst teacher I ever had. However, I think this story became a life lesson as I decided I would always try to find ways to confront injustice."

LORRAINE, AS A TEENAGER

"Growing up, I was the kid who always did what she was told. My sisters acted out but I toed the line. The first time I remember someone violating my trust was in college. I was on the student council and enjoyed it because I could sit back and find out what was going on in school. There was an election for president of the council, and I quickly became aware that some of the current council members were attempting to 'fix' the election. They tried to include me in their scheme but I refused because I thought they were wrong. They were discovered and were abolished from the council. So many of them left, that I became president."

ABOUT THIS CASE STUDY ————————————

As children, Sally and Lorraine learned their lessons well. Sometimes all it takes is stepping back and thinking about a situation to recognize "B" behaviors. It took three courageous people to expose Desiree's destructive behaviors. Essential ingredients in fighting back are coordination and the willingness to work with others to get the job done.

Slow Response to Fighting Back

DENISE

"I worked at a large wellness clinic. When I look back at the low point in my career, I think of my boss, Sherry, who single-handedly destroyed our well-run program in a short period of time. I was a senior staff person on the hiring team for a new director, which to this day just kills me. In my defense, Sherry was our only candidate. We had been without leadership for many months and were feeling desperate. From Sherry's first day on the job, we were off on the wrong foot. If I said something was black, she would say it was white. We agreed on nothing, and I can honestly say I had never felt this level of disrespect from a supervisor before. I was really taken off guard.

"All the staff members were struggling with Sherry's arrogant attitude. One day a supervisor, Camille, went home and found a message from Sherry on her voicemail stating she had moved one of Camille's staff to another position and she would not be replaced. Camille had walked right past Sherry on her way out of the building that day, and Sherry hadn't mention a thing. Human resources (HR) told Camille that if she wanted to quit because of Sherry, HR would support this decision.

"Every one of the seven employees who worked most closely with Sherry had résumés out within a month of Sherry starting in the position. One of the workers, who gave two week's notice, had called in sick most of her two weeks. Sherry called her and told her to 'suck it up and finish her time out.' The worker had a doctor's note for having bronchitis.

"Sherry led daily staff meetings and she failed to announce whenever a staff member resigned. An administrative assistant went to HR to complain about Sherry and was told Sherry 'is just a poor communicator but she really is a nice person.' Dr. Jones, the head physician in the program, said she was also thinking of leaving. She reported waking up at night thinking about how Sherry was mistreating the staff. Dr. Jones said she found herself snapping at members of her family, which was not something she would normally do.

"Sherry had a habit of pitting staff and clients against each other. The clients expressed concerns about the high turnover, worrying and wondering what was happening to their program. Sherry met alone with some of the clients and later met with staff to report that the clients were upset about how the staff members were sharing their problems, related to agency politics, with them. Staff members were shocked by Sherry's comments, knowing they had been completely professional with clients.

"My former student, Molly, was applying for a staff position. Sherry conducted the interview alone, even though she didn't share a similar educational background with Molly and had little knowledge of the position. Molly reported afterward that she felt like Sherry was interrogating her. During the interview, Sherry badgered Molly about 'which side she would take if she got the job, the staff's side or Sherry's side.'

Sherry asked Molly, 'If you take this job, what do you think you will hate the most about it?' Molly said later she had no clue how to respond to such a 'negative statement.' At the end of the interview, Sherry told Molly how no one likes her and how no one welcomed her with open arms when she first started at the company. Molly was speechless and couldn't believe how inappropriately Sherry was behaving. Molly didn't get the job.

"An outside provider called for Caroline, a staff member at the clinic. The front desk was paging over the loudspeaker for Caroline to take the call. After several pages, Sherry picked up the call and said she was taking all of Caroline's calls in another department. Sherry asked the caller what she wanted, and the caller said she really needed to speak to Caroline. The caller asked when Caroline would be available. Sherry told the caller Caroline no longer worked there, and she told the caller never to call again and have someone paged. The caller contacted Caroline at home that night to tell her what happened.

"My department was short-staffed because of the high turnover, and I told Sherry we needed to develop a hiring plan. Sherry agreed, but when I asked her to meet, she said she didn't have time. Sherry would leave me voicemails saying she would like to meet and told me what time. When I arrived at the prescribed time, she would tell me she couldn't meet. At the end of the day, when my blood pressure was sky high, Sherry told me she wanted to be there for me and asked me what I needed. I told her I needed to know the plan for filling the vacant positions. Sherry said she needed to have more meetings and didn't have answers yet. I told her having a plan for filling positions would alleviate some of my anxiety. Sherry said, 'I don't want you to be fearful.' I replied that every day I was fearful with the state of our clinic.

"Staff members were being fired, jobs were being eliminated, and people were quitting daily. Sherry had been there two months, and every system we had developed over the previous five years was crumbling. She would complain that I didn't keep her informed. Due to the increasingly short staffing, I was carrying a double caseload, time was tight, and Sherry told me to delegate. She placed a pile of medical releases on my desk with a note telling me to get signatures. She stressed that it was urgent. In an attempt to delegate, I took the forms back to Sherry and asked if perhaps this was a task better suited for medical records. Sherry took the releases out of my hands and threw them on her desk, saying, 'Fine, I will do them!' Sherry then turned from me to focus on something on her desk. I was surprised and shocked by her reaction and didn't know how to respond. Later in the day, Sherry came to me and told me she thought she should apologize because she may have been too rough on me that morning.

"I had been through difficult agency transitions before but never something like this. HR made me participate in counseling sessions with Sherry to 'work through our issues.' After these sessions, I would watch Sherry leave the building to go have lunch with the head of HR. Soon after that, I resigned. When I told Sherry I was leaving, she just sat there and said nothing. It looked like she was about to cry. A few weeks later, she was fired."

DENISE, AS A YOUNG GIRL

"In fifth grade, students had the opportunity to be on patrol (helping other students cross the street). It came with responsibility, an orange sash, a silver pin, and a bit of prestige. The process was to 'try out' for patrol as a fourth grader by spending time with the current fifth graders on patrol and being rated by them on a scale from one to five (with five being the best). I did my rounds and was rated highly by everyone until my last corner. My neighbor was on the corner along with another boy I was not as familiar with. My neighbor gave me a five and the other boy gave me a one. I didn't make patrol because of this boy. He didn't even know me.

"My neighbor didn't stick up for me. He laughed, sympathetically, and said he didn't know why the other boy did this to me. He knew it was wrong but he didn't do anything about it. I felt completely confused and powerless. Any time I saw that other boy throughout middle school and high school, my blood would boil. He never even acknowledged me again. He didn't seem to have any remorse for what he did. It was like screwing up someone's life was just a typical part of his day. The other day I saw him on Facebook and wanted to write and ask him why he did such a mean, senseless thing to someone he didn't even know."

ABOUT THIS CASE STUDY

It's not easy to know when enough is enough. Denise's story about her boss, Sherry, highlights Denise's initial attempt to problem-solve and pin down solutions to problems with her superior's unstable behaviors. Unfortunately, the situation escalated too quickly. Sherry's impulsive behaviors and rapidly changing emotions are hallmarks of borderline behaviors. Ideally, borderline "B"s need to be held to a defined structure. But since Sherry was the director, Denise needed someone else to help establish that structure and hold Sherry accountable. Denise was never able to establish a stable base of support for herself because too many of her colleagues had left the agency. The story is a great example of the chaos that's created when a borderline "B" takes control of a group. Just when you think you have something settled, they'll upset it again.

When you are feeling totally crazy and out of control, you must question the presence of a borderline "B." Sherry kept the chaos at a high pitch by continuously changing roles from perse-

cutor to rescuer to victim. Even when Denise told Sherry she was leaving, Sherry immediately switched to her tearful victim face.

Denise's story about being voted out of patrol left her feeling helpless and out of control. It is clear she wanted to avoid this feeling in her job. Although Denise made heroic attempts to intervene and stabilize the situation, the cards were stacked against her. She felt that she had done her best to fight back before leaving the agency. Paradoxically, Denise's leaving might have precipitated Sherry's firing.

Pushing the Drama Toward Resolution

ROSE

"I had worked for 12 years as a mid-level administrator in a large healthcare facility that was partially funded by private donations. One section of our department dealt with donations from donors who liked what we were accomplishing. I was the supervisor for Darin, the person who accepted and recorded the donations. Because there were so many donations, several different accounts were set up and a committee approved disbursement of the money. Darin always seemed to resent me as his boss, however, he befriended those with more power. Darin found ways to get what he wanted within the organization. Even though Darin worked for me, he had a much larger office than I did, and others actually thought he was my boss. When a new CEO was hired, Darin convinced the CEO to become his boss, even though the CEO was not directly supervising anyone else at Darin's level.

"I'm not sure when I started to suspect Darin of mishandling money. However, after he began working for the new CEO, Darin would withhold donations that would ordinarily have been distributed to different departments at regular intervals. I began to watch Darin more closely and notice that he seemed rather loose with his handling of the donations. He would convince the head of the donations committee to sign blank checks for him. Over the course of a year, I reported my concerns to the CFO, the COO, and finally to the CEO. They merely said they would check into it but nothing changed. My complaints were ignored by all of my supervisors.

"About eighteen months after I had filed my first complaint about Darin's behavior, I was suddenly notified that my position had been eliminated. I was left with a house payment, no job and no income. I decided I had an obligation to file a complaint with the Department of Justice. After they investigated my complaint, Darin was fired and charged with embezzling a large sum of money. I decided to file a lawsuit under the whistleblower law. It is now four years later and my lawsuit is still pending. I have another full-time job and have taken a second job to pay for my legal fees. I reported Darin's behavior because it was the right thing to do. I'm happy Darin has finally received justice and hope it will come for me as well."

ROSE, AS A YOUNG GIRL

"I was eight or nine years old when relatives from out of state came to visit us. One of my cousins, who was older than my father, played a game of cards with me. I realized he was cheating and I became furious. As he kept on cheating, I became increasingly angry with him. After throwing my cards down on the table in total exasperation, my dad sent me to my room. My father's unjust reaction changed my relationship with him for the rest of my life."

ABOUT THIS CASE STUDY ——————————————

From the time she was young and stood up to her older cousin for cheating at cards, Rose seemed to have a strong sense of what was right and what was wrong. She also had developed a sense that authority figures were not always right and should-n't always be trusted just because they were older or were in charge. Through all of her personal pain, Rose has retained the conviction that she did the right thing.

The World of Art

Artists must create a body of work and then sell themselves and their work. Because of the strong possibility of rejection, an artist must find ways to protect her ego. Because of this, it would seem that the arts community might harbor its fair share of "B"s who have developed an inability to see reality in their behaviors. Some artists stay out of the "B's" nest by avoiding public places unless they need to promote their work. Other artists willingly enter the drama.

DRAKE

"One of the artists I featured in my gallery would regularly come in to tell me that the reason his art wasn't selling was because of the location I, the owner, had placed it within the gallery. Initially, after the artist left the gallery I would question myself to see if I was being fair. After going through this scenario many times, however, I finally had enough grief and told the artist to remove his artwork from my gallery."

ABOUT THIS CASE STUDY

Drake knew that nothing would have satisfied this complaining "B," and he exercised his power as gallery owner to decide which artists would be in and which would be out.

MISTY

"I am a professional artist who was new to a community, so I volunteered my time to help a curator of a local art museum. Observing the curator, I noticed that she paid a lot of attention to certain visitors and volunteers while ignoring others. After a while I could identify the prominent people in town simply by noting the people the curator chose to converse with. As I became busier with my art, I stopped volunteering but whenever I ran into the curator I would greet her. Often she didn't acknowledge my presence. I mentioned her behavior to other artists and they just brushed it aside saying, 'That's the way she is.'

"A while later I entered a show at the museum because the judge had been one of my mentors and I wanted to show her the progress I had made. I chose my best piece of artwork and entered it in the show. I was upset when my piece was not juried into the show. Although I wanted feedback from my old mentor, I didn't want to upset her if indeed she thought that my piece wasn't good enough for the show. So I kept my disappointment to myself. I remained upset for over a month and couldn't bring myself to resume my artwork.

"One day I received a call from my mentor on another matter and I finally used the opportunity to ask her for feedback on why my piece didn't make the show. My mentor expressed profound surprise, saying that she remembered the piece and had juried it into the show. My mentor proceeded to call the curator and ask why my piece didn't end up in the show. The curator stumbled for words but could give no explanation. My mentor then asked the curator to call me to apologize. When I received the phone call, the curator took no blame but simply said, 'I am sorry that an error occurred and your piece didn't make the show.' I was left feeling manipulated and was especially upset when I again realized that the other artists quietly tolerated the curator's behavior and never called her on it."

ABOUT THIS CASE STUDY

Misty's mentor chose to fight back by calling the curator and questioning why Misty's artwork hadn't been placed in the show. She is to be commended for asking the curator to apologize to Misty. The curator's unwillingness to take personal responsibility for keeping Misty's work out of the show was an example of the arrogant and cold behaviors of a narcissistic "B." However, the mentor's willingness to take action allowed Misty to return to her art.

ARIEL

"I interact with many shop owners who sell my art. Justine, a shop owner, was always ready with some nasty comments when I brought in my pieces. Although I dreaded going there, my pieces sold well at her shop, so I continued to bring them in. One day I brought in some ceramic vases I had created and lined them up on her counter. She immediately said she didn't like them. So I began gathering them up, and when I was near tears she asked me what I was doing. I said I was taking them back since she didn't like them. I continued to repackage them. She then started a back-and-forth with me, saying she maybe liked a part of this one or that one. She didn't like this but she would try that. So I had her choose four pieces.

"Justine then asked me if I had brought in some of my ceramic tiles. I told her no, because the prior year she had told me she didn't want any pieces like the ones I had in other shops, and I had my tiles in other shops in the area. Justine said I should remove all of my pieces from last year and she would like four sets of my tiles. As always, I left her shop feeling violated. I later spoke with several other artists who said they were treated the same way when they brought their pieces to Justine.

"Gracie, who had opened a new shop in an adjoining town, said she had brought pieces to Justine and was treated like dirt. She told me Justine said one of her art pieces looked like plastic. Gracie said she now owned three shops and was competing with Justine. I left pieces in Gracie's new shop and was treated with respect. After a lot of reflection, I emailed Justine and decided to take control of the situation:

> Hi Justine,
>
> I am going to stick with my original plan and sell my tiles exclusively at Gracie's shop this summer. If you still want those four sets, I'll consider it a "special order" and will be able to send you those when you send me payment of $60 each. This is how I always handle special orders. Let me know if you want them or if you would rather refer your clients to Gracie's shop to get tiles.
>
> Thanks,
>
> Ariel

"In response to my email, Justine emailed me back, saying she was sorry that I wouldn't be bringing in my tiles. First she noted how she had sold several of my pieces the same day I delivered them. She then tried to entice me back by offering me a special consignment fee. However, I didn't take her bait. Instead, I wrote her another email:

Hi Justine,

Thanks for your quick response. I'd prefer to just keep my tiles at Gracie's shop, so it would be best to just let your clients know where they can get them. Thanks,

Ariel

ABOUT THIS CASE STUDY

Ariel fought back against Justine's narcissistic behaviors by talking to other artists and getting Ariel's behaviors out in the open where they could examine them. This helped Ariel realize she was not alone. Finally, Ariel established firm boundaries with Justine. It is obvious in Justine's email how she's trying to draw Ariel out of her newly established boundaries and lure her back. In fighting back against a "B," you can expect their behaviors to escalate. Note how Ariel re-stated her terms.

Using Clear Language

CELIA

"I have lived in a nice neighborhood with my sister Pearl for years. A year ago, Buffy moved next door. Pearl and I were friendly toward her in a neighborly way. Buffy was always friendly to our faces. Recently I discovered Buffy has been telling lies around town about Pearl and me. The owner of a local restaurant we frequent told Pearl that Buffy told him we were in financial trouble and couldn't pay our bills. This is completely false. Pearl and I have learned that Buffy took out restraining orders on several patrons of another restaurant, saying they were abusive to her. The restraining orders were dismissed as unfounded. It is clear to me now that this woman attacks others for the behaviors that she perpetrates on them. A month ago I asked Buffy to please stop telling lies about Pearl and me. I even discovered Buffy had told the proprietor of another business that Pearl and I have taken unfair advantage of another neighbor. Where does she get this stuff?

"The other day I had enough of Buffy's lies, and when she started her friendly chatter as Pearl and I were unloading groceries, I stopped her from speaking further. I calmly but firmly told Buffy that after being so nice to her and clearly asking her not to lie about Pearl and me, I discovered she was still lying about us. After summarizing the details of the lies, I told her I didn't like her anymore, I didn't want her to speak to me, and I didn't want her to talk about Pearl and me anymore. I told her she was untrustworthy and I that could no longer tolerate her lies. She replied, 'I don't want to argue with you.' I told her there was nothing to argue about.

"Buffy then wrote a letter to the neighborhood association saying that Pearl and I had abused her. The president of the neighborhood association took Buffy's letter seriously and responded with a letter to Pearl and me. Buffy has subsequently moved from the neighborhood."

ABOUT THIS CASE STUDY

Celia did all the right things in dealing with the lies of this neighborhood "B." It is important to meet this kind of coercion with equal force, and that's what Celia did with language that was clear and concise. This is another example of the need for a witness when you confront a "B," because it is a sure bet the "B" will try to retaliate by blaming you for something you didn't do. Hopefully Buffy will stay away. If she returns to cause more trouble, however, Celia and her sister will need to unite with others to set collective boundaries against Buffy's histrionic lies.

Know Your Strengths

COLE

"I was a new principal at a junior high school. A shift was in progress when I started, since the following year the school would change to a middle-school concept with just grades seven and eight. One third of the staff would have to leave, and by union edict it would be determined entirely by seniority. Teachers made decisions in teacher-led committees, so I set up teacher-led committees to decide schedules, and there had to be 80 percent consensus.

"One of the reasons I went to the middle-school level was because the curriculum structure was changing to core teams of teachers. It created an opportunity to set aside a planning hour in which the teachers would get together. This was very threatening to many teachers because they had to talk to colleagues about what they were doing.

"Jim and Lisa, two 50-year-old teachers, had been running the school for many years and frequently intimidating younger teachers. One day, while entering a team meeting, Lisa turned to me and said this had better go all right or else. I immediately told Lisa she would need to meet with me the following day, and I told her to bring her union representative.

"Another teacher, Roy, was sexually inappropriate with eighth grade girls. He would compliment them for what they wore. One day a girl forgot her assignment, and Roy made her take off her shoes and he took them. I told him I needed to speak to him about his behavior. He pulled out his tape recorder, and I had to speak into it. I had been a union representative for years, so I knew the tricks. The next time Roy came into my office with his representative, I had my supervisor there. I had purchased the largest tape recorder I could find and I put it on my desk. When he started his recorder, I started mine. I reviewed the complaints of two parent calls and three or four students who had come in feeling uneasy about him. I documented that and wrote him a step-one reprimand. I put a letter in his file, and we went to our separate corners.

"Roy's undoing was when he started saying inappropriate things to a young student teacher. He had been looking down her shirt, and she came into my office to report this. It was unusual for a student teacher to speak out, but she did. After that, word got out. Another female teacher, who had been intimidated by Roy, brought another matter to my attention, and we gave Roy a step-two reprimand. I managed to drive Roy out because he was losing support from the rest of the teachers, and he realized I wouldn't leave. The game you play is to get them to leave. They are certain that you can't get rid of them because few principals ever take that step. The teachers at that school had a strong teacher union, so it would be a full-time job to get rid of someone. The union tells the teachers who are on probation, 'You don't want to talk to the principal. Stay under the radar for three years so you can become vested.'

It was my first year in the district and I was trying to learn the politics. Everyone knew that the middle school was the 'union school' and all the 'goonheads' went there. In the second year, I politely and professionally went after the union president. When my evaluation came up, I heard that the union president reported that I had been causing friction, and the superintendent reprimanded me. The superintendent had told the assistant superintendent I should go easy on any union issues. Although I wasn't told first-hand, I was told to not 'make the phone ring downtown.'

"After that, I decided to focus on anything that would improve the overall climate of the school (and would not upset the applecart). The superintendent would demote administrators who took on issues involving the union. Subsequently, the board worshipped him because no teacher problems ever came to the board. The superintendent's long-range strategy was to create as little friction as possible so he could more easily pass referenda. I was under him for seven years.

"I learned to get smarter about fighting and found ways to get the teachers to work together. They knew I understood what teaching was about and that teaching was full of frustrations. So, when I saw a teacher's legitimate need, I would go to bat for that teacher. And when the old-guard would try to bait me at a faculty meeting, I wouldn't take the bait. When one tried to create a scene, I would say we'll talk about his or her issue after the meeting. I told the teacher I wouldn't talk about personal issues in a public forum and would set an appointment later.

"I had been a staff development coordinator before I went to that school. Consequently, when I went into rooms to observe the teachers, I scripted the whole thing and pointed out things that were good and things that needed to improve. Teachers were used to someone coming in for a few minutes and leaving. I tried to be in a coaching mode.

"One of the more curious things I observed was in the move from being a teacher to being an administrator. All of a sudden I didn't know anything. I had taught high school for 18 years and I had been out of teaching for three months, but all of a sudden I was perceived as not knowing anything. They were used to administrators behaving in a certain way, and as soon as you held a certain standard out there it was incredibly threatening to even the good teachers. Good teachers would think I was going to find something wrong with their teaching.

"Ultimately, my experience as a principal made me lower my expectations for what I could accomplish. I had to learn the games being played by the superintendent and realize I had limited power to change things within my school. However, I used the power I had as a principal to encourage the teachers to monitor and improve their teaching. I was also able to insure the teachers didn't intimidate or abuse other teachers or students."

ABOUT THIS CASE STUDY

From the superintendent who didn't want to hear about problems in the schools to the teachers who didn't want to look at their performance, Cole found himself in the middle of a "B's" nest. It would have been easy to blame the teacher's unions for all of the problems in this story. However, the shirking of responsibility by the superintendent who didn't back a team effort for addressing the problem teachers created the perfect cover for the "B's" nest to expand. The intentional blindness of the school board members and those who voted for them protected the nest. The unwillingness of even the good teachers to welcome honest feedback was another guard function that protected the few teachers who exhibited "B" behaviors. In this case, it took a village to create and protect this "B's" nest.

Cole's observation was notable that when he became principal, the teaching staff suddenly questioned his ability to teach. Change is an opportunity for "B"s to make their moves. They take advantage of the normal fear that is engendered by change to convince those involved that there's a problem. The uncertain newness of Cole as principal enhanced the teacher's normal fears and allowed some of the old-guard teachers to try manipulating both the teachers and Cole.

SUMMARY

THESE STORIES ARE EXAMPLES OF WHY IT'S NOT ALWAYS enough to stay away from the "B's" nest. Standing back to avoid being stung often promotes more stinging behaviors. While we have a primary obligation to protect ourselves by not tolerating abuse from others, we also have a human obligation to help those around us who are being abused.

We have taught health professionals and students for many years. Many of our students related stories of being harassed or put down by other health professionals. We would always tell them the same thing: they had a right to *not* be abused. Sometimes, all it took for them to act against the abuse was a word of encouragement and the assurance that we would help them end their role as a victim by discussing legitimate ways to resolve their problems.

It is important to note many "B" stories are not simple and cannot be simply told. Most are full of twists and turns and tangled webs of influence and alliances. Attempting to engage in righting an injustice that is precipitated by a

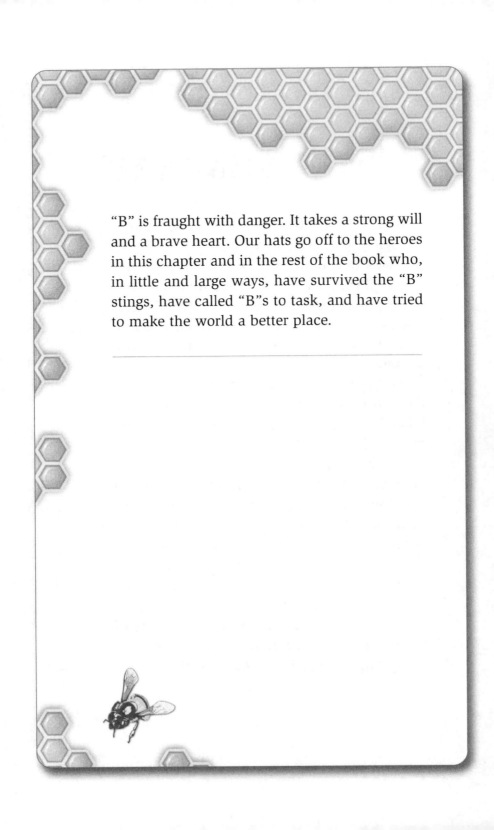

"B" is fraught with danger. It takes a strong will and a brave heart. Our hats go off to the heroes in this chapter and in the rest of the book who, in little and large ways, have survived the "B" stings, have called "B"s to task, and have tried to make the world a better place.

CHAPTER TWELVE

Surviving the "B" Stings

*"If you know the enemy and know yourself, you need not fear
the result of a hundred battles. If you know yourself but not the enemy,
for every victory gained you will also suffer a defeat. if you know
neither the enemy nor yourself, you will succumb in every battle."*

SUN-TZU, FROM THE ART OF WAR
(TRANSLATED FROM CHINESE BY LIONEL GILES, M.A., 1910)

The intent of this book is not to focus on "B"s but rather on those who have been stung. However, survival is contingent on understanding the behavior of "B"s as well as knowing yourself. The most important thing to remember in surviving a "B" sting is that "B"s lack a moral center that causes them to exhibit destructive behavior patterns. Some people perpetuate the stings by wondering why "B"s don't love them back. These "wonderers" can live their entire lives not realizing "B"s are incapable of loving them and are therefore unable to reciprocate with real compassion. Some people change into what they think the "B" will accept or do things to make the "B" love them more, but this only leads to more heartache. "B"s have a void that cannot be filled, no matter how hard one tries.

Another fact of "B" morphology is that you cannot help "B"s unless they want to be helped. Because of something that occurred in their developmental past, "B"s wall themselves off from accurate self-reflection. "B"s won't want help unless they are in a crisis situation and they desire something beyond their reach. Even then, as soon as they regain their footing, they'll attempt to pull you back into their "B's" nest. A "B" who really wants to change will seek professional help from someone who specializes in treating personality disorders. You cannot help them. If you think you're the person who has just what it takes to change a "B's" behavior patterns, you should examine your own streak of narcissism.

We know the temptation is great to rationalize your need to rescue. "He can't help it." "Look at how he was raised." "She can be so sweet, and I feel sorry for her." "He is so nice to me." "He can't be that bad." We repeat. *Unless you are a specially trained therapist, you cannot change a "B."* What you can do is to set in motion the steps that will enable you to survive, either by leaving the "B's" nest or by establishing clear boundaries for what you will and will not tolerate. You can also plan how you will stay out of the "B's" nest in the future.

Understanding Your Blind Spots

A blind spot is an area in our psyche that causes us to see someone's good qualities while ignoring their destructive qualities. Some people have very large blind spots and only see goodness in everyone. The size of our blind spot is fed by a mindset or belief that we develop for what we assume is normal. Throughout our lives we develop a human ethic for how people should behave. The instructors for our personal code of ethics are our parental figures, our teachers, our spiritual leaders, and our good friends. We learn to define their behaviors and what they teach us as *normal*. Sometimes those people we trust mix manipulative behaviors with compassionate behaviors, and that fuels our blind spots.

In learning to understand "B"s, we compare behaviors of those in our expanding social repertoire with the behaviors of people we have learned to trust. Many people fall within a normal range, and that collective ethic supports our society. When we mature and discover that some people we trusted are not trustworthy, it causes confusion in our ability to judge the behavior of others.

We all have blind spots when it comes to judging others because the ethic we have developed becomes our norm. One of the most common examples of a blind spot playing out is when a person who has been abused by a parent seeks in a mate someone who demonstrates the positive qualities (charm, good looks, talent) possessed by the abusive parent. Because she hopes she can rewrite her past, she doesn't notice the manipulative qualities in her potential mate that were also qualities of her abuser. She is stung when her relationship deepens, the power shifts, and she becomes emotionally dependent on that person. The person abused by a parent finds that she's fallen into the same pattern she had hoped to escape.

Someone else might try to duplicate a loving relationship that he had, and in his quest to find someone with the same qualities ends up turning a blind eye to the early warning signs that his love interest isn't the person he imagined her to be. The abuser is often a "B" who shows only his good side in the early stages of the relationship, and only after a deeper commitment develops does his "B" side emerge.

ILENE

"My first husband swept me off my feet. He was charming and loving and acted like he desperately needed me in his life. But as soon as the wedding was over, he began physically and mentally abusing me. We had a son together, and after that I got out of the marriage because I was afraid he would kill me and/or my son. I finished my degree and became a teacher. I never regretted leaving my husband. I recognize now I have a blind spot for someone who comes on strong, is intelligent, and who always takes charge of a situation the way my father always did."

Understanding Your Soft Spots

Soft spots are a combination of our talents and desires and the vulnerabilities they create when someone uses them to manipulate us. If you are a reflective person, you learn to reduce your vulnerability by realistically assessing your capabilities and matching them to your desires. We hone our self-assessments by reflecting on our encounters with others throughout our lives. We all make mistakes, and it's only when we reflect on those mistakes that we learn and move forward in our development. Self-reflection makes us aware of our desires and things that attract us. If we don't accurately self-reflect, our desires can become our Achilles' heels, or soft spots. Soft spots are our areas of vulnerability that essentially allow others to have power over us. We know we have them but don't always recognize them soon enough to avoid being stung.

All of us have soft spots, and many "B"s instinctively know how to target them. Our soft spots are qualities that make us unique. They are part of our personalities. If these qualities are readily observable to others, we're more vulnerable to "B"s who might use our soft spots as fodder for their games. Sometimes others can see our soft spots better than we can. In the previous example, Ilene was able to move forward from unconsciously seeking a strong and intelligent man. Her understanding of her blind spot, a charming man, led to increased awareness of her soft spot, her desire to be needed by someone. The most effective way to avoid being repeatedly stung is to know your blind spots and soft spots. The second way is to develop an awareness of people who exhibit the behaviors that compose your blind spots and those who regularly target your soft spots.

ROSS

"I had been working with Jenna for many years as we moved up the corporate ladder on different paths. Initially, Jenna had been nice to me and seemed supportive of my career advancement. But as she moved up, she seemed less helpful, and several times I was aware of lies she had told others about me. In my presence, she always praised others and never mentioned my accomplishments. I had given my all to the organization and felt proud of my many achievements.

"When a request for nominations for a national management award was issued, I knew that it was tailor-made for my achievements. I was surprised when Jenna suggested I nominate someone else for the award. I encouraged Jenna to nominate that person and told her I thought my achievements fit the award and I was going to nominate myself. I ended up winning the award. Jenna never congratulated me, but other colleagues and my friends did."

ABOUT THIS CASE STUDY ⎯⎯⎯⎯⎯⎯⎯⎯⎯⎯⎯⎯⎯

It is clear that Jenna knew Ross's soft spot was genuine pride in the quality of his work, and Jenna tried to use it as a power chip to deflate Ross's success. One of our most important tasks in life is getting to know ourselves. It is not easy to endure subtle and not-so-subtle putdowns by our friends or colleagues. Jenna underestimated Ross's level of self-esteem. Ross knew himself and had developed a support system that didn't include Jenna.

The Carrot Versus the Stick

Some people masterfully use manipulative behaviors to exploit our blind spots and soft spots. These behaviors become the "B's" power currencies. High-functioning "B"s will generally use more collaborative or engaging tactics, that appear cooperative, to engage us. This makes it easier to target our blind spots and soft spots. If we're lonely, the "B" will engage us in social activity. If we desire to move up the corporate ladder, the "B" will help us out. If we need to feel special, the "B" will comply by showering us with compliments and special favors. If we're turned on by excitement and new adventures, the "B" will titillate us with opportunities for wild times. If we respect integrity, the "B" will praise us for it and list the occasions in which he has demonstrated integrity. If we have strong spiritual beliefs, the "B" will espouse those values. If we seek loyal friendships, the "B" will pretend to be our friend. Once the "B" has our attention and our trust, he'll use the power he has gained to obtain whatever he wants. If we feel more connected and less lonely because of the actions of a "B," we will become loyal to that "B."

Some people with less finesse will use the same power currencies to target our blind spots and soft spots. However, they'll use
them in coercive ways to force us into submission. If we are lonely
or insecure, the "B" will make sure we're not invited to a social
activity. If we desire to move up the corporate ladder, the "B" will
lie about us to someone higher up. If we need to feel special, the
"B" will offer a favor to someone else in our presence. If we are
turned on by excitement and new adventures, the "B" will brag
about his adventures with *others*. If we respect integrity, the "B"
will accuse us of being unethical. If we have strong spiritual
beliefs, the "B" will degrade our spirituality. If we value loyal
friendship, the "B" will befriend our friends and exclude us.

GINA

"I love my mother, but she has always been very critical of me
and my other siblings. I promised her I would care for her when
she was old, and I'm fulfilling that duty. She is mentally sound but
has some mobility problems. She likes people and needs to be around
them. She refuses to go to any social functions, however, and wants
me near her constantly. Consequently, I cannot get my own work done
and have stopped activities I enjoy because my mother lays a guilt trip
on me when I leave the house for more than a half hour. She complains I am abusing her when it's the other way around. I have tried
talking to her and telling her about my needs but she won't listen. I
have tried using her behavior to point out her inconsistent thinking,
but I don't think that is helping either. It is really all about her and
always has been."

ABOUT THIS CASE STUDY

Gina's mother knows Gina's soft spots all too well. She entered the "B's" nest as a victim and imposed guilt by using Gina's soft spots as her power currencies against Gina. In this case, it's Gina's sense of responsibility and a need to care for others. This coercive tactic draws natural caregivers into the "B's" nest in the rescuer role. Once they are drawn in as their rescuer, the "B" changes to the role of persecutor. Nothing you do for the "B" will be good enough or will satisfy her sense of superiority and entitlement.

People who are natural caregivers have the most problems managing "B" behaviors, and the "B"s they are caring for know this. Caring for an aging parent "B" or an ill sibling "B" or an adult child "B" can be some of the most difficult relationships to manage. It might seem impossible to leave these relationships. However, this does not mean you cannot firmly establish your terms for care. These terms of care are your boundaries, and it's essential to spell out the consequences for violating your boundaries. If your boundaries are violated, you must re-state them and carry out your specified consequences. Refusing to play the role of rescuer does not mean you cannot be a caregiver. It means that you are recognizing your own needs.

Gina needs to assess her strengths, realize her limitations, and convey those to her mother and everyone involved in the situation. Gina should be firm about the help she needs from others, and accept that help. *In establishing boundaries with a loved one, it's useful to solicit help from a counselor, family and friends. If your loved one is a "B," she will fight back with all she has.*

Understanding Hot Spots

Sometimes you find yourself in a situation that reaches so deeply into your core you react immediately with either rage or withdrawal. Someone has touched your hot spot. These opposing reactions are the modern-day equivalent of fight or flight. In the "civilized" world of adulthood, organizational decorum and social graces, you are expected to restrict your reactions to a limited repertoire of pleasantries, data and discussion. When someone causes you to have a visceral reaction, it's important to know what button they are pushing and to reflect on why your reactions are so intense. It is likely you have come in contact with a "B" who has characteristics of other "B"s in your life who stung you. Unfortunately, when you're caught off guard by a "B" who intentionally or unintentionally triggers your hot spots, it's difficult to maintain your cool.

While "B" behaviors aren't always the trigger for our hot spots, our hot spots leave us vulnerable to "B" behaviors. Some "B"s look for peoples' hot spots and target them to devalue those who blow their cool. If they can trigger an irrational reaction to a difficult problem, it allows them to slip their own ideas into the mix. This is the basis of political attack ads. If ads can trigger a society's irrational hot spots, a politician will have the public crying for solutions to problems that might not even exist.

IKE

"On several occasions I have had a severe reaction to arrogant males. It caught me off guard the first time it happened. I attended a meeting at work as an observer. A man from an outside organization started speaking to our staff members with such extreme condescension I could feel myself literally having a physical reaction. I started sweating and rolling my eyes and clenching my fists. By the end of the meeting, I was uncharacteristically responding to this man with firm and direct comments. I went back to my office ranting about this man, and also a little concerned about my reaction. Where were these feelings coming from and why did they seem so out of my control?"

IKE AS A YOUNG BOY

"Growing up, my father was always putting me down. It was subtle, and I always thought there was some truth to the things he said. I grew up not ever thinking I was smart enough or good enough. I entered my professional life with very little confidence or assertiveness. Over the years I've recognized where these qualities have stemmed from and now I'm much more aware in my interactions with my father. I try not to buy into his comments. I recognize it's a flaw in him and it's not my issue."

CELESTE

"I have a lot of energy, and when I accepted my job as a program developer, I saw a lot of opportunities for advancing the scope of the company. I worked many extra nights and weekends to create new programs and to assure that they were on solid footing when they began. I don't expect to receive praise for doing my job. But as a middle child who had to fight to be acknowledged, I firmly believe if I do something extraordinary, I should at least be recognized for my achievements. After several years I noticed I was not getting the raises I thought I deserved. After going through the proper channels with my advancement requests, I finally met with the CEO to ask for a raise that I thought was well deserved.

"To my surprise, when I listed all of the programs I was instrumental in developing and the millions of dollars those programs had brought to the company, the CEO had a quizzical look on his face. When the CEO acted like I was out of line for asserting my achievements, I literally shouted, "Who do think did all of these things?" His expression of surprise and my expression of rage clearly took both of us aback. I quickly realized one of the managers in my department, who was very charming, fast-talking, and determined to get ahead, had likely been taking credit for my achievements. A week later I received my raise. I felt bad that I had lost my temper because this kind of reaction was out of character for me, but the lack of appreciation for the extra work I had done deeply hurt me. Realizing another manager in the department was taking credit for my work really pushed my buttons."

CELESTE, AS A YOUNG GIRL

"My cousin and I had just finished making matching white outfits when we joined our friends to play outside. One of the boys in our group became angry with another boy and physically attacked him. A third boy picked up the jacket of the boy who was being attacked and threw it into a mud puddle. I felt sorry for the boy who was being attacked, so I went to retrieve his jacket. He saw me and pushed me into the puddle, ruining my new outfit. I will never forget the shock I felt at trying to help someone and having that person attack me."

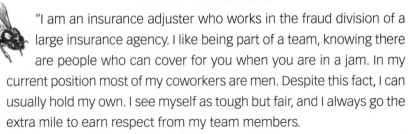

KIT

"I am an insurance adjuster who works in the fraud division of a large insurance agency. I like being part of a team, knowing there are people who can cover for you when you are in a jam. In my current position most of my coworkers are men. Despite this fact, I can usually hold my own. I see myself as tough but fair, and I always go the extra mile to earn respect from my team members.

"A year ago, Owen, another adjustor who was new to this type of investigation, was assigned to my section. Owen quickly made it clear that he neither wanted to take direction from me nor work with me. I had met the candidates who applied for the job and had favored another candidate over Owen because I had heard of Owen's reputation for schmoozing the bosses and for lying. Owen was a friend of my boss's because they had worked together for another insurance agency. My boss had left that agency during a financial scandal and Owen remained his friend. Like this new investigator, my boss is also widely known as a liar and a bully when he wants things done his way. Despite their personalities, I show my coworkers respect and expect the same respect from them.

"When Owen started, we classified the investigations into two categories and agreed he would work in one category and I would work in another. Although I wondered what he did with his time, I wasn't his supervisor so I paid little attention to him. He never came to me for information or advice on any of his cases, and whenever I spoke to him he would make some nasty remark to me. Several times he referred to me as 'Twiggy.' I never reported his behavior since I didn't want to sound like a whiner. One day my boss called me into his office along with Owen and another departmental supervisor. For the next hour my boss and Owen berated me while the other supervisor looked on.

"Owen accused me of not sharing cases with him, but he had many open cases and hadn't closed one of them in the year he had worked with us. He had never asked me for any new ones. The other supervisor watched the whole thing unfold with a wry smirk on his face. I was so angry I couldn't speak. I felt like a pack of wolves was attacking me. For the first time in my life I understood how workplace violence could occur. I had assumed that my boss and the supervisor, whom I thought I knew, respected me as a colleague. I have never felt so disrespected and angry at the way I was treated.

"The next day, after I had calmed down, I went to talk to my boss, who refused to acknowledge that the team had ambushed me. I told my boss he needed to get someone from human resources (HR) to mediate the situation. That was all I said because he didn't want to talk about it. I was hesitant to get HR involved because I was afraid it might come back to haunt me. Later that day, I spent an hour and a half talking to the supervisor who witnessed the event and I thought he started to understand why I was so upset. However, the next day he acted like he didn't have a clue."

KIT, AS A YOUNG GIRL

"In second grade my teacher told me I would be punished for talking out of turn in class. She made me stay in during recess, and I remember the sounds of the other children playing and laughing outside the window. The only problem was I had not talked out of turn in class and didn't know who had lied to say I did. I was angry because this felt completely unfair to me."

ABOUT THESE CASE STUDIES —————————————

Ike, Celeste and Kit were all surprised when someone hit their hot spots. Ike had already realized he was susceptible to the denigrating behaviors his father used on him. Despite that, he was surprised at his white-hot reaction to this man who was putting down his colleagues. Celeste and Kit took great pride in their work and their accomplishments. In Celeste's case the "manager B" took credit for much of Celeste's work and was charming enough to convince the CEO she had done it all. Celeste had done a good job but was not rewarded for it. The CEO unknowingly triggered Celeste's hot spot when he acted surprised at her purported accomplishments. Although Celeste's reaction was excessive, she had a good rationale for her anger and she was finally rewarded.

In Kit's case, it's likely the new adjustor intentionally targeted her soft spot, which was the need to feel a respected part of a team. In doing so he unintentionally hit her hot spot, which was falsely accusing her of neglecting her job. In the meeting, Kit was likely caught between two "B"s as a guard looked on. She unsuccessfully confronted a "B" and the guard in an attempt to set the record straight and clear her name. She was right in realizing that going to HR could put her in a bind. If Kit secured a reputation as a complaining female in a male world, it would potentially hinder her future chances for a promotion. However, it would also establish a record of what had happened. Since Kit's colleagues "didn't get it," the harassment will likely occur again in the future.

Interventions for Survival

Surviving a life of potential "B" stings reminds us of the three children we introduced in chapter one: Mia, Gabriela and Isabel. We wonder how to protect them from being psychologically injured or even destroyed by "B"s. It's impossible to teach a formula for avoiding "B" stings because "B"s, like bacteria, are everywhere and continuously adapt to changing circumstances. The strength of a "B's" need to protect his self-image at all costs can be a powerful force when you, by choice or by accident, enter a "B's" field of vision.

The will to survive "B"s seems to be stronger in some people than in others. And although the art of survival seems to come more naturally for some, you can learn to protect yourself by becoming aware of the patterns of "B"s. "B"s can surprise you in any situation, and it is impossible to prevent all stings. Surviving our encounters with "B"s involves four interventions:

- Avoid a "B's" sting
- Extract yourself from the "B's" nest
- Treat your wounds
- Prevent future stings

Avoiding a "B's" Sting

The first step in avoiding stings is to evaluate how it felt to be stung. To do this, you need to admit to having been stung. Although "B" behaviors are widespread, some people continue to believe they have never been stung. Occasionally these deniers are also "B"s who cannot engage in self-reflection. Alternatively, they could be perpetual rescuers or guards who are helpful to the "B." We have worked with numerous deniers. Perhaps they were

385

abused as children and have an innate ability to self-protect by finding ways to avoid rocking the boat. Perhaps they have learned to interpret a "B's" behavior in a way that doesn't feel threatening or offensive. It's also likely they have learned to view "B" behaviors as normal. Assuming you are not one of the permanent guards or rescuers and can recognize and admit to having been stung, you'll need to learn how to avoid future stings.

It is nearly impossible to avoid being stung without being motivated by the pain of a previous sting. Recognizing the painful feeling you are left with makes you want to avoid future stings. Mia, Gabriela and Isabel, like all the children from previous chapters, were stung in different ways when they were quite young. As a parent, mentor or teacher, it is important to create a trusting environment for children and others to recognize and discuss the circumstances of these stings. Through this mechanism, a child or adult can begin to learn the basic patterns of "B" behaviors and recognize places where they tend to build their nests. In chapter eleven, Isabel's parents and teacher set the stage for her expression of distress and subsequent self-protection from a classmate who was being inconsiderate.

The most effective approach to avoiding future "B" stings is to realize you can protect yourself. Sometimes that includes staying out of the way. An effective mechanism for avoiding the "B's" nest is to get in touch with the circumstances of being stung. Did the "B" act in certain ways before you were stung? A "B" might come on too strong, elevate you to best-friend status when you are not, praise you too much, ignore you in favor of someone else, charm you, say something condescending, act arrogant, disregard the rights of others, exhibit inconsistent behavior, talk behind your back, say one thing and do another, or exhibit cruelty toward an animal or a human. Was there any warning before you were stung? Does the person's behavior remind you of the behavior of a "B" who stung you in the past? Are you feeling some of the same feelings you felt before being stung in the past? Think! Listen to your gut and your instincts.

We have heard many descriptions of what it feels like to interact with a "B": "It feels like a one-sided hug." "She stood there like a stone." "I feel like I am always walking on eggshells." "No matter what I say, she can't hear me." Unfortunately, these people probably experienced the feelings early on in the relationship but chose to ignore them.

If you are in a work situation with a boss who is a "B" and you want to keep your job, you'll need to understand the behavior patterns of your "B" boss. You'll need to find ways to work with your boss while trying not to get stung. On some level, you have to learn to play the game. It's not that you're selling out. It relates to having the patience to strategically position yourself to act when it is most appropriate and you have the best chance of having an impact. Strategic positioning also includes keeping your options open to leave the situation.

PATRICK

"My boss Reggie is intelligent but dangerous. I have always been in Reggie's good graces and have learned over the years to work with him by using light humor and banter. I have seen Reggie turn on people and it's always for the same reason: he is intolerant of others who disagree with him. With the slightest disagreement, Reggie's tone becomes condescending and the tenor of his voice increases until he feels as though his viewpoint has triumphed. If someone dares to challenge him in public or in private, Reggie will question the person's ability to be caring and respectful. Unfortunately, Reggie's position in the agency allows him to use his opinions to control the careers of many employees. Watching coworkers challenge Reggie is like watching them repeatedly bang their head against a brick wall. Many employees have eventually left the agency after being demonized by Reggie.

"I have weathered many changes in this agency by adopting certain behaviors. Timing is everything, and I do not react negatively or urgently to changes. I let things unfold and talk to Reggie with humor, allowing him to reach conclusions that make sense for him. I fly under the radar as much as possible, often saving comments or questions for private sessions with Reggie. Making progress takes time, since forcing your way doesn't work with a boss like Reggie, because he'll become defensive and resistant. I know if I try to rescue someone who is being demonized by Reggie, Reggie will turn on *me*."

ABOUT THIS CASE STUDY ──────────────────────

It appears that Reggie, as both rescuer and persecutor, will go to any lengths to protect those he likes and will create unending difficulties for those he doesn't like. Patrick is quietly refusing to become Reggie's victim. He is also using Reggie's penchant for rescuing people by assuring he does not approach or antagonize 'Reggie the persecutor.' He only approaches Reggie when Reggie is in his rescuer role. Sometimes Patrick needs to put his ego aside in the short term to protect himself in the long run.

The rules you set are your boundaries. They are the lines you will not cross. You have a right to be respected no matter who is abusing you, and that should be your most basic boundary, no matter what other rules you set. If you can't stay out of the "B's" way, you can try to contain the "B's" behaviors so you can at least accomplish what you have to do. If there is a con-

tentious issue and you don't have time to play the game, you'll want a witness to your interaction with the "B."

It is extremely helpful to create allies who recognize the "B" behaviors and who will also commit to not tolerating them. Allies also help validate your feelings. Knowing others recognize what is happening can help keep you from feeling crazy. Whether the "B" is a boss, a coworker, a friend, a sibling or a parent, it is important to have a band of allies who are willing to express their intolerance of the manipulative behaviors. It's much harder for narcissistic "B"s to act arrogant and entitled when more than one person is reflecting back their rude behaviors. It's difficult for a borderline "B" to play one person off against another if both people are singing the same song. It's not easy for an antisocial "B" to tell you a fabricated lie if several people can reiterate the true facts of the situation. And it's more difficult for a histrionic "B" to command all of the attention if you collectively demonstrate that others are also in need of attention."

Once you familiarize yourself with the patterns of "B"s, staying out of a "B's" way after you have been stung once is relatively easy to do if it's a casual relationship. However, if the "B" is a family member or you are in a long-term relationship, either personal or job-related, it is much more difficult to avoid repeated stings. In any long-term relationship it is critical that you decide what behaviors you're not willing to tolerate and to be firm in communicating that to the "B." Establishing clear boundaries is one of the best ways of avoiding a "B" sting.

KELLY

"I applied for a position as administrator of a large state agency and was called for a round of interviews. I was then asked to meet with the governor since it was a governor-appointed position. In the interview I told the governor that I wasn't a member of his party, that I didn't vote for him, and that I wouldn't campaign for him; however, I was prepared to do the job for which I was applying. I was amazed when he actually hired me for the position.

"Two years later the job was going well. However, as the governor started to plan his campaign for his second term, things began to change. He called me to his office and said I needed to contribute money to his campaign and host a certain number of fundraising efforts. I told him, 'No, I won't do that.' I reminded him of what I had said in my first interview. I thought for sure that I would be fired on the spot. However, he didn't bother me for the next two years.

"Despite being left to do my job, I knew the writing was on the wall and realized that I would have to leave. When I landed a national position, he gave me a good reference. After he gave the reference he called me into his office and said, 'Why are you abandoning me?' I thought that was rather odd terminology. I didn't know if he was playing a game with my head or if he was serious."

ABOUT THIS CASE STUDY

The main point of this story is to demonstrate how to establish your personal and professional boundaries with clarity. If Kelly had not done that, she would have found herself trapped in a situation that she clearly didn't want to be in. Kelly was aware that a politically appointed position is always tenuous and had probably learned from past experience that establishing her boundaries at the beginning of a job was essential. It is not clear if the governor was exerting subtle "B" pressure on Kelly. However, Kelly was feeling that pressure. It's a sure bet that the governor was used to dismissing his staff, and not the other way around.

Extracting Yourself from the "B's" Nest

People with anxiety disorders are like onions. Their behaviors bother them more than they bother others. People with personality disorders are like garlic. Their behaviors bother others more than they bother them. It is important to distinguish when you are dealing with garlic. It is most likely garlic when you've done everything you can to improve a situation to avoid a "B" sting, and yet the situation persists. In fact, sometimes the harder you push to make things better, the harder the "B" pushes back. If you feel that you have done your best but aren't making progress, it's time to think about moving on and protecting yourself and your health. Staying in the situation or relationship will only eat at your soul and possibly destroy you in the end. It is often a much healthier alternative to move to a different agency, a different department, a different friend, or a new family situation. The art of quitting involves knowing when to leave.

The Importance of Timing

It is not always the right time to fight a battle with a "B," and it's not always the right time to leave. Sometimes you are on the periphery of the "B's" nest and other times you find yourself in the center. At different times in your life, you are going to have different levels of energy and different kinds of courage. Perhaps you have allowed a bad marriage to go on for years because you were in survival mode. You might have let a questionable friendship continue because you were starting a new job, dealing with the death of a parent, or starting a family. These are times when you might not have the energy to make new friends. Often it takes a shift in the balance of a relationship to create a crisis that forces you to reassess that relationship and decide to either stay or move on.

Shifting the Balance

A shift in the balance of a relationship can be caused by something significant like starting school, a promotion, the death of a loved one, or a pregnancy. However, the balance in a tenuous relationship with a "B" often changes because of something small, like making a new friend, being praised for an accomplishment, canceling an engagement, or not noticing someone who expects to be noticed. Sometimes it doesn't take much to change the pattern of your relationship with a "B" or the "B's" relationship with you. When you notice a dramatic change in someone's behavior toward you, look around for changes in your own behavior, either large or small. Then look for patterns in how the other person behaves toward you. If those behavior patterns seem exaggerated or don't make sense to you, you might be engaged with a "B."

Whenever you recognize a series of negative behavior patterns that seem unrelated or out of proportion to the stated cause, it's a good time to rethink your relationship with the person engaging in them. It's also a good time to restate your boundaries. If that doesn't work, plan your withdrawal. Determining your alternatives serves you well when you need to move on. Knowing you have options is a liberating experience when you feel trapped in a seemingly impossible situation.

ROY

"My wife, Sharla, and I had an ongoing friendship with another couple, April and Wally. This relationship changed quickly the second time we invited them to our condo in Colorado. The first time they came it was just the four of us and they had our full attention. Before they came they asked what the expectations and rules of the condo were. We thought that was a very nice gesture. We actually wondered what made them so insightful. The second time they came we invited another couple to spend a few days at the condo during the same week that April and Wally were there.

"But April and Wally refused to even interact with them. Their behavior was totally bizarre, and left us feeling confused about our friendship. Sharla and I both felt bad about the weekend. We continued to socialize with April and Wally but things were never the same. After much head-scratching at their behaviors, we decided this couple was threatened by us having other close friends in our lives."

BETTY

"Several years ago, my husband John and I met Lynne and Dick, and we seemed to get along. We enjoyed our conversations with them and also enjoyed meeting their friends. We also spent time at a house they had on a nearby lake. We recently spent a month's vacation in Florida, staying in a house we had rented in the past. Lynne and Dick were there for the winter and we spent time socializing with them. During our stay, my sister and brother came for a week and we spent a lot of time with them. Our car was vandalized twice during the month, so that also kept us busy. Lynne and Dick were very authoritative on how and where we should get our car fixed and how to file the insurance claim. We told them we had already taken care of it. It felt like we were their children.

"Toward the end of our stay, we were getting anxious to return home so we left three days early. When we reached home, I received an email from the man who owned the house we had rented. He said how much he enjoyed seeing us again. He mentioned he had run into Lynne and Dick at a garden center and Lynne asked, 'Wasn't Betty just awful to be around?' He said. 'No, actually she was very pleasant.' Our landlord included an email Lynne and Dick had sent to him stating how I was full of negative energy because I wanted to leave early and that she felt sorry for my husband. She also stated she was glad that we were gone. I honestly don't know what set them off. However, the more I stewed about it the more I was determined to send Lynne an email expressing my feelings. Here is my response to Lynne and Dick:

> We recently received your ugly, mean and misinformed email forwarded from our Florida landlord. We both would have appreciated you talking directly to us instead of communicating with a third party. Our joint decision to leave Florida when we did should have been of no consequence to you. It's hard for us to understand why you took our departure so personally, resulting in this email as well as other verbal comments about our presence. Lynne, both of us appreciate honest and respectful communication but this time you crossed the line. With time you may regret such language; unfortunately, your choice of words has done permanent damage to our friendship.

ABOUT THESE CASE STUDIES

Roy and Sharla and Betty and John had strange encounters with people they thought were their friends. The narcissistic

"B"s masqueraded as friends and showed their true colors when the actual circumstances of the visit didn't match their expectations to be the center of attention. Both couples were left wondering what precipitated the critical behaviors of their "friends." In reality, the critical behaviors were likely precipitated by very small changes in circumstances that lessened the adulation the "B"s were expecting.

The Need for Patience

Sometimes we have to do what we think is right and then patiently stand back and see what happens. Perhaps patience involves waiting for the right time to leave a "B's" nest, whether it involves a job, a spouse, or an unhealthy friendship. If you are getting something you need from a relationship, you might choose to contend with the "B's" behavior. However, if the relationship is draining your strength and you are giving far more than you are getting, it might be time to leave. Leaving a long-term relationship is never easy but if done willingly, it puts the power on your side and, in the long run, helps you heal.

When you decide to leave a bad situation, it is optimal to do it thoughtfully and calmly. When a "B" is involved, however, this might not be the best approach. While it is good to know why you are leaving and where you are going, trying to discuss that with a "B" is like walking in quicksand. So make your plans and get on with your life. No matter how much you explain, the "B" will never understand why you left and might try to lure you back into the nest. If the "B" is physically abusive, or if you sense any danger to yourself or your loved ones, it's wise to leave as quickly and as quietly as possible.

SAM

"My mother was very hot and cold. One minute she would tell me I was the best child and the next day she would turn around and tell me I was the worst child. I became an overachiever, always trying harder to please my mother. As an adult, I decided to keep my distance from her because I never knew where I stood with her. Being with her caused me too much pain."

LOUISE

"Although I was years from retirement, I decided to leave a job I loved because the person who had stabbed me in the back many times was about to become my boss. After a period of active grieving, I assessed my education and my strengths and then looked at alternatives. Leaving turned out to be a good decision with stimulating challenges and new opportunities for my career."

JOHN

"I retired early because I couldn't bear to witness what the administration was doing to the staff. I had tried for years to intervene in their behalf but was unable to make my voice heard. When one of my staff members was fired and I was not even part of the decision-making process, I had had enough and submitted my resignation. The top administrators were the most immoral people I had ever encountered and they did not want anyone with ethical behavior to get in their way. After I left, I found other people who had also been stung by these administrators. Together we fought privately to have the administrators removed. Our success didn't help us, but hopefully it helped those who were left at the agency."

ABOUT THESE CASE STUDIES

Sam, Louise and John assessed the patterns of "B" behaviors and assessed their own strengths. They each used their personal power in different ways to leave untenable situations that involved "B"s. One example was of someone who left when she was comfortable in the knowledge that she had contributed something positive to the situation. Others left knowing they could do more to improve the situation from outside its influence.

Treating Your Wounds

We do not mean to imply that purposely exiting the "B's" nest or changing your relationship with a "B" is an easy task. When all is said and done, the aftermath has to be managed. The "B"s have either forgotten about their encounters with you or transformed their memories into something that suits their needs. However, you are left with the pain, the suffering, and the fear of being stung again. The suffering can last years or a lifetime.

It is common for someone who has endured a "B" relationship to experience sleeplessness, exhaustion, weight loss or gain, agitation, anxiety, tearfulness and fear. Physical problems such as high blood pressure, stomach pains or headaches can also emerge. You will need to pay attention to your body and get help for any ailments you encounter. This is the time to eat good food, exercise, engage in meditative activity, and make new friends or connect with old ones.

It is also common for those who've been stung to blame themselves, thinking they could have done something differently. A secondary sting can come from hearing people talk about the person who stung you as nice or competent or generous. Hearing such talk can cause you to spiral down into self-doubt. These doubting behaviors are part of the lesser stings we apply to ourselves after a "B" has stung us.

CARMINE

"Sometimes it feels like I have fallen off a cliff and am trying to claw my way back to where I was. It feels like she is standing on the edge of the cliff, stepping on my hands."

LILY

"After ending my friendship with Angie, I heard another woman talk about Angie as such a cool person. I started to worry that Angie really was a cool person and there was something wrong with me or that Angie had changed and was now light-hearted and fun (instead of negative and deceptive, which is how I knew her). I need to remember this woman only sees what Angie wants her to see. On the surface, Angie could be fun, helpful, kind and generous.

"I spoke with another friend of mine who was having a similar experience with someone she had befriended, and we realized the patterns were the same. Somehow we worry that these deceptive people will move on and magically change. We worry that the next person they befriend will get the relationship we longed for."

ABOUT THESE CASE STUDIES ————————————————

Carmine and Lily are still mired in grief and self-doubt. They need emotional support and a dialogue with either a trusted friend or a therapist who will encourage them to transform their self-destructive thoughts. Once they do that, they can treat their wounds.

Getting Past the Pain

Some approaches for getting past the pain are to map a strategy for survival and measure your success against that strategy. Make an effort to meet new friends. Get a new job. Obtain more training. Find a substitute family. Pursue a creative outlet to work through your feelings. Learn new exercise routines. It is important to track your progress.

Consider how much you grew from the experience of being caught in a "B's" nest. Think of what you gained from the relationship and see it as a steppingstone to a better life. When you feel you can't restore the balance in your life, it might be because the balance was an illusion. The "B" probably had more control than you realized. You want to go back to that moment where you thought the balance was real but you can't get there. This is the time to recall the moment where you decided to move on, reset your expectations, and reestablish your plans to control your own future.

TOBY

"Sometimes I feel like I am on an icy road, spinning my tires and sliding backward. I need to turn around and go another way."

MARK

"For years I worked together with a colleague in an environment filled with overwhelming egos. We retired at the same time, and some years later I ran into him. He said after he retired he experienced three to four months of very bad dreams, and said he almost thought he had post-traumatic stress disorder (PTSD). As I thought about our conversation, I realized I had been having the same feelings. I felt like I had been in a prizefight for 10 years. I wondered if you really could have PTSD from trying to work with people who had hidden agendas and who played politics to stroke their own egos."

ABOUT THESE CASE STUDIES

Toby and Mark are demonstrating self-insights about their pain and the need to get past it. Mark's feeling of having PTSD is common in people who have survived stings from "B"s. When those experiences have been long term, the effects can linger for years. Many clients and friends have told us about their experiences after leaving a situation in which a "B" has stung them. One of the most common experiences we hear is of recurring nightmares. Another is a feeling of wanting to get even with the person or of wishing them harm. It's hard to listen to someone you care about launch into a vitriolic verbal attack on a "B" who stung them, because it's evident this person is still suffering. It's even more difficult to listen to them talk longingly or nostalgically about the "B" after witnessing their pain.

Expect Blowback

Once you realize you are in the "B's" nest and want to exit, you can expect the "B's" anger will likely ensue with the intent of engendering guilt in you. The "B" will exhibit a variety of expressions like anger, phony tears, self-righteous indignation, and the silence of exclusion. You will be left with your guilt and your feelings that you might be wrong. You might also fear for yourself, your reputation, your job or your family. These fears act as powerful deterrents to keep you from confronting or giving constructive feedback to the "B." The more you are aware and ready for these blowback behaviors, the more effectively you will be able to treat your wounds. Do not let these blowback behaviors keep you from planning your strategy for survival. Chart your course for change and move forward with your plan.

Preventing Future Stings

People who repeatedly engage in manipulative behaviors rely on their inconsistent behavior to keep you off guard. They disguise their inconsistencies with their superficial rationality. In any setting where you must continue to interact with "B"s, it is very important to clearly define behavior expectations. To the extent that your stature in the organization or relationship will allow, it is important to be straightforward with those who exhibit "B" behaviors. Do not joke with them or leave things open-ended. Keep records of important conversations and agreements. Repeat what you heard them say and ask them to confirm it or repeat it to you. This becomes a verbal record you can track. Praise work well done and don't let bad work or mistakes slide because you're afraid of the repercussions. If you're a supervisor, accurate and specific performance evaluations are critical.

A Strong Team as Prevention

A group of good friends can be critical when you need to establish boundaries with family members or loved ones. Likewise, a well-functioning team can be a helpful vehicle for setting boundaries, for stating your needs, and for giving constructive feedback to a manipulative coworker. A team can also be helpful in giving emotional support when the manipulative person is your boss. Administrators who are "B"s often give lip service to good teamwork when, in reality, they don't support the maturation of the team. Instead, they promote guard "B"s who they can depend on to gather information on the inner workings of the team.

It is important for administrator "B"s to have the illusion of "total control," as the thought of a team with participative leadership is very frightening to their sense of self. A cohesive team has a strong voice against such a boss, and that cohesiveness will prevent pitting one team member against another. A well-developed team can also use the talents of specific members to tailor their interactions with a "B" administrator.

Assess Your Responsibility

It is important for all of us to assess our contributions to the behaviors of "B"s. While it feels safe to ignore stinging behaviors by a "B," ignoring their behaviors also condones them. When parents let their children get away with manipulative, deceitful behaviors or cover for them when they engage in such behaviors, it's a ticket to trouble. Whether we are dealing with children or adults, we must expect people to take responsibility for their actions. We must also assess our responsibility if we notice manipulative behavior that's harmful to others. By ignoring "B" behaviors, we are more likely to minimize or tolerate those behaviors in the future, perhaps not even noticing when they recur.

Dr. Amy Bishop was arrested for shooting six of her academic colleagues at the University of Alabama. According to a *New York Times* report, there had been multiple clues throughout Bishop's life that she exhibited "B" behaviors.[62] When she was 21, she had shot her 18-year-old brother. Allegedly, she could be pleasant and friendly when she wanted to be. At the smallest slight, however, her behavior changed and she reportedly became mean and aggressive.

Bishop had hired a lawyer and filed a discrimination complaint against the university. Allegedly, she frequented a firing range in the weeks leading up to the shootings. Her husband admitted accompanying her to the shooting range. It was not reported if he questioned his wife about why she was practicing her marksmanship.

We have a tendency to concentrate on our own small circle of relationships. However, when we encounter "B"s, it's useful to think in terms of how much damage their manipulative behaviors can do to the whole. Unlike the perspective of "B"s, it's not just about us. It's about the community around us. Thinking in a broader context can help us decide to effectively address the "B" behaviors.

---

[62] Dewan, Saul & Zezima, "For Professor, Fury Just Beneath the Surface," *New York Times.*

SUMMARY

THEY HURT YOU BY EMBARRASSING, INVALIDATING OR ignoring you, and then when they realize you are hurt, they make up excuses for why they hurt you or they question why *you* hurt them. They will continue to hurt you to justify their excuses and think you are pathetic for not fighting back. In response, you are filled with self-doubt, guilt, avoidance, ideas for revenge, passive aggressive behaviors or painful silence. This is the nature of our relationships with people who repeatedly engage in manipulation.

We are all wired as social animals to want status and influence. We have a need for recognition because it gives us a survival advantage in a social group. However, a strong desire for recognition from a "B" can become pathological, blinding us to behaviors that will eventually become destructive to us and to the collective whole. If the "B" decides that having someone *normal* around him will provide a front for him to exercise his "B" behaviors, we want to make sure that we don't become that special *normal* someone.

We hope this book has fostered a recognition and understanding of the behavior patterns of those who repeatedly manipulate others. We also hope it has helped you discover better ways to manage your responses to "B" behaviors and to being stung. The message we hoped to convey is that accepting "B" behaviors as part of reality doesn't mean we should support or ignore such behaviors.

As we noted in chapter one, we all engage in some manipulative behaviors. When those behaviors become repetitive and lead to social dysfunction, however, suspect that a "B" is in the mix and be watchful. The behaviors would have to form very specific patterns over time to be categorized as a personality disorder. But that is not our concern. We are merely concerned about avoiding being stung by repeated patterns of manipulative behaviors. Manipulative behaviors exist on a continuum from occasional to repetitive to specific patterns of behavior. Such behaviors are also on a continuum from mild to psychopathic. Hopefully, most of the manipulative behaviors we encounter will be in the mild-to-moderate range. However, some "B"s have the capability, when stressed, to extend their behaviors into the psychopathic realm.

It is essential to have a sympathetic understanding of what drives "B"s and their behaviors. It is critical to know what behaviors should be ignored, what behaviors to deflect, and what behaviors must be addressed. When a manipulator stings you, it might be divine to forgive, but it's downright foolish to forget. Remembering helps us to see maladaptive behavior patterns and alerts us to take appropriate action.

The stories in this book have provided examples of stinging "B" behaviors in many spheres of life. The stories also demonstrated how those who were stung dealt with their psychic injuries. Because some people have a limitless repertoire of stinging behaviors, it's only by observing their repetitive behaviors that you can recognize them, protect yourself, and fight back when you have the opportunity to do so. The ability to identify these patterns early in a relationship can protect you from being stung.

If you recognize manipulative "B" behaviors early and act accordingly to address them, you might be able to save your group, your organization, or yourselves the pain of untangling the messes "B"s create. Since "B" behaviors may be pervasive, it's wise to choose your battles carefully. As helpful as it is to recognize "B" behaviors, it's equally helpful to recognize the individual needs you have that attract you to someone who repeatedly exhibits such behaviors.

Bibliography

A Christmas Story. Directed by Bob Clark. Hollywood, CA: MGM, 1983.

Avlon, John. *Wingnuts: How the Lunatic Fringe is Hijacking America*. New York: Beast Books, 2010.

Berne, Eric. *Games People Play: The Basic Handbook of Transactional Analysis*. New York: Grove Press, 1964.

Biography.com. "Bernard Madoff Biography." Accessed July 25, 2011. www.biography.com/articles/Bernard-Madoff-466366

Blanco, Carlos, Mayumi Okuda, Crystal Wright, Deborah Hasin, Bridget Grant, Shang-Min Liu, and Mark Olfson. "Mental Health of College Students and Their Non-College-Attending Peers: Results from the National Epidemiologic Study on Alcohol and Related Conditions." *Archives of General Psychiatry* 65 (Dec. 2008): 1425–37.

Capote. Directed by Bennett Miller. Hollywood, CA: Sony Pictures, 2005.

Carter, Jay. *Nasty People: How to Stop Being Hurt by Them without Stooping to Their Level*. New York: Barnes and Noble, 1989.

Chicago Tribune. "Highlights: Rod Blagojevich (2008-2011)." Accessed July 25, 2011. www.chicagotribune.com/topic/politics/government/rod-blagojevich-PEPLT007479.topic

Dewan, Shaila, Stephanie Saul and Katie Zezima. "For Professor, Fury Just Beneath the Surface." *New York Times*. Page A1. February 20, 2010.

Diagnostic and Statistical Manual of Mental Disorders (4th ed.) Washington, DC: American Psychiatric Association, 2000.

Drinka, Theresa J. K. and Joel Streim. "Case Studies from Purgatory: Maladaptive Behavior within Geriatrics Health Care Teams." *The Gerontologist* 34 (1994): 541–547.

Fatal Attraction. Adrian Lyne. Hollywood, CA: Paramount, 1987.

Fromm, Erich. *The Heart of Man: Its Genius for Good and Evil.* London: Routledge and Kegan Paul PLC, 1965.

Glasser, William. *Choice Theory: A New Psychology of Personal Freedom.* New York: HarperCollins, 1998.

Goldfarb, Zachary A. "Staffer at SEC Had Warned of Madoff: Lawyer Raised Alarm, Then Was Pointed Elsewhere." *Washington Post*, July 2, 2009. Accessed July 25, 2011. www.washingtonpost.com/wp-dyn/content/article/2009/07/01/AR2009070104223.html

Golding, William. *Lord of the Flies*. New York: Berkley Publishing, 1954.

Goldman, Adam and Mike Baker. "Brother Defends Accused Terror Head." AP *NewsBreak*, July 31, 2009.

Gross, Raz, Mark Olfson, Marc Gameroff, Steven Shea, Adriana Feder, Milton Fuentes, Rafael Lantigua, and Myrna Weissman. "Borderline Personality Disorder in Primary Care." *Archives of Internal Medicine* 162 (Jan. 2002): 53–60.

Harvey, Jerry. "How Come Every Time I Get Stabbed in the Back My Fingerprints Are On the Knife?" *The Academy of Management Executive* Vol. 3 No. 4. (1989): 271–77.

High School Musical. Directed by Kenny Ortega. Hollywood, CA: Disney Channel, 2006.

Hogan, R., R. Raskin and D. Fazzini. "The Dark Side of Charisma." *Measures of Leadership* (Edited by K. E. Clark and M. B. Clark). Greensboro, NC: Center for Creative Leadership (1990): 343–54.

Holy Smoke. Directed by Jane Campion. Hollywood, CA: Miramax, 1999.

House of Cards. Written by James Jacoby. CNBC, aired on January 18, 2009.

Janis, Irving. *Groupthink: Psychological Studies of Policy Decisions and Fiascoes.* Second Edition. Florence, KY: Cencage Learning, 1982.

Janis, Irving. *Victims of Groupthink: A Psychological Study of Foreign-Policy Decisions and Fiascoes.* New York: Houghton Mifflin, 1972.

Jonestown: The Life and Death of Peoples Temple. PBS documentary, 2009.

Kantor, Martin. *The Psychopathy of Everyday Life: How Antisocial Personality Disorder Affects All of Us*. Westport, CT: Praeger, 2006.

Keltner, Dacher, Deborah Gruenfeld and Cameron Anderson (2000). "Power Approach, and Inhibition: Research Paper No. 1669." *Research Paper Series* (December 28, 2000). Stanford University Graduate School of Business, Palo Alto, CA.

Kernberg, Otto. "Factors in the Psychoanalytic Treatment of Narcissistic Personalities." *Journal of the American Psychoanalytic Association* 18 (1970): 51–85.

Kivimaki, Mika, Marko Elovainio, and Jussi Vahtera. "Workplace Bullying and Sickness Absence in Hospital Staff." *Occupational and Environmental Medicine*: 57 (May 2000): 656–60.

Langan, Patrick and David Levin. "Recidivism of Prisoners Released in 1994." *Bureau of Justice Statistics Special Report*. U.S. Dept. of Justice Office of Justice Programs. June 2, 2002. NJC 193427. http://bjs.ojp.usdoj.gov/index.cfm?ty = pbdetail&lid = 1134.

Lenzenweger, Mark, John Clarkin, Frank Yeomans, Otto Kernberg, and Kenneth Levy. "Refining the Borderline Personality Disorder Phenotype Through Finite Mixture Modeling: Implications for Classification." *Journal of Personality Disorders* 22 (Aug. 2008): 313–31.

LEO Weekly. "History Repeating? As Former U of L Dean Robert Felner Faces the Feds, Colleagues and Students Shed Light on His Turbulent Past." August 13, 2008. Accessed on July 25, 2011. http://leoweekly.com/news-features/major-stories/features/history-repeating

Lester, Gregory. *Personality Disorders in Social Work and Health Care*. Brentwood, TN: Cross Country Education, 2005.

Living With Michael Jackson: A Tonight Special. By Martin Bashir. London: Granada Television, 2003.

"Love and Death: The Story of Bonnie and Clyde." *Biography*. A & E Home Video, 2000.

Lowen, Alexander. *Narcissism: Denial of the True Self*. New York: Touchstone, 2004.

411

Maccoby, Michael. "Narcissistic Leaders: The Incredible Pros, the Inevitable Cons." *Harvard Business Review.* Jan.–-Feb. 2000. Accessed on August 14, 2011. http://www.maccoby.com/Articles/NarLeaders.shtml

Mean Girls. Directed by Mark Waters. Hollywood, CA: Paramount Pictures, 2004.

Mendoza, Martha. "Sexual Conduct Mars Military Recruiting." *Associated Press.* August 20, 2006.

Mulvaney, K. "Robert Felner's Trail of Deceit Passed Through URI." *The Providence Journal.* April 11, 2009.

Nelson, D. A., C. C. Robinson, and C. H. Hart. "Relational and Physical Aggression of Preschool-Age Children: Peer Status Linkages Across Informants." *Early Education and Development: Special Issue on Relational Aggression in Early Childhood* 16 (2005): 115–139.

Page One Kentucky (blog). "Robert Felner, the University of Louisville, Open Records Requests Galore—An Interesting Look at the Situation." July 14, 2008. Accessed on July 25, 2011. http://pageonekentucky.com/2008/07/14/robert-felner-the-university-of-louisville-open-records-requests-galore-an-interesting-look-at-the-situation/

Page One Kentucky. "Breaking: Felner and Schroeder More Than Friends? And Other Updates On the Scandal." July 28, 2008. Accessed July 26, 2011. http://pageonekentucky.com/2008/07/28/breaking-felner-and-schroeder-more-than-friends-and-other-updates-on-the-scandal/

Page One Kentucky. "Robert Felner Sentenced 63 Months in the Pokey." May 17, 2010. Accessed on July 25, 2011. http://pageonekentucky.com/2010/05/17/robert-felner-sentenced-63-months-in-the-pokey/

Payson, Eleanor. *The Wizard of Oz and Other Narcissists: Coping with the One-Way Relationship in Work, Love, and Family.* Royal Oak, MI: Julian Day Publications, 2002.

PBS documentary (2009). *Jonestown: The Life and Death of Peoples Temple:*

Porter, Stephen, Leanne ten Brinke, and Kevin Wilson. "Crime Profiles and Conditional Release Performance of Psychopathic and Non-Ppsychopathic Sexual Offenders." *Legal and Criminological Psychology.* 14, (2009): 109--118.

Rodriguez, Gregory. "Haiti Quake Brings Dose of Reality." *Los Angeles Times.* January 18, 2010.

Schneider, S. S., T. Deeby, D. C. Gilley and G. DeGrandi-Hoffman. "Seasonal Nest Usurpation of European Colonies by African Swarms in Arizona, USA." *Insectes Sociaux* 51 (2004): 359–64.

Smith, Sally Bedell. *Diana in Search of Herself: Portrait of a Troubled Princess.* New York: Signet, 2000.

Stinson, F. S.; D. A. Dawson, R. B. Goldstein, S. P. Chou, B. Huang, S. M. Smith, W. J. Ruan, A. J. Pulay, T. D. Saha, R. P. Pickering, and B. F. Grant. "Prevalence, Correlates, Disability, and Comorbidity of DSM-IV Narcissistic Personality Disorder: Results from the Wave 2 National Epidemiologic Survey on Alcohol and Related Conditions." *Journal of Clinical Psychiatry* 69 (2008): 1033–45.

Stout, Martha. *The Sociopath Next Door.* New York: Broadway Books, 2005.

Suskind, Patrick. *Perfume: The Story of a Murderer.* New York: Washington Square Press, 1986.

The Breakfast Club. Directed by John Hughes. Hollywood, CA: Universal Studios, 1985.

The Corporation. Directed by Mark Achbar and Jennifer Abbott. Vancouver, BC: Big Picture Media Corporation, 2003.

The Huffington Post. "Robert Felner, Former U of Louisville Dean, Sentenced to More Than 5 Years in Prison." May 18, 2010. Accessed on July 25, 2011. http://www.huffingtonpost.com/ 2010/05/18/robert-felner-former-u-of_n_579871.html

The Jacksons: An American Dream. Directed by Karen Arthur. Hollywood, CA: De Passe Entertainment, 1992.

The Jonestown Institute, http://jonestown.sdsu.edu.

The Source on Women's Issues in Congress. "House Subcommittee Examines Sexual Assault in the Military." Vol. 11, No. 19 (2006)

The Today Show. Interview of Harry Markopolos. March 1, 2010.

Thomas, Pierre, Yuni de Nies, and Devin Dwyer. "White House Crashers: How the Salahis Strolled Past Secret Service," *Good Morning America*, Nov. 30, 2009. Accessed July 25, 2011. http://abcnews.go.com/GMA/white-house-crashers-michaele-tareq salahi-past-secret-service/story?id = 9202817&page = 1

Twenge, Jean M. and W. Keith Campbell. *The Narcissism Epidemic: Living in the Age of Entitlement*. New York: Free Press, 2009.

University of Massachusetts at Amherst. "UMass Researcher Finds Link Between Lying and Popularity." *Science Daily*. Dec. 14, 1999. Accessed July 25, 2011. http://www.sciencedaily.com/releases/1999/12/991214072623.htm

Walden, Jennifer. "Michael Jackson, the World's King of Pop, 1958–2009." *A Nip and a Tuck: Medscape* (blog). July 14, 2009. http://blogs.medscape.com/jenniferwalden

Wallace, Mike. "Liar, Liar." Feb. 11, 2009. *60 Minutes*, CBS News. Accessed July 25, 2011. http://www.cbsnews.com/ stories/2000/01/28/60II/main154661 .shtml?tag = mncol;lst;1

Wilson, Bee. *The Hive: The Story of the Honeybee and Us*. London: John Murray, 2004.

Witness to Jonestown. MSNBC Films, 2008.

Index

A

Achilles' heels, 36, 317–18
Alcohol abuse, 9
Antisocial behaviors
    examples of, 19–21, 75, 77, 109, 112,
        143, 150, 315
    friendships and, 97
    occasional, 17
    strategies for coping with, 176
Antisocial personality disorder
    behavior patterns of, 7, 8
    characteristics of, 6
    prevalence of, 11–12
Anxiety, 9
Apologies, 310–11, 346–47
Artists, 359–63
Attorneys, hiring, 176
Avlon, John, 288

B

"B" behaviors. *See also individual behaviors*
    accepting, as normal, 52, 334
    apologies for, 310–11, 346–47
    changing, 30–32
    in childhood, 39–52, 60–61, 158, 218,
        347–49
    continuum of severity for, 14–17
    coping with, 45, 56–57, 251–52
    denial and, 266–68, 272, 276,
        283–86
    effects of, 13, 18–19, 42, 397–99
    encouraging, 240
    fighting back against, 238, 319–25,
        336, 339, 352, 369–70
    in groups, 203–34
    masking, 32, 36
    recognizing, 18–19
    selective devaluation and, 106–8
    stress and, 54–55, 235
    tolerating, 287–89, 299, 306, 308–10,
        316–17, 328–31, 402–3

Berne, Eric, 52–53, 336
Bishop, Amy, 403
Blagojevich, Rod, 27
Blind spots, 372–74, 376–77
Blogging, 139–40, 318–25
Blowback behaviors, 401
Bonnie and Clyde, 267–68
Borderline behaviors
    boundaries and, 118
    examples of, 24–26, 117, 137,
        186–87, 294, 356
    friendships and, 97
    occasional, 17
Borderline personality disorder
    behavior patterns of, 7, 8
    characteristics of, 6
    prevalence of, 12
Boundaries
    establishing, 118, 143, 177–81, 211,
        388–89, 390–91
    with family members, 129
    loose, 126
Boyd, Daniel, 267
"B"s
    apologies by, 310–11, 346–47
    blind spots targeted by, 372–74, 376–77
    dead, 162–68
    definition of, 18
    helping, 371–72
    hot spots targeted by, 379–84
    on the Internet, 139–42
    passively collaborating with, 339
    protectors of, 55–56, 316
    punishing, 315–16
    roles played by, 53–55, 335–36
    seductiveness of, 33–36, 241, 310
    soft spots targeted by, 372–78
    vulnerability to, 35–36, 66

CASE STUDIES